Kelenoh

The last High Priestess of the Temple of Hera on Samos who possessed the knowledge of ancient wisdom

Kelenoh

*The last High Priestess of the Temple of Hera on Samos
who possessed the knowledge of ancient wisdom*

Hillie Kuipers

MOUNT OLYMPUS PUBLISHING

First Dutch Language Edition 2008

First English Language Edition 2016

Translation by Jan Lips

Cover Design and maps by Misty Taylor

Editing by Misty Taylor, Manola Carter and Maria Rybaczyk

ISBN 978-0-9958177-0-8
ISBN 978-0-9958177-1-5   eBook

Body, Mind and Spirit / Spirituality / Occultism / Past Lives

Mount Olympus Publishing
302 – 2005 Luxstone Blvd
Airdrie, AB T4B 3J9 Canada

www.mountolympuspublishing.com

Printed by CreateSpace

Dedicated to my children Sonja and Erik

Table of Contents

Acknowledgements

This book would never have happened without a number of people, for whom I am most grateful.

Lammert Gosse Jansma, I would like to thank you for reading the Dutch manuscript and making all the improvements necessary for a good story.

My daughter Sonja, who always was available to listen patiently to me when emotions ran high during my writing, and who helped me to improve the manuscript.

My son Erik who stood ready every time when called upon.
I love you both.

I am especially grateful to those involved in the production of the English language edition of the book:
Jan Lips from Canada, and Misty Taylor, Manola Carter and Maria Rybaczyk from the USA.

Hillie Kuipers
Samos, Fall of 2016

Foreword

The book you are holding in your hands contains a most extraordinary story. It is a story that would be the dream of every fiction writer with all the ingredients of a sweeping and spellbinding narrative. Love, hate, passion, jealousy, power, intrigue, science and invention, religious practices, occult powers, and life and death.

But this story is not fiction. It is the tale of a life as lived by a High Priestess in Greece in the 6th Century BC, as it is re-lived and re-told through visions of the past and mental transportation back in time by the author, revealed to her over the course of many years.

My cousin, who lives on the Greek island of Samos, thought that I might be interested in reading this material, written by a Dutch woman she had met. The title of the book was *Kèlenòh*, and the author, Hillie Kuipers. After I received my copy and started reading, I could not put it down.

I found the story fascinating—intriguing from beginning to end. And given that I have been a student of the occult and esoteric wisdom for decades, the story was also believable—in fact, it confirmed many of the things I had long believed to be true, as well as illuminating various religious practices in times long past I was not aware of.

After finishing the book I began to think that many of my friends would be interested in learning of the story of *Kèlenòh* because of its esoteric value. The story contains deep spiritual insights and teachings concerning many aspects of life, not only as applied in the time of ancient Greece and Egypt, but it seems just as relevant to this present day and age. Then it dawned on me one day that I could share this incredible story by translating the book into English. I contacted Hillie and she was thrilled with the prospect of having her book published in English, since we both understood that the story of Kelenoh's life in 6th century BC deserved to be shared with a much wider audience.

The training Kelenoh received in the Egyptian temples of Karnak at the hand of the High Priest Yufaa enhanced the natural abilities she possessed from birth—reading people's auras and their thoughts and feelings; the ability to heal illnesses and help resolve people's personal problems, even influence the weather, and communicate directly with the gods. It was up to her to use these powers for the good of all people that were entrusted to her. What hindrances did she have to conquer to be victorious and what were the pitfalls in her own character had to be overcome are an integral part of this gripping narrative.

See for yourself how it all unfolds. I promise you, this story will keep you riveted, as it did me. I was filled with empathy for the characters in the story. I asked myself, what would I have done if I had been in Kelenoh's shoes (sandals in this case) or for that matter in the shoes of any one of the other characters. I found that I came away with a far better understanding of life in ancient Greece and Egypt, and Kelenoh's story made me realize the many valuable lessons to be learned in studying the past, lessons that can be applied to present-day life.

Hillie Kuipers' story made the past come alive in ways that one can only dream of! Be a part of the dream, for a clearer reality of your own.

Happy reading.

Jan Lips,
Translator

About the writing of Kelenoh

It all began innocently enough. In 1986, Hillie Kuipers was invited to accompany her friend and former husband on a vacation for three weeks to the Greek Island of Samos, a place she didn't know anything about.

As soon as she stepped off the plane onto Samos, everything felt and looked very familiar; the smells, the vistas, the mountains. To her astonishment, something strange began happening. She started seeing and having mental pictures flash across her mind, which, in her opinion, couldn't be real. They were visions of a Samos during ancient times.

At first she was confused, and not at all sure what it all meant or why. Eventually, for her own sanity, she decided to write everything down in a notebook. Thus, over the span of many years and many return trips to Samos, a story began to unfold.

Several of the events she had seen in her visions were not common historical knowledge but, to her relief, were later confirmed by people with more in-depth knowledge of the island during antiquity, from existing historical facts, and modern excavations. These validations gave her the confidence that what she saw were actual events from the past. Eventually, years later, she began to accept that the woman she saw in her visions, the High Priestess of the Temple of Hera, was a previous embodiment of hers. Up until then she had considered reincarnation to be a strange notion and hadn't given it much thought.

Around 1999, 13 years after her first visit to Samos, she began compiling all her visions in an orderly manner and started writing a book about what she had seen and experienced.

After Hillie finished her manuscript, she couldn't find a publisher. A close friend advised her to change her story from first person format to third person. It took Hillie six months to convince herself to start all over again and rewrite her book. That was in 2005.

She had finished the first page when, out of nowhere, she heard a sentence in her head, 'The sand of the desert is hot under her bare feet.' She ignored it and kept writing what she intended to write. However, the sentence kept repeating itself. Finally giving in, she got a blank piece of paper and typed the sentence on it, if only to make that bothersome thought go away. She paused for a brief moment after completing the sentence, when suddenly she was transported to another time and place. She was in the desert and she was Kelenoh.

The whole story unfolded in this way, writing faithfully for two hours every day what she experienced over the span of the next two years. The story of Kelenoh – the last High Priestess of the Temple of Hera on Samos. She, who possessed the knowledge of ancient wisdom.

The first publisher she contacted after that, accepted the completed manuscript, *Kèlenòh.*

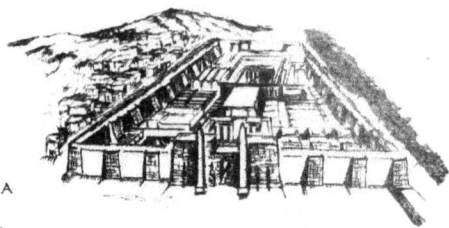

MEDITERRANEAN SEA

EGYPT

MEMPHIS

SINAI DESERT

NILE RIVER

TEMPLE COMPLEX
OF KARNAK

VALLEY OF
THE KINGS

RED SEA

AFRICA

NUBIA

PYTHAGORAS'
HIDING CAVE

SAMOS

PYTHAGORAS'
TEACHING CAVE

TUNNEL OF
EUPALINOS

TEMPLE COMPLEX
OF HERA

POLYKRATES'
PALACE

TURKEY

EASTERN AEGEAN SEA

GREECE

Chapter 1

The sand of the desert is hot under her bare feet as she stands there, dreamily looking into the distance at the impressive buildings shimmering in the light of the setting sun. Shivering for a moment from the evening winds and beginning to feel cold, she wraps the shawl firmly around her shoulders. Even from this far distance, the pillars of the temple are tall and the walls enormous, the Temple of Karnak is impressive. Kelenoh again turns her head, this time to the left, and sees far away the temple complex of Luxor, now covered over in a splendid orange glow.

It is so quiet here without the daily sounds of the temple, and it suddenly dawns upon her how far she went. She knows Yufaa will be very upset because he does not allow her to go into the desert by herself. Yufaa is the high priest, training her to become a high priestess. Every so often she just needs to escape and be alone for a moment; his strict rules and those of the temple sometimes oppress her.

Kelenoh is twelve years old, slender, tall for her age, with an oval face, surrounded by a large mop of black curls and deep blue eyes.

Disregarding the punishment awaiting her later, she closes her eyes and calmly sits in a meditative pose on the warm sand, cross-legged, with upraised hands on her knees, just as Yufaa has taught. How easy it is to meditate here. She is feeling so safe and secure that not even a snake she hears slithering by, disrupts her peacefulness.

As she starts breathing deeper, clear images of the temple complex of Hera on the Island of Samos appear. These images of her home are accompanied by a deep feeling of homesickness arising within her. Then she can't help but smile at seeing the people she loves most, getting ready for the night. She giggles at seeing Cassandra, one of the priestesses, looking around and knowing she is present. Then Cassandra says to Selene and Theano, the other priestesses, "Kelenoh is here." The three hug each other. Now, Kelenoh feels reassured, knowing that she can return to Samos at any time, if and when she desires to do so.

Still smiling, she opens her eyes and is alarmed at seeing just how dark it has become. Hurriedly she gets up and races back to her temporary home. Reaching the threshold of her house, panting, she stops to catch her breath before entering in. As she looks through the door into her bedroom, she can see Yufaa's tall figure standing in the corner of the room by the light of the fires burning in the bowls. His arms are crossed as he angrily stares back at her with his large brown eyes, showing a dislike for her tousled curls. She notices how the gold chain he is wearing, with a turquoise winged scarab pendant, is sparkling in the light of the fire bowls that made the necklace stand out splendidly against his deep brown skin.

He opens his mouth to address her, but before he can utter a word, she exclaims, "I have been to Samos!"

His angry look fades, replaced by a twinkle in the eye. "Take a seat and tell me."

Yufaa, having spent five years in silence as part of his training, can easily get annoyed with her chatty personality. He has thus become an austere and reserved man. When he does speak, it is in short, plain sentences, clear, and to the point.

From a stone jug, Yufaa pours a cup of water from one of the holy ponds of the temple. Offering the cup to her, she thankfully accepts it and thirstily begins drinking. The water is sweet and fresh tasting, like the lotus flowers growing in the pond. Sensing that Yufaa is intently staring at her, she instinctively begins to drink more slowly. There is still so much to learn.

He nods toward a chair and she obediently goes and sits down. "I am sorry Yufaa, but I had to go into the desert for a short time. There are always people here and I wanted to be alone. It was such a beautiful evening and the desert was splendid! Did you see how beautiful the sunset was?"

She looks at him, impatience beginning to appear on his face. "All right, I will tell you about Samos. I did exactly what you told me, and it actually happened on its own. I saw Cassandra, Selene and Theano. I was so happy, and they felt me too. I heard them say so."

While telling her story, she re-ties her hair and strings the ribbon around her head again. Yufaa looks at her and simply says, "Good." She hands him her cup and he fills it again. "Tomorrow morning," Yufaa continues, looking at her with probing eyes, "when the sun rises, I will meet you at the Temple of the Listening Ear. Sleep well." He leaves the room.

Kelenoh hears him order Kawari to go and help her get ready for the night. Kawari is a girl from Nubia, given to her by Yufaa when she first arrived at the temple to receive her training.

Kawari enters the room laughing, with a bowl of perfumed, warm water. Her dark brown skin shines in the light coming from the fire bowls. She has a small round face. The whites of her small, clear eyes stand out prominently on her face. Her linen dress is draped around her somewhat small round body and her hair is covered with a cloth. She is shorter than Kelenoh, but they are both the same age.

Kawari is helping her undress, get into the tub and washes her, while talking non-stop about all the day's events at the temple. Kelenoh enjoys this daily ritual. All clean and fresh, Kawari towel dries her, rubs oil all over her body and then helps her put on a night dress. Totally relaxed, Kelenoh slides under the fine linen sheets on the bed. Kawari then hands her a cup of warm date wine and asks, "Would you like a sheep's fleece to cover you during the night? It will be very cold."

Sleepily, Kelenoh nods. Kawari then walks to the corner of the room, opens up the chest, grasps the fleece, returns and spreads it over the bed. "Sleep well, Kelenoh. I will see you tomorrow."

Feeling very content, Kelenoh drinks her wine slowly. Done, she snuggles deep into her bed and falls asleep to the echoes of the distant gong, calling the priestesses to their nightly ritual bath in the holy pond.

The Temple of Karnak is vast. It is mostly surrounded by and contained within a continuous protective wall. In the interior of the complex are minor temples throughout and one can enter some of these minor temples from the open desert. This is the case for The Temple of the Listening Ear. It is small and ancient. One comes in from the outside, entering into an open square vestibule which has an obelisk on top of its roof. At the portico is the entrance to the u-shaped courtyard and its magnificent small garden. At the back wall is the main entrance to the actual temple.

Kelenoh enters the sacred grounds looking splendid. Her hair is orderly; it is pulled back and held in place by a ribbon around her forehead. The clean, white linen dress she is wearing falls elegantly around her slender body. She is tall for her age but not yet a woman. Through the portico, beyond the garden, the temple door is wide open, and sitting there is Yufaa, looking straight at her. She walks toward him, all the while observing the new surroundings.

He looks her over and receives an image of what she will look like in ten years. Satisfied, he smiles. Kelenoh, not aware of what Yufaa is thinking, tenses up, but continues walking forward full of expectations, knowing that she will be learning something new today. As she walks in through the door, he motions her to sit in front of him. She does so and calmly awaits instruction.

"We are now sitting in the middle part of the upper most area of the U, the open rooms to the left and right sides will amplify what you hear. You are presently sitting on a round, raised platform. It is imperative that you remain here and not go and sit elsewhere, otherwise there will be a disharmony. You have already mastered the technique of meditation, now it is time you learn how to listen to your own self. As you receive the answers, know it is the Listening Ear redirecting your thoughts back to you. Listen to it!"

Kelenoh focuses attentively. Never had she heard such a long sentence come from his lips before. Although she doesn't really understand what he means, she knows that what he is telling her must be important.

"I will leave you alone. Know that when I close the temple, it will be dark. Don't be afraid of what you will hear and feel. Those are only your own thoughts. Be very aware of that." When Yufaa walks out and shuts the door, it is pitch dark and very silent.

Assimilating Yufaa's words, she positions herself in a meditation pose and closes her eyes. Immediately, she smells the scents of Samos wafting through her consciousness, promptly accompanied by an overwhelming feeling of homesickness churning in her stomach. Terrified, she instinctively opens her eyes, but all is black nothingness.

What was that? Oh yes, her own thoughts, returning to her through the Listening Ear. But then, what is she supposed to think about? As waves of uncertainty washed over her, that sense of homesickness grips her even more. Frightened, she promptly gets up and begins feeling her way toward the door. She wants out, but the door is locked shut. Unable to open the door, panic sets in. She bursts into tears and slumps down to the ground.

Kelenoh, with arms outstretched before her, attempts to walk back, her hands grasping in the darkness. Suddenly, her foot hits the round platform hard and she falls to the ground as the pain she feels comes over her in waves. Crawling up on the platform, she sits down on it, and is relieved in finding the middle again.

As that feeling of panic lessens, she hears within her thoughts, "Who am I?" Though knowing that thought to be good, she can't help but sense uncertainty closing in on her from everywhere.

Then she says out loud, "I am Kelenoh. Help me."

A voice replies, "You are Kelenoh, listen to yourself."

Realizing what was happening, she forces herself to become quiet. Remembering the meditation technique she learned, she repositions herself and begins to breathe slowly and deeply; in-breath/out-breath, in-breath/out-breath. Soon, the melodic tempo turns into the very air itself and she finds herself floating on her back, arms spread, gently being rocked back and forth, in and out to the rhythm of her own breathing. The sensation is so pleasant, she doesn't want it to stop.

Then her thoughts take over again. I am not supposed to be thoughtless within this temple, that won't teach me anything. All of a sudden, she finds herself back again on the hard platform and her foot is hurting.

She hears a soft laughter and thinks, oh, this is a good thought. But what is good and what is bad?

"Kelenoh, nothing you think or find is good or bad. Everything is good," she hears.

She readjusts back into her meditative posture in order to feel more certain. "So, everything I think and feel is good?"

"Your thoughts have great power, greater than you can ever imagine. So you must be careful about what you think and what you feel, for one thought is not the same as another. Everything you think and feel will return to you. When you have wicked thoughts, they will return to you wickedness. When you feel love, it will be love that returns to you. When you feel fear or anguish, fear and anguish will come upon you. It is you, yourself, who decides what you think and what or how you feel. You always have free choice in the matter. This is a given, not only for you, but for every human living on earth."

Kelenoh heaves out a deep sigh. The sigh returns to her as a tempest and she senses her body leaning sideward from the force of the wind. She bursts out in laughter and is filled with happiness. Then she thinks, "I want to be a child a little longer. I want to play, have fun and run as I have done until now. Why do I have all of these lessons and all of this responsibility?"

"Kelenoh, there will always be a child within you. Remember this when you have difficulties in the future. When those occasions arise, recall this happy, childlike feeling you are in now. In this life you are called to do great things, and there will be consequences. That is why you have these lessons in accountability."

Kelenoh thinks, "Where am I to be called?"

"You came to earth to help and heal people. That is why you have been brought to Karnak, to be educated and prepare you for your destiny."

The temple door opens wide, letting the light in. Instinctively, Kelenoh shields her eyes from the blinding light. She sees the tall contour of Yufaa's silhouette standing there, laughing at seeing her tangled hair. "Did you sigh? Come, I will take you to the courtyard." Kelenoh doesn't know what to say and so silently follows him.

She sits down on a low wall and is amazed at how low the red sun is in the horizon. Is it evening? Did she really spend the whole day in the temple? But how could it be, the time seemed so short?

"Here, have something to drink," Yufaa says.

Realizing how dry her throat is, she eagerly takes the cup, emptying it with just a few gulps. She looks at Yufaa. This time there is no annoyance in his eyes because of her haste in drinking, instead there is understanding.

Kelenoh closes her eyes. She feels empty and exhausted, yet so filled to overflowing that, for a moment, she doesn't know what to do with herself.

"I know you feel confused now. In the coming weeks you are not allowed to eat, only drink. Think about all you have heard and felt today. I will leave you alone this week. In case you have any questions, send Kawari to me, and I will try to answer them."

For a little while longer they sit together, silently enjoying the beautiful, full-orbed setting sun, until Kelenoh begins to shiver terribly from being tired and cold.

"Wonderful, I was waiting for this," Yufaa replies. "The feeling in your body is returning. I will take you home now."

Kawari is already waiting for her at the house and when they enter, the smell of lavender permeates the air. She sees the steam rising from the bowls prepared with the bathing water. Yufaa nods to Kawari and then leaves. Kelenoh, unable to speak and barely move about by herself, allows Kawari to undress and then to bathe her. Even Kawari is silent.

Kelenoh is grateful for Kawari's gentle care and feels a great fount of love radiating from her, which in turn produces a thankful, loving laugh from Kawari. Even though Kelenoh is still feeling foggy and still isn't able to think properly, she again hears the voice from the temple, "When you feel love, it will return to you."

This evening she doesn't get any date wine but only a cup of lukewarm water. As soon as she has finished, her body becomes limber, and Kawari helps her into bed. Upon touching the sheets, she immediately falls into a deep, dreamless sleep.

Chapter 2

Kelenoh wakes up to a still, dark silence, making her think she is back at the Temple of the Listening Ear. As the room starts to become illumined with daybreak, she sees her trusted objects all around and realizes she is actually lying in her own bed. She looks at the two chairs, then at the beautifully decorated chest in the corner, and then looks at the large dresser. On top of the dresser are a multitude of small boxes, some of which contain ground minerals for eye paint. There are also wooden hair combs, small alabaster bottles with body oils, ointments for her face, as well as her treasured bronze polished mirror with an ivory handle.

Inside the dresser are her linen dresses, and the pleated linen cape, which she is only allowed to wear during temple festivals. Making the pleats for the cape is a lot of work. First, the wet linen is placed over a wooden plank with slots in it. Then the cloth is evenly pressed down in between the slots, and left until the fabric is dry. In this way, the formed pleats become part of the actual structure of the fabric.

Kelenoh begins to smell a delightful scent and looks about the room. The walls are painted red-brown with beautiful lotus-flower motifs. Hanging on the walls are garlands of fragrant flowers. As she looks at them, she instantly recalls that yesterday they had been changed for fresh ones.

She feels different today, she is not the same as before. As she contemplates this new awareness, Kawari enters, all happy and smiling. She is carrying a bowl of water, ready to wash Kelenoh and then dress her.

Chatting in her usual way, Kawari talks about the gossip she recently heard in the kitchen. Every now and then, in between stories, Kawari glances at Kelenoh, but Kelenoh, with her head too full, can hardly pay any attention to anything Kawari is saying.

Kawari finishes and leaves. Kelenoh sits alone, drinking her cup of water. Her mind is still racing so she forces herself to become silent within. Having no idea what is happening, she decides she must speak to Yufaa about this. Maybe he knows what is going on. She calls Kawari and asks her to go and get Yufaa.

When Yufaa enters, she can't help but smile at seeing him standing there still totally wet, his loin cloth dripping with water from his cleansing ritual in the holy pond. Priests must wash themselves in the holy pond twice a day, and twice during the night. Karnak has two such ponds. The largest one is at the main temple in the middle square. It is walled in by rock walls, and each wall has two bays with stairs. The smaller pond is situated at the Precinct of Mut. Both ponds are fed by underground springs.

Kelenoh can see tiny hair stubble on Yufaa's head and feels a little bad for having summoned him. He hasn't even shaved yet. She knows that priests remove all the hair from their body in order to be clean, so that no lice or other vermin can nest there. She begins to understand why Yufaa has at times detested her wild locks of hair.

"What would you like to ask?" That is how she knows Yufaa; a man short on courtesy, without the use of superfluous words and straight to the point.

"I feel so strange, I don't know why that is."

Yufaa takes a seat in front of her, the chair creaking a bit under the weight of his large body. "I will explain. At the time of your first menstruation on Samos, you were brought to Karnak. After that first menstrual cycle, your body began to change, to grow up. Now, after what happened in the temple yesterday, you are beginning to mentally grow up." His large dark brown eyes looking lovingly at her as he speaks.

"That is also the reason that I am not giving you any difficult tasks this week. What you must do this week however, is not eat any food and speak as little as possible. This new feeling you are dealing with has to peacefully conquer a place in your head, in your heart, and all within yourself."

She nods. Even though she doesn't totally understand, she instinctively knows that what he says is true. Her head is so full she doesn't even know what else to ask.

"Just do your meditations. Direct your meditation toward the Voice of the Temple. Visit the Temple of Mut every day. At the back of the temple is the holy pond. It is in the shape of a U. Go to the pond and sit down in the center of the u-shape; in this way the surrounding arms of the pond embrace you. Meditate there."

Yufaa stands next to her in silence. It is as if he has something more to say, but has to think about it. "I told you that I would not give you a task to do this week, but because you are learning quickly, and internalizing what is most important, I will give you a task anyway. You are allowed to go outside the temple walls, on the condition that you take Kawari with you."

Kelenoh nearly jumps up from her seat, and for a moment is a child again, radiating with happiness as she looks at Yufaa with eyes full of wonder.

"There is a harbor with three inlets that belong to the temple complex of Karnak. The three inlets each have a straight and open connection into the Nile River. You are allowed to walk the causeway of the middle inlet all the way down to the river. Once there, sit down at the left-hand side on the bank of the Nile River. There, the water flowing in from the left, converges with the water coming in from the right, forming a u-shape. Sit inside of the u-shape. As at the pond of Mut, it will accelerate your process and bring you back into harmony."

"Don't just listen to the Voice of the Temple of the Listening Ear, but also listen to the sounds of the pond and of the surrounding area. When you go to the river, listen to the sound of the Nile and everything else you may hear there. Become one with the water and its surroundings."

Yufaa arises and looks at Kelenoh who sits silently in her chair with a bowed head. He feels a strong love for her. Kelenoh, sensing this, looks up to him and laughs meekly. It is not the full laugh that Yufaa is accustomed to hearing. He replies to her soft, uncertain little laugh with the encouraging words: "You are doing well."

Yufaa departs and goes to inform Kawari about her tasks regarding Kelenoh. Then he must go and shave.

Kelenoh sits in her chair pondering what she just heard. She is allowed outside the temple walls! Immediately, the urge for freedom begins to pull on her. But then, for a moment, she begins to doubt if she can perform what Yufaa has asked her to do.

Having a fervent longing to be alone in order to think about what happened yesterday in the Temple of the Listening Ear, and about what Yufaa just told her, Kelenoh decides to go to the Temple of Mut, to sit there and see what transpires. Now feeling more certain of herself, she rises from her chair and walks out of the house into the warm sunshine of daylight. Before long she arrives at the Lane of the Sphinxes, and shortly thereafter reaches the Temple of Mut.

The Precinct of Mut is a separate, walled section with a large pylon (gateway) for its entrance. She walks through, turns left and then turns right, continuing on toward the back end of the temple. Soon, she begins to see the u-shape of the holy pond. She stops for a moment and looks around. To the left is a somewhat smaller temple. It is the Temple of Chonsu Pa-Chered. Beside it is a small annex which is the treasure house of the Temple of Chonsu Pa-Chered. There are palm trees all about the grounds and the air itself is permeated with the smell of the water from the holy pond. While taking in the sight of it all, she deeply inhales the scented air. Delightful!

Kelenoh reaches the back of the Temple of Mut, turns right and sees where she can pleasantly sit by the pond. To the right in front of her, and on the opposite side of the pond, is the Temple of Ramses III. It looks rather neglected because of the peeling paint on the walls. Not many people visit this temple any more. Now there is only one priest left, and he is very old.

She sits down and nestles herself into the sand, then looks around to see if she has placed herself near the middle of the pond. She has. The sand is hot, but the palm tree behind her provides some shade and coolness. There are lotus plants floating on top of the pond. Nearby, a few ibises stand in the water, searching for food with their long narrow beaks. For the first time in two days, Kelenoh begins to feel a peace come over her.

She adjusts her sitting position into a meditative posture. Enjoying the moment, she inhales deeply. She looks around and listens to all the sounds around her. The rustling of the wind in the palm trees. The ripples in the water formed by the splash of the small waves lapping against the banks. The lotus flowers swaying back and forth to the rhythm of the small waves and the long thin beaks of the ibises moving through the water. Kelenoh takes all of it in.

She feels protected with the high wall of the temple behind her.

When she closes her eyes it is dark. All of a sudden, she is back in the Temple of the Listening Ear. "Your own responsibility," she hears. A momentary feeling of panic grips her. Can she deal with this responsibility? The tasks she has been called to perform are certainly huge. Instantly, she begins to feel herself becoming very small and that she is disappearing into the sand.

"You are doing well," she hears Yufaa's voice repeat in her head.

Now her body seems to be rising out of the sand. "I am still a child, how am I supposed to do all of this?" she says out loud.

The voice from the Temple says, "Don't be afraid! We will help you step by step."

Then there is silence. Yet she is keenly aware of the many sounds all about her. Enjoying these sounds, she lets them penetrate her being. They give her a feeling of belonging, and she has an inner knowing that she is exactly where she is supposed to be.

Slowly, she opens her eyes and is astonished to see how low the sun is in the sky. Again, she realizes that when she meditates, time either flies by or does not exist at all. Feeling chilly, she gets out of her meditative pose and stands up. She is immediately drawn to enter into the water. Kelenoh undresses, and naked she enters into the pond. It is pleasantly warm and the chill in her body disappears as she lets herself be gently rocked back and forth by the water, just like the lotus flowers. Suddenly and unexpectedly, she bursts out with an exuberant laugh, which reverberates out to the high wall, then echoes back. This only makes her laugh all the more.

The old priest of the Temple of Ramses III hurries out to look. He is most surprised to see a naked girl lying in the water laughing out loud. Reverently, he brings his hands together in front of his chest, bows his head, greeting her with a blessing. A smile appears on his wrinkled face.

Frightened, Kelenoh suddenly becomes very aware of her
body and dives back into the water. She realizes on that instant
that she is no longer a child but is becoming a woman. Only Kawari
has seen her naked up to this point here in Karnak. When she
pokes her head out of the water and looks around, the old priest
is gone. She gets out of the water, finds her clothes and quickly
dresses. Feeling more secure now that she is not naked, Kelenoh
begins to relax. She leaves the sacred pond and area of the temple
and slowly walks back home.

The following morning Kelenoh wakes up full of anticipation.
Today she will go to the Nile River. Kawari comes in and is elated
to find out that she too will be going to the Nile. Kawari leaves
quickly, making her way to the kitchen. Soon she is back carrying
a large bag with small stone bottles of water and other things for
the day. She notices that things have changed and that she has to
get used to this new Kelenoh, who has become so serious and who
doesn't want to run anymore.

They walk together between the houses to the large pylon at
the front of Karnak. When they pass through the gateway, in the
distance they can see large boats moored at the harbor of Karnak.
They continue walking on through the small lane of sphinxes
leading to the river. Upon arrival at the banks of the Nile, they wait
a moment as Kelenoh looks around. Her whole body starts tingling
and all her senses become flooded with a pure joy.

Far away to her left, on the other side of the river, in the middle
of a farmer's field, she sees two large, 20-meter statues standing
across from the Temple of Luxor. They are statues of Pharaoh
Amenhotep III, called the Colossi of Memnon. Yufaa has told her
that when the Nile floods, the statues seem to be floating on the
water. She is so happy to see them for herself.

Behind the statues, the mountains can be seen where the
Valley of the Kings is located and where many Egyptian pharaohs
are buried. The deserted village Deir el-Bahari, where the masons
who built the tombs of the pharaohs used to live, is also located in
the same valley. She really would like to go visit this valley one day
to see all those magnificent tombs.

She looks to her right past the harbor of Karnak, and there, though not visible, past that part of the desert, is the city of Thebes. Kelenoh looks all around absorbing the whole environment. She takes a deep breath and ponders how beautiful it is here. The sun is hot.

While Kelenoh is absorbed in her surroundings, Kawari is erecting a small shelter made from a woven palm-leaf mat with two poles in the front. She thrusts the poles into the sand, then begins loading the back end of the sloped mat with sand so that the shelter doesn't blow away.

Kelenoh looks at Kawari's shelter and admires that she placed it in the exact location Yufaa told her she should sit at. It is an open area with a papyrus bush at the water's edge. She sits down under the small shelter and looks out at the water lapping against the river shore. After a little while, she begins to feel as if she is rocking back and forth, back and forth.

She is amazed by all the various sounds she hears all around her—the cormorants, the pintail ducks, the pelicans, and many more birds she doesn't recognize, along with a choir of frogs—sounds that had probably been there all along, but she had shut out without even realizing it.

Now, it is as though an orchestra, an avalanche of loudness, comes down over her. The resounding vibrations make her shake all over. Feeling the need to shelter herself from it all, Kelenoh covers her ears with her hands. Then, through the clatter, she hears a voice, "Listen!"

She forces her body to become quiet, and listens. Now the noise changes into a melodic, soothing symphony and she realizes that behind the cacophony of sounds, there is a harmony she has never heard before. Then the sound becomes one with her surroundings.

Kelenoh opens her eyes and sees Kawari standing there with a cup of water, looking somewhat dismayed. She had been looking forward to a nice day trip, but instead has been utterly bored, waiting for Kelenoh to open her eyes.

Kelenoh, at seeing Kawari's face, laughs. Kawari reacts by smiling broadly and then immediately starts chattering away about the splendid boats and the men who had waved at her, how she had waved back, and about the fishermen in smaller boats passing by. Kelenoh listens silently, then she slowly gets up and says, "We are going home."

Kawari, disappointed, and without saying a word, begins packing up their things, and then the last thing that she does is break down the small shelter. Kelenoh, sensing what Kawari is thinking, would like hug her, but can't seem to get herself to do so. Something did happen to her today. Yet, she still hasn't been able to grasp why she is not her usual, spontaneous self.

They walk back in silence. Kelenoh filled with what she has seen, heard and felt. Kawari walks behind, sulking with disappointment.

When they arrive back home, Yufaa is standing in her little house. They look at each other. Yufaa nods and says, "Good." Then he leaves and returns to the temple to do his work.

In the days following, Kelenoh alternates between going to the pond, and going to the Nile. It is on the last day of her week of silence, while she is meditating at the Nile, when it happens. She feels herself become one with her surroundings, as if disappearing within them. She is the water. She is the sand. She is the papyrus plant. She is a bird. She is everything! As she is fully enjoying just being, a deep, overpowering love floods over and within her. She opens her eyes and begins to laugh out loud with abandon.

Kawari is startled awake from her nap. She looks wide-eyed at Kelenoh standing there, who leans down and hugs her. Kelenoh takes Kawari by the hands, lifting her up. She grabs her by the hips and starts dancing. Kawari is in a near stupor. First of all, Kelenoh hadn't spoken to her for a whole week, and now all of a sudden she is laughing, dancing and being the cheerful Kelenoh she has always known!

With the reverie over, they begin to pack their things together. Kawari, a little troubled, thinks, 'All week long she leaves me alone, and now she is even helping me to pack!'

Laughing loudly Kelenoh says, "Kawari, I love you!" Kawari, not understanding a thing, quietly shrugs her shoulders.

Kelenoh starts running. Kawari tries to keep up but is burdened under the weight of all she is carrying. Suddenly, Kelenoh stops. Kawari bumps into her and immediately falls backward to the ground. Laughing at such a sight, Kelenoh falls down beside her and soon their laughter is resounding through the desert. They both stand up, hug each other, wipe the sand off of their clothes, then arm in arm, busily chat all the way back home.

Kelenoh sees Yufaa approaching from far away, his stately gait still astonishes her. He is always himself and is always in control. Yet, as he gets closer, she sees something in his face she hasn't seen before. He is agitated and his body is tense. When they are standing across from each other, he looks deep into her eyes and after a little while nods. He strokes her cheek with his right hand, leaving it there but for a moment. She catches the scent of holy oils; it smells like cedar and myrrh. As the high priest, Yufaa is the only one allowed to enter the Holy of Holies. The only other person who can enter besides himself is the pharaoh.

Every morning he opens the sealed doors of the altar, greets the godly statue and brings offerings of perfume, incense and flowers. With the little finger of his left hand, he anoints the forehead of the godhead with the holy oils. Then he puts makeup on its face and then undresses the statue. Next, he dresses the god again with clean ceremonial clothing, leaves food, and a large new bouquet of flowers, whose very fragrance is a reminder of the godhead's majesty. When Yufaa leaves the sanctuary, a priest of the temple sweeps the floor so that no trace of their presence is left behind, after which Yufaa again seals the doors.

All this goes through her mind as she catches the scent coming from his hand. She also has the realization, that this is the very first time Yufaa has ever touched her. Tears of emotion well up in her eyes and when she looks at him, she sees, he is also emotional. By his touch, Kelenoh suddenly understands that she too is one of them. A feeling of pride and joy fills her and they look at each other in silence.

Yufaa then says, "You are ready for your next task. This one will be difficult for you. You have to isolate yourself for one year. During that time, you are not allowed to see or to talk to anyone except the gods."

Kawari, who is standing behind Kelenoh, lets out a scream. She had totally forgotten about Kawari. Quietly, she looks at Yufaa and says, "Good, take me there." Just as with her previous tasks, Kelenoh is wholly obedient and without even thinking about it, does what Yufaa asks of her.

When they reach the first of the large pylons of the long passageway, Kawari begins to cry. Kelenoh tries to comfort her,

"You may live in my house during that time. I will be back before you know it. Go now." Kawari turns around and walks away, weeping.

As they walk through, she sees that all the openings of the pylons line up until the last one in the far distance, ending at the Temple of Thutmose III. They continue under the second pylon, and then walk on until they come to the large portico. Kelenoh holds her breath in awe because she hasn't been here before.

The hall is grand. The pillars are made in the form of a papyrus plant. They look like splendid, stylized, giant stone papyrus bushes. She feels very small as they walk through the hall. Yufaa continues walking beside her in silence. They reach the third pylon. Behind this pylon, she sees four large obelisks with the titles of their pharaohs and their dedication to the gods on them. The pointed tops of the obelisks represent the ground on which the Sun God was standing when creating the universe.

When they go through the fourth pylon, she sees two more large obelisks. After the fifth pylon, they arrive at a square, a dark space. Kelenoh blinks her eyes for a moment while adjusting to the dimness. She sees an opening on the other side of the hall that leads to a courtyard built by the pharaohs of the 11th Dynasty. The buildings around the courtyard are looking old and dilapidated. They cross the courtyard reaching the large memorial Temple of Thutmose III.

Kelenoh halts. She hesitates, unsure whether or not she wants to enter. Yufaa gives her a little time. He stands before the temple's entrance, waiting quietly. Kelenoh takes a deep breath and walks toward him. "Good," she says, "I am ready."

Yufaa takes her inside. It is dark. Mounted on the walls are burning torches as well as a few fire bowls. She smells a delicious aroma of incense. When her eyes become accustomed to the dark, she sees the splendid painted walls with beautiful flowers and birds on them, and the green papyrus plants with ibises in between the stylized lotus flowers. The colors of white and blue stand out from the red-brown background. The ceiling of the temple is supported by two rows of slender, straight pillars covered with gold leaf. The ceiling itself is blue and painted with glistening stars. The beauty of it takes her breath away.

When her eyes are totally adjusted to the dark, she sees that the colors are flaking off, that the temples of Karnak are not being well cared for. Kelenoh's pondering is interrupted by two priestesses, putting bowls of steaming water on the floor in front of her. Kelenoh is then bathed and dressed in a clean new linen garb.

When she is ready, Yufaa enters with food. Since she hasn't eaten for a whole week, the smells hurt her stomach. In front of her, he places a delicious bowl of warm vegetables with onions, leeks and lentils, along with other bowls of melon, squash, cucumber, dates and figs. He has also brought her a bowl with fresh bread. She notices that the bread is not the usual heavy barley bread, but the fine bread made of spelt. The bread is sweetened with dates and honey. For the first time in a while she also gets a cup of delicious, warm date wine.

"Eat and drink," Yufaa says, as he sits down across from her. Slowly, she eats her food. When she is finished, Yufaa calls for a priestess to come and remove the bowls. Yufaa sits cross-legged, waiting quietly as Kelenoh washes her hands and face, then maneuvers to sit herself across from him, also cross-legged. Still and silent, she waits somewhat anxiously for what Yufaa has to tell her.

"What you experienced at the Nile today is one way to find new strength when you are exhausted. Becoming one with nature and your surroundings gives you a lot of energy. You will need this practice in the future, so be sure to remember it. Soon, I will bring you to the room where you will stay for one year. While you are in there, examine yourself. Get to know your strong and weak sides. Learn to accept and love yourself. Only then can you give yourself to someone else totally in the fullness of love. Self-knowledge is another way to acquire more energy. Be aware of that."

Yufaa is quiet for a minute so she can absorb what he has just told her. Kelenoh heard everything he said, but because of the food, and because she has been outside the whole day, she has become a little sleepy. Feeling like she is going to fall asleep at any moment, she forces herself to stay awake.

Yufaa sees this and says, "Come, we will first do something else." He leads her to a table on which sounding bowls are positioned. "Lie down."

Thankfully, Kelenoh lies down and closes her eyes. Yufaa starts striking the bowls. Low tones, alternated by high tones. The sounds of the singing bowls penetrate her deeply, making her body vibrate on the inside. This harmony of sounds makes her relax completely and soon she falls into a deep sleep.

When she wakes up, the torches and fire bowls are almost extinguished. Yufaa takes a torch from the wall. He holds it close to his face, the fire lighting up the white of his eyes. "Come," he says, taking her by the hand.

She gets up and he leads her toward a descending stairway. With her hand in his, Yufaa leads her down the narrow stairs. They arrive in the vaults of the temple. With his torch, Yufaa lights the torches that are hanging against the walls.

Kelenoh sees a long, narrow hallway that branches out in several directions. It looks like a labyrinth. It doesn't take long before she loses her sense of direction. However, she sees Yufaa knows exactly where they are going.

He stops at an opening and takes her inside. He lights the torches that hang against the walls in the holders, and also lights the fire bowl. It is a square room without any color. It has only a bed, a table and a chair. Other than that, the room is empty. In a corner of the ceiling is a hole. She goes over to it, looks up, and sees an unclear little bit of sky.

"That is an air shaft. It provides the room with fresh air from outside." She hears Yufaa say this, but his voice sounds different, hollow and with an echo. Fear floods over Kelenoh and she gasps for air. Yufaa walks to her and takes her hand in his.

"Come, sit down." He leads her to the bed. Shaking, Kelenoh sits down. Does she really have to stay here for one year, in this silence?

Yufaa feels her fright and says, "Look at me." He takes both her hands in his and feels how they tremble and are cold. Kelenoh looks at him with wide, open eyes, then begins to feel his calm energy flowing through her. She begins to breath slower. Yufaa sits on his knees in front of her. They look at each other in silence for a while. Then Yufaa starts talking.

"Be not afraid, Kelenoh. The gods will protect you. Your future is already established in time. Nothing will happen to you. You are here to get to know yourself. Use this time to learn to handle yourself. This room is in the core of the vaults under the temple. The room is open and is connected to everything around you. This spot will help you. It will help you to reach the core of your true Being. It is not unlike the Temple of the Listening Ear where all thoughts return to you from left and right. This room and the spaces around you are meant to deepen your thoughts and feelings. Even as in the Temple of the Listening Ear where you had to sit in the middle, it is important that you stay in this room, otherwise you will disturb the harmony."

"Every day there will be food, drink, and fire brought in. You will not see the people who bring it. They will place it in front of the opening. You are not allowed to talk to them. There will also be a period of fasting. At that time they will only bring water. You will have to spend your fasting time in the dark. So there will not be any fire. You will know when the time of fasting starts and I tell you now, that when that time comes, you will know and understand you need it."

Kelenoh is listening to his words but doesn't know what to say. Her head is full of thoughts and questions, so much so, that she can only remain silent. Yufaa's firm hold on her hands has helped her to calm down again, and the cold she had felt has disappeared.

Yufaa encouragingly gives both her hands a little squeeze and continues, "Kelenoh, every person is a dual person. You have to resolve that duality within yourself. Your male and your female side; your strong and weak sides, must be united. Make sure to find that union."

Yufaa lets go of her right hand and places his left hand on her forehead, blessing her.

"I impart to you strength, insight and wisdom. It is already in you. Now just let it out."

A wave of warmth and of love streams through Kelenoh's body. Her eyes tear up, and she sees that Yufaa is also crying, but silently. Without any sound, he slowly rises, turns around and leaves.

She is alone!

Chapter 3

The silence which enfolds her is as thick as a blanket. She sits down in a meditative posture on the bed and with her thoughts tries to create her own space so that within, she can breathe freely and move around unrestricted.

She is disoriented by the sudden change. This morning she was sitting at the Nile River with Kawari, and now she is realizing how much she misses her. Kelenoh looks around the small room and with a vehement hand gesture, wipes the tears off her face. The small space and the silence give her the feeling that she is choking, and in her mind, she desperately tries to make the room larger, but to no avail.

She gets up, frightened, places her right hand against the wall and walks the perimeter of the room by sliding herself along the wall. Afterwards, she notices that she doesn't have the courage to move away from the wall to walk toward the middle of the room and go sit at the table. Fearful, she keeps her back against the wall. It is as if she is glued to the very wall itself.

She is alone!

The word 'alone' sticks in her mind. Then she realizes that the word alone actually stands for "all-one." What is she doing here again? She is indeed "all-one." With her back against the wall she shuffles to the exit and wants to leave.

She wants to call Yufaa and tell him that he should come back and get her. She wants out! She doesn't have to stay here for a whole year! Her throat is so tight from fear that no sound comes out, and tears of desperation flow down her face. She is standing by the room's entrance, trembling, and for the first time smells the musty odor hanging in the air.

The light is behind her, so as she looks ahead, it is just a black hole of nothing but darkness. She can't get out and doesn't even know the way if she could get out. Overtaken by a feeling of panic, falls to her knees, covers her face with her hands and starts sobbing. The sounds of her crying are returning from all sides as a loud echo. This frightens her so much, that she lifts up her head, stops crying and sits quietly by the opening. The sound then begins to weaken until a deep silence surrounds her.

Kelenoh gets up and shuffles alongside the wall back to the bed and sits down. She contemplates the words Yufaa told her about finding the core of her being and to unite the duality within herself. She asks out loud, "Who am I?" She lies down on the bed and falls asleep with this question on her mind. She dreams about the Temple of Hera on Samos and hears a voice saying, "Start at the beginning."

Upon waking, her fearfulness has disappeared. She quietly looks around the room and realizes that the space is what it is, no bigger, no smaller. She gets up from the bed and walks to the air shaft and looks up. It is dark outside. Dark? But her feelings are telling her that it is day now. Is her sense of time messed up, or is it that within these vaults there is a different notion of time?

Suddenly she notices several objects in the opening. There is a basin with water to wash herself, a high bowl with a lid to relieve herself, dishes with food, a small stone bottle with water, a bowl with fire, new torches and a clean linen dress. For the first time in her life she has to wash and dress herself.

She undresses, folds her dirty dress neatly and lays it in the opening. Then proceeds to clumsily wash herself with the warm water. There is no perfume in it, just plain water, though she does smell a hint of lotus flowers and knows it is water from the holy pond. When she is dressed, feeling clean and fresh, she gets a sense of pride from having done the task herself.

She starts walking toward the opening and steps in a puddle of water. She looks at the floor and sees little pools of water everywhere. How did Kawari do this? And before that, how did her dresser in the Temple of Hera do this? She goes and takes her dirty dress from the opening, returns and begins to wipe the floor dry with it.

Even though she is not hungry, she puts the dishes with the food on the table anyway. "Start at the beginning," she hears again.

"At the beginning? Do you mean at my birth?"

"If possible even before then, Kelenoh. It would be wonderful if you could recall that."

Kelenoh sits down on the floor and closes her eyes. She is now on an island, hearing the ocean. Which island? A woman is walking toward her. She is an older woman. Kelenoh sees on her head some grey hairs in between the black hairs. The woman looks sad. Who is she?

The woman walks to the harbor and looks out over the sea. She is waiting for someone, but whom? Kelenoh joins her gaze and sees a small boat approaching from afar. It is a small fishing vessel. When it gets closer, Kelenoh sees a man who sits straight up in the small boat. He sees the woman and a smile appears on his face. His face is wrinkled and his hair is grey. He comes ashore and embraces the woman. They stay like that for a little while and Kelenoh can feel a deep love between them. Why is the woman full of sorrow?

The man goes to the boat and takes out a small net which doesn't have many fish in it. Kelenoh sees the fish glistening in the sun. He takes the small net in his left hand, and wraps his right arm around the woman. They walk away together, all the while having a lively conversation.

He is tall and robust. She is slender and a little shorter. There is a pride and stateliness radiating from both of them. They walk up a mountain and Kelenoh sees a small village near the top. There is a small house at the edge of the village. The man and woman enter.

Kelenoh hears the sound of laughing children coming from the village. The woman comes out of her small house, stands there sadly listening to the children's voices. They themselves do not have any children. That is the sorrow of the woman. She re-enters the house.

Kelenoh doesn't know exactly what to make of it. Who are these people? What place or island is she looking at?

"Your future parents, and the name of the island is Karpathos," she hears.

Moved, she takes this information in for a moment. My parents? And where am I?

"Think and see."

Kelenoh becomes very tranquil, it is a tranquility that she hasn't ever felt before. She becomes smaller and smaller, and has the feeling that she is disappearing. It resembles what happened to her at the Nile, the sense of being merged with everything. Something starts to tremble. She is a cell, a minuscule small and vibrating cell.

Suddenly, there appear rays of light and energy. Two godlike Beings of Light radiate their light and energy into that small cell. So much energy in such a small cell. Kelenoh looks with astonishment at what is happening.

Suddenly it is dark and she hears a rustling and a pounding sound. She has been placed in the abdomen of her mother. It is nice and warm, and she feels safe and protected. She grows, and hears the voices of her parents. The heavy bass voice of her father and the laughter of her mother that roars throughout the small house.

"How are you born?"

Kelenoh feels how she glides easily through the birth canal. Happy shouts erupt; they enter her being as a thunderous avalanche. Then she feels many hands on her little body. They are women's hands that all want to touch her. Feeling fearful and unsafe, she starts crying. The transition of that moment was too quick and too great for her.

The women start singing and she is placed on the bare abdomen of her mother. This feels familiar. She smells the scent of her mother. After a short time of adjustment, the singing and the soft warm stomach causes her to quietly fall asleep. She is covered with a sheep's fleece.

"I was born on Rhodes," she says out loud, startled by her own voice returning as an echo.

She opens her eyes and doesn't know where she is. She now is back in her own grown body and it feels strange. Then she hears, "Kelenoh, you are safe with us."

Remembering again where she is, she gets up, goes and fetches a new fire bowl from the opening, then comes back and puts it in the room. She decides not to light the new torch because through the light shaft, she can see that it is dark outside. It is night.

She goes and lies down on the bed and tries to sleep. But, the gods are not done with her yet. They ask, "Why were you born on Rhodes?"

Kelenoh thinks and in her mind she answers, "Because the men of the island are often away fishing. It is the custom on Karpathos that pregnant women are brought to Rhodes to deliver there."

She is a baby again. Now she is feeling that she is being wrapped in cloths. Her mother is holding her and she can see her radiating face looking at her. Then she feels movement. The women and her mother are walking over a road that leads to the harbor. There is a boat ready to depart. It is a small boat with a small shelter under which her mother goes and sits down.

Kelenoh feels that she is falling asleep because of the soft rocking of the boat. When she wakes up, Kelenoh sees a tall man smiling at her. It is her father. He grabs her mother at her hips and starts singing and dancing all the while she is laying in the arms of her mother. Frightened, she starts crying. Her father picks her up and puts her against his shoulder. With a soft voice he sings to her. She feels a great love from this tall man.

Kelenoh feels herself growing. She is very happy in that small house with her parents. There is much love and lots of laughter and singing. Suddenly, she sees that her mother cries a lot, and doesn't understand it.

She is now three years old and is playing outside in the yard when a stranger approaches. He is not as tall as her father, but he is as wide. He is still young. His black curls frame a broad and open face.

She looks at him and sees a pair of clear brown eyes looking back at her. It is Pythagoras, the mathematician and philosopher of the island of Samos. She recognizes him, but she doesn't know why. Full of confidence and as a matter of course, she walks up to him, puts her small hand in his, and together they walk away, she without looking back.

Kelenoh looks at this scene and sees that her mother follows them. Her eyes are filled with tears. The sorrow of her mother touches Kelenoh deeply in her soul and she now understands why it was that her mother had cried so much. She had known that she was going to be picked up and taken away.

Kelenoh feels the tears rolling down her cheeks as she looks at the scene. A deep love fills her, and with her thoughts, she sends out this love out to the woman who bore her. She wipes the tears off her face and looks again at the vision.

In the harbor of Karpathos, Kelenoh sees a ship anchored there. It is a strange ship, one the likes of which she has never seen before. It has the head of a large bird at the bow; in the middle is a raised large square sail, and the back of the ship turns up in a curve forming a head of a snake.

She boards the ship with Pythagoras. She has no idea where they are going but is happy and runs across the deck in between all the men who are seated at the oars. Pythagoras catches her and says, "We are going to Samos, I will bring you to the Temple of Hera."

Kelenoh doesn't know what he is talking about, but it is all right, she feels safe. A little later she falls asleep in his arms. When she wakes up, she sees an island looming far in the distance. "We are almost there," Pythagoras says.

Kelenoh sees a multitude of people standing at the harbor, and as the ship moors, she hears music and singing. Walking on the seashore hand in hand with Pythagoras, she hears him say, "Here she is. Her name is Kelenoh."

"I still remember that," Kelenoh says out loud.

She is again frightened by the sound of her own voice which has such a strange and hollow echo.

"I remember all those people and their happy faces. They all wanted to touch me."

She shakes her head for a moment and realizes that she is in the vaults and that her large body is in her way, and that just as it was yesterday... was it yesterday? She has difficulty getting back to her present reality and is lost for time. The room is dark. The fire has gone out. She stands up and feeling her way along the walls, walks over to the air shaft. She looks up and sees that it is light outside.

At the opening of her living area, she sees a faint light of fire flickering there. She feels her way along the wall to there and sees that there is a fresh bowl with food, stone bottles with water, and new torches.

Eagerly, she takes the small stone water bottle and puts it to her lips thinking, it is good that Yufaa doesn't see how she hadn't taken the time to pour the water in a cup. As she is placing the fire bowl in the room, there arises a fragrance of lavender incense. Yufaa! Would he be feeling what she is experiencing? Kelenoh senses his protective love and for a short time feels less lonely. She lights the torches and attaches them to the wall. Hungry and grateful, she starts to eat her meal. Finished, she readies things, and then falls asleep.

🏛

Having no sense of day or night, Kelenoh fills her days with meditation, eating and sleeping. She experiences a sort of total timelessness. Sometimes the silence is so intense, that she will start to sing. Initially, she couldn't bear to hear the sound of her voice echoing back. Yet, she continued to sing and eventually, behind her voice, she could hear those harmonious tones, like when she was at the Nile and heard the cacophony of birds. Now it is as if she is surrounded by voices singing with her.

She begins to dance, dancing herself into a trance. This time the scent of herbs and flowers envelope her. She begins to feel the warmth of Samos. She is back on the island again.

The small girl walks among the people with pride and is laughing happily. She touches the people who reach out to her with their hands as she walks over the Procession Road with Pythagoras. It is the road that crosses the grounds of the Temple of Hera.

Suddenly, it is all becomes too much for her; all those people with all their personal smells and energies. She looks for Pythagoras' hand and tries to hide behind him. He picks her up as they walk on toward a large mansion. When they enter, Kelenoh sees a large hall, in the middle of the hall there is a fully laid out table and there are flowers everywhere she looks.

Pythagoras puts her down and talks to the people around him. Kelenoh looks wide-eyed at the women all dressed in white. Along three walls of the large hall, there are soldiers sitting at other tables. These are the soldiers who protect the temple complex.

She is hungry and runs to the large table in the middle of the hall, and then climbs up on a bench. All of a sudden, all around her laughter breaks out. Stiffened from fright, she sits stock-still on her knees. She looks to Pythagoras for help. He stops speaking mid-sentence and walks over to her, lovingly embracing her, says, "Don't be afraid, Kelenoh." He sits down beside her and says, "Let's eat first, I will address the people later."

Kelenoh doesn't hear what he says. She received a plate of food from the woman sitting beside her and hungrily begins to eat, which again causes a roar of laughter from the others. Kelenoh startles, looks around and sees that Pythagoras is now standing behind her. He sings a song of Victory before the meal. After he finishes singing, Kelenoh sees that everyone begins to eat. There is such a buzz in the large hall. She feels everyone around her is excited and happy.

After the meal, Pythagoras gets up and starts singing again and this time the women join in. Kelenoh feels the vibration of the song go right through her and she starts clapping her hands, then she gets up from the bench and starts dancing. Suddenly the dining hall becomes deathly quiet as everyone around is looking at her.

Then she is picked up by Pythagoras and held high in his arms. She feels the safety he provides. Pythagoras then begins to speak and because of his deep voice, Kelenoh falls asleep against his shoulder.

Kelenoh looks at this scene and tears well up in her eyes. Oh, how much she misses this man. At that time, she didn't hear any of the words he spoke, but now she listens to him.

Pythagoras tells all of the oracle, Pythia, whom predicted that a girl with black hair and blue eyes would come to the temple, and that he had found her on the island of Karpathos.

"This child," she hears, seeing Pythagoras place a hand on her head, "has the gift of vision. She can heal, and when she has completed her training, will have the power over life and death. She will also be able to influence the weather. When I am away, I want you to treat her as a normal child. Let her be a child. Let her play and enjoy life as much as possible. Let her adapt slowly to the rhythms and disciplines of the temple. I want her to live in a separate house, not together with all the priestesses, but with the three priestesses that I will elect now."

Kelenoh feels the tension in the hall. Pythagoras walks with her around the table. "Cassandra, Selene and Theano, you will live in the house with Kelenoh. Cassandra, you are eleven years old now, so you will be the leader. You are very capable, and when you have any questions or problems regarding anything, you can always depend on Hestia, who is currently the head of the temple."

Kelenoh looks around and sees the familiar face of Hestia at the head of the table. She sees Hestia nod in the direction of Cassandra.

"Selene and Theano, you are six and seven years old now. I charge you to help Kelenoh get accustomed and to be as sisters for her. That goes for you as well, Cassandra."

Kelenoh sees that for a brief moment, he rests his hand on the head of Theano. She is small for her age, slender with a small oval face, black curls and brown eyes. She looks up at Pythagoras radiating, it is as if her face lights up by her happiness.

"You, Theano, take care of her clothing and food. Make sure she gets everything she needs."

Selene has fair curls, a round face, and brown eyes. She sits beside Theano and despite the fact that she is younger, she is taller than Theano.

"Selene," Pythagoras says, laying his hand on her head as well, "you are destined to be the little sister of Kelenoh in all aspects. Listen to her, talk to her, play with her, and be there for her."

Kelenoh sees Selene look at her and stroke her back for a moment, she then nods in acceptance to Pythagoras.

Then, Pythagoras walks over to Cassandra who is sitting upright at the table. He puts his hand on her head and Cassandra, with a thinking frown on her forehead, looks at him earnestly. Upon seeing this, Kelenoh bursts out with laughter. Cassandra is built strong. She has brown eyes and her round face is framed with black curls. She is not tall for her age.

"You Cassandra, besides having a leadership role, also have the task of caring for the home and the well-being of Kelenoh. Make sure everything runs smoothly."

Kelenoh feels the tears running down along her cheeks, and then suddenly, she finds herself back again in the vaults. After seeing the young Cassandra, Theano and Selene, a deep home sickness for them and for Samos comes over her. Sobbing, she crawls to her bed and cries until she empties herself.

After she is somewhat recovered, she washes her face and thinks about the moment when she left Samos. She thinks of Cassandra with her sweet and soft face, now tall and slender with arms that always made her feel safe. Theano, still the shortest of the three, who always lovingly washed and cared for her. The sweet Selene, tall and strong, always laughing, the one whom she could always share her stories and problems with.

She sees them standing on the quay of the harbor of the temple complex, waving goodbye as she leaves Samos. A terrible loneliness suddenly descends upon her and she doesn't know what to do. She wants to get out of this room, to see people and the light of day. Wanting to leave the room, she runs toward the opening and bumps into something. As Kelenoh is falling backward on the ground with a bang, she hears a very loud, "No!" Carefully, she gets up. Hurt and in pain, she starts crying again, but softly this time. She lies down on the bed and falls asleep.

When Kelenoh wakes up, she feels that her hip is sore. Slowly she gets up, puts her hands up in the air, and thanks the gods who stopped her. She knows she has to get through this. After her prayer of thanks, she asks out loud, "May my pain disappear?"

A warmth streams through the painful area in her hip, and the discomfort disappears. After washing herself, which she can now do without wasting too much water, and putting on clean clothes, she feels a lot better.

Hungry, she starts to eat. After the meal, she clears up the room and puts everything by the opening. She goes and looks through the air shaft and sees that it is night. She deeply inhales the fresh outside air a few more times.

Sitting down on the floor in meditative posture, she is back on Samos. She sees herself sleeping in the arms of Pythagoras. He is standing at the entrance of the dining hall with Cassandra, Theano and Selene at his side. He pronounces, "I will now take her to the house where she will live. Take good care of her. I address all of you because this time, I will be away from Samos for a longer period."

When Pythagoras goes outside with her, the sun feels warm on her back. He turns left, away from the dining hall and walks the road that crosses the temple complex. In the distance, right beside the road, Kelenoh sees a long rectangular building with a flat roof and an opening facing the road.

They arrive there and Pythagoras enters into a small kitchen with a hole in the ceiling for the smoke. He passes through the kitchen. Behind the kitchen, there is a small room that contains a long table positioned against the wall. At the front of the table is a long bench and a chair pulled up at the side. He turns right. Through the opening, Kelenoh sees a large square room with two burning fire bowls set high on poles, both flanking either side of a big bed. On the opposite side of the bed, there is a dresser with a large polished bronze mirror. The walls are bare except for the brackets that hold the torches upright, but they are empty now.

Pythagoras puts her down on the bed and tells Selene to stay with Kelenoh. He leaves with Cassandra and Theano. He passes through the small room with the table, and then on to three smaller rooms. These are the rooms for Cassandra, Theano and Selene. In each room there is also a bed, a high fire bowl, and a dresser with a bronze mirror on top. There is incense in the fire bowls and the aroma smells wonderful throughout the house. Pythagoras again approaches Kelenoh, lays his hand on her head and blesses her. He then leaves. As Kelenoh watches him go, tears roll down her cheeks. Will she ever see him again? Aware of her crying, she is brought back into the vaults of the temple at Karnak.

Many years have already passed since she last saw Pythagoras and she is thankful to the gods that she was allowed to experience these moments again. It becomes clear to her that there was a great purpose and reason as to why she had been brought to the Temple of Hera on Samos. What is it that they expect of her? She has the power of vision, she can heal, and when she has completed her training here in Egypt, she will also have the power over life and death, and be able to influence the weather.

Is that really true? Will it be like that? Isn't it a true fact that all people are able to see the colors that she sees around others? Are not all people able to feel the emotions of others? Can they not also remove the pain of people with a single glance? Are other people not able to do this?

Slowly, it begins to dawn on her that, no, not all people are endowed with these abilities. Now she understands better why she was the one who received so much attention at the Temple of Hera which, until now, had seemed normal, but in truth, it was not at all obvious.

When Hestia told her that after her first menstruation she would be taken to Egypt to receive further training, she was torn by sadness. She didn't want to go, but Hestia told her that, yes, she had to go to Egypt because one day she was going to be the high priestess of the Temple of Hera.

Kelenoh begins to understand that there is more to her life than meets the eye and that it is not common for a person to see and feel what others experience. She arises and lights the fires. This is what Yufaa meant by understanding yourself. Was she at that time not allowed to hear all of this? Is that why, as a little girl she had fallen asleep as Pythagoras was telling the people of the Temple of Hera about who she was? It was as if the pieces of the puzzle began falling into place.

Sitting down at the table, she thinks back to her time at the temple of Samos. She sees it all now with totally different eyes.

Again, she begins to see herself running across the temple complex together with Theano and Selene. She remembers the joy of her existence, the feeling of happiness when she would stand still looking at the small flowers that were growing all around. She now understands why the color of a flower would become brighter when she touched it. Why people wanted to touch her all the time, and the happiness on their faces, that at first were often full of sorrow before they had touched her. Now she knows why it happened. She had taken all this for granted, thinking that everybody just liked her, and therefore wanted to be close to her.

All of a sudden she sees herself running, turn a corner and is suddenly standing eye to eye with a peacock. She hears the fearful scream that a peacock utters. Once again she can feel her own fright. The peacock spreads its feathers and utters a few more screams. Horrified by the sound, she puts her small hands over her ears. Theano and Selene come running to her rescue. Selene puts her arm around her and presses her against her own body as protection. Now she understands why she can't stand the screams of a peacock.

Theano and Selene take her home. Cassandra gives her a massage with lavender oil and she is able to totally relax again. Cassandra always did this when she had been frightened or afraid.

She sees herself growing up to the daily rhythm which had been established in her life. In the morning, when the sun rises, she, with the priestesses, would walk to an old small temple that has within it a statue of Hera. The statue is at first hidden when you enter the temple because it stands in its own separate space, in a dark recess.

She joins the priestesses as they sing together songs of victory for the new day. She then looks to Hestia, who is the only one allowed to touch the statue. As Hestia cleans the statue with a long brush, she is saying something but Kelenoh cannot hear it. Hestia continues cleaning the statue and Kelenoh smells the sweet fragrance coming from the brush. When Hestia lays down flowers by the statue, the singing of the priestesses stops.

After that, they all go to the dining room and eat breakfast. There is a lot of laughter at the temple complex and Kelenoh remembers the cozy chatter. After breakfast the priestesses form groups and each group has their own task. One goes to the vegetable gardens. Another takes care of the flower gardens. Some go back to the temple to tend to it and to receive people that come from the islands to ask for help with the problems they are having.

A few of the priestesses go to the small Temples of Apollo, Artemis, Aphrodite, and Hermes, where they perform the same tasks as do the priestesses of the Temple of Hera. The soldiers, who protect the priestesses, are the ones that do the heavy work around the temple complex. They maintain the Sacred Road, the straight Procession Road, all the buildings, take care of the olive groves, and the lygos trees at the River Imbrasos. It is a small river that flows along the temple complex. Kelenoh runs from one group to another trying to help wherever she can. The atmosphere is peaceful and cheerful and there is lots of singing while they work. Every evening at sunset, the priestesses go to the beach to dance and sing.

She then sees the grand Festival of Hera in which everyone on the island participates. All the people walk the Procession Road to the Temple of Hera, turn left and then walk along the Sacred Road to the beach. Six soldiers, carrying the statue of Hera, walk at the front of the procession. Then follows Hestia with a lygos branch in her hand. Cassandra walks beside Kelenoh, and both walk behind Hestia. Theano and Selene follow behind them. Subsequently come the priestesses in rows of two, and then the men, women and children of the island. All the women are carrying something with their arms, baskets with vegetables, flowers and grains.

A part of the offerings are burned on the altar, and the remaining gifts are offered to the sea. Songs of Gratitude are then sung for the abundance of food. The lygos trees at the complex are holy. It was under these trees on the banks of the River Imbrasos, where the Goddess Hera had been born. It is also here, where she met her husband Zeus and had intercourse with him for the first time.

The memories that Kelenoh revisited and felt, brought a smile to her face. She is once again back in her own body. Looking at herself, she sees that the small body has disappeared. Gratitude wells up within, knowing that she has reached a turning point and that now she can move on into the present.

She is very hungry; it is as if she hasn't eaten in days. She gets up and quickly walks to the opening, grabs a plate with food and hungrily devours her meal.

Chapter 4

Why is she running like that? This question keeps popping up in her head. Was she in a hurry, or was it just for fun? Did she just not want to waste any time in life? Even here in Karnak she ran at every opportunity. Kelenoh ponders the question. She receives an answer from the gods.

"Life is precious. You enjoy it intensely, and you make the most of every moment, getting out of it all you can. In experiencing the joy of life so often, you feel the urge to jump, dance and run. These urges happen on their own, naturally. It is in your blood."

"Time, as you experience it on earth, does not exist in our realms. What is important is what each person puts into the time they have been given. You determine how you feel. Nobody else can do that for you. You, Kelenoh, have made the choice to be happy and to enjoy life."

Kelenoh thinks about the answer for a moment and says out loud, "It is an easy choice for me. I am well looked after. I have no care in the world. I have enough to eat and drink. How is it for people who have worries, or an illness, or no food?"

"This principle applies to all people, rich or poor, those who are ill or in good health. Everyone has free will; it is the ability to choose how one feels. Everyone is placed, or born, where it is good for his or her own development. The setbacks that people experience, however bad they may be, are not of importance. What is important is how the individual will deal with it! This is a lesson each one has to learn. The choice is always within the individual."

"So when your child is ill, or your house burns down," says Kelenoh, "or you are hungry, or someone you love is murdered, you can choose not to feel sorrow or hate?"

"Emotions, Kelenoh, like hate, sorrow, and fear, are a part of life. It is okay to experience these emotions and then let them go. That makes you grow. It is your choice as to what you will do with these emotions. When you keep entertaining them and are unable to let them go, you will continue to hate, stay sad, or fearful. By doing this, you take away the space to grow, to learn to forgive, to be happy, to feel love, and to trust people."

Kelenoh stands up, raises her arms, and allows a feeling of gratitude to flow through her. Yufaa is right, every human being is a dual being. There are contradictions in the emotions one can feel, such as hatred and love, fear and trust, sorrow and happiness. You can feel all of them, but it is up to each one as to which feeling to choose.

For Kelenoh it is now clear how this works. She raises her arms and starts to sing and dance. Now she can laugh at the hollow sound her echo produces and instead concentrate on what is behind the echo. She does this until the harmony within herself and with her surroundings is present. She remembers what she has heard in the Temple of the Listening Ear about the power of thought. It confirms all she has heard just now. She has the choice, the free will, the ability to decide how and what to think, as well as the choice on how to deal with her emotions and all the feelings that accompany them.

The Temple of the Listening Ear had made her aware that it is she who determines all her thoughts. Here in the vaults this Truth is reinforced, and it is clear to her that she herself determines how and what to think and feel, and that every person on earth does the same for himself or herself.

She also now clearly understands that you are allowed to experience your emotions in order to grow, that this is a necessary part of the process. When you don't experience the emotion, you won't be able to recognize it and to let go of that emotion building up at the time, let alone recognize the feeling that is connected to it.

Kelenoh sits down at the table and, with a sigh of deep relief, smiles because of this insight and because of the feeling of happiness that is streaming through her.

Since the first day that she set foot in this space, she realizes the arrogance she had held in thinking that Yufaa was wrong, that she wouldn't need a whole year in the vaults. She had felt so alone. And in order to deal with the feeling of loneliness, she imagined that the word alone really meant: all-one. That the word all-one was full of everything within and outside of herself.

After a while, she began to realize that she didn't feel alone or afraid any more. The gods were with her at all times. She is not alone! The fact is that she is not only all-one within herself, but she is all-one with the cosmos. Inspired by her new understanding, Kelenoh gets a cup of water and prepares herself for a deep and restful sleep.

After her initial insights, times passes on and nothing more or new occurs. Kelenoh meditates, eats, and feels in harmony with herself. She dances and sings in the place where she has been taken to stay for a year of complete aloneness.

Sometimes, when she walks to the air shaft to take in a few deep breaths of fresh outside air, the question arises, how long have I been here? Her notion of time has totally disappeared. Has it been a few weeks? A few months? One day? She doesn't really know. She lets go. Day has become night and night has become day as she experiences her life confined to the small dimly lit room, where she remains alone with her own thoughts and feelings.

Kelenoh sits down to do her daily meditation. Suddenly, she sees a small girl running along a sandy path. In the distance, she sees a wooden bridge with white painted railings and a large forest beyond it. The girl is bare foot. Kelenoh sees something familiar in her, but she doesn't know who she is. The environment is unknown to her. Wondering, she looks more closely at the little girl and sees her fall down on her knees and fold her tiny hands. Then the vision disappears.

Kelenoh opens her eyes and asks the gods, "What did you show me? I don't know who this little girl is."

"Kelenoh, we have shown you something from your future. You will be that little girl. You are living in another country, far from here. The reason we showed you this is to help you understand that time doesn't exist for us, and in truth it doesn't for you either. All the lines of your many lives run parallel to each other. Therefore we have total insight into your Being. You have, as you know, had many lives already. There will be many more before you will be able to join us forever. At the time of your last life, your soul will have had all the experience it needs and desires, and then you will be one of us."

"The little girl you just saw will be one of your last lives. For now you are Kelenoh, and the task that you have volunteered for is difficult. Direct all your attention and love toward this life. Get to know and love yourself. This is the only thing you have to do. What has been, and what will come is nothing to be concerned with. We will take care of the larger and unseen whole of your journey."

Having listened to the gods, Kelenoh remains in a meditative pose, sitting quietly on her bed for a long time. The grandeur of those words is enormous. She realizes that this is not only true for her, but for everything alive on earth. She notices herself becoming smaller and smaller. What does she stand for? Who is she that she is allowed to hear this from the gods?

"Kelenoh, don't belittle yourself. Everything that is alive on earth is of equal value to us. We deem nothing or no one on the earth to be more or less than the other. We have showed you this so you might know how this works by and for us."

"Man, woman," she hears all at once. Then she remembers what Yufaa had told her about the male and female side in herself, and how they must become united.

His voice suddenly speaks, "When only the male energy in yourself dominates, you will get out of balance. The same is true when only the female side dominates. Try to unite these energies. Find a balance between them in order to produce a well-balanced energy flowing through you."

Kelenoh looks at herself, spreads her arms, tilts her head back a little, and says out loud, "Be one!"

The room is dark as she walks to the opening to get new fire and food. She feels cold, but isn't hungry at the moment. With her hands she feels about the floor and stumbles upon a small stone bottle of water and clean clothes. She takes them inside and places the clothes on the table. She takes the bottle of water and pours the water in a cup while putting her finger on the inside rim of the bottle, so as to not pour out too much water at once.

The time of fasting has arrived. She had forgotten, but now remembers what Yufaa said about it. He said that she would know when her fasting was about to begin, and that she would have a need for it at that time. He is right. The only need she has for now is to just be.

She lies down on the bed and before falling asleep thinks about all she has heard, seen and felt. When she wakes up, the silence around her is almost audible. She feels peaceful and calm. Now and then a flash of joy moves through her.

It is not easy to wash herself in the dark, but she takes all the time she needs. When clean, while examining her own thoughts, she puts on fresh clothing and drinks some water. Are her thoughts good for her? Is she good for herself? Suddenly a power streams into her, so forceful that she almost falls over. Then a large, white light fills her body. The white light is so blinding and intense, that she must close her eyes. It lights up the whole room. Through her eyelids she can see the white light in the room gradually diminish, and from her body all colors of the rainbow radiate out.

She opens her eyes and with grateful wonderment beholds all the beautiful colors. She trembles as she stands up because of this powerful force within her. Kelenoh looks at the colors moving around her as ribbons. The colors then start whirling around with increasing speed until they are no longer discernible as separate colors. The force is so intense she is knocked down to the floor and passes out.

When she regains consciousness, it is dark in the room. She gets up and feels her way to the air shaft, takes in a deep breath of outside air and notices that it is light outside. Her sense of time is completely gone and she has no idea how long she has been there. Her head and body feel light, accompanied by a sense that she is floating.

She takes a cup of water and makes herself erect, then positions her feet firmly on the ground and a little bit apart. She closes her eyes and focuses on the earth. Slowly, her body becomes heavier again. It feels as if her body has grown. When she opens her eyes, she looks straight into the eyes of Yufaa with a burning torch standing there in the opening.

Quietly they look at each other. Yufaa speaks, "Kelenoh, I came to get you. Your time here is over."

As she walks toward him, Yufaa attaches the torch to a bracket on the wall. He puts his hands together in front of his chest, and makes a light bow toward her. It was akin to the same kind of bow that the old priest made to her at the Temple of Mut when she had been swimming in the pond.

Standing in front of Yufaa she notices that she is grown taller, because now there is no need for her to tilt her head backward in order to look him in the eye. Yufaa takes the torch from the bracket, and in silence, with the torchlight illuminating the way, leads her through the long, narrow hallways. Kelenoh realizes that she has to get used to walking again. They continue on, the echo of their footsteps gradually lessening. When they reach the stairway, Yufaa pauses. He raises the torch and asks, "Are you ready?" She nods and follows Yufaa up the stairs.

They arrive in the large hall of the temple dedicated to the memory of Thutmose III. Because of its vastness, Kelenoh becomes dizzy for a moment, stops to rest and begins to breathe deeply. Yufaa waits until she recovers. Upon seeing that color has returned to her cheeks, he says, "Come."

They walk through to the other end of the large hall and arrive at the courtyard. For the first time in one year, Kelenoh sees the open sky and feels the wind. It is evening. She feels Yufaa's love because he had chosen this time of day so that she wouldn't have to face full sunlight.

Kelenoh spreads her arms, inhaling in the outside air. She throws her hair back letting the wind play with it. Off in the distance she can hear the priestesses singing, and also the melody of sistrums and of bells. These sounds make her shiver. It is as if both the singing and the music are inside and beside her all at the same time.

Yufaa approaches, then stands beside her and says, "I know that the sounds penetrate hard and deep. Listen to the singing and the music. Give it the space it deserves." Kelenoh closes her eyes and slowly the sounds fade into the background.

They walk through the vestibule, then under the pylons, finally arriving at the large hall with the pillars. Kelenoh feels dizzy again from seeing the giant bunch of stone papyrus plants, and the immense height of the hall itself. She leans her body against a stone pillar, preparing herself before continuing, because she knows that there are two more pylons to go under before they will be outside. She starts walking slower, pacing herself. Yufaa looks back at her, imparting an encouraging smile. When they pass through the last pylon, Kelenoh can see the lanes with the sphinxes, and beyond the large harbor of Karnak.

The light and colors are overwhelming. The evening sun's splendid orange glow is reflected in the sand. The water is dark blue with thousands of sparkling diamonds on its surface. The boats are rocking back and forth in the wind. There are the green palms and in the far distance, the green papyrus bushes along the Nile. All this rushes at her with such intensity that her body becomes limber and she falls down to the ground unconscious. When she wakes up, Kawari is standing there bending over her with a cup of water in hand.

She has a big smile on her face and is crying tears of joy. Kelenoh feels a deep love and happiness and she also starts crying as all tension flows out of her. Slowly, she gets up and looks at Kawari with amazement. What happened to that small round little girl?

In front of her stands a splendid, slender young woman. They both look at each other in astonishment. Laughing and crying at the same time, they fall into each other's arms. Yufaa looks on with a smile and then he instructs them to stop because Kelenoh needs to go home to sleep and recover.

When they arrive at her home, Kelenoh is awestruck by all flowers and garlands everywhere. She is again feeling overwhelmed by all of the colors and smells. She leans on Kawari in order to not fall over. Once inside the house, she sees that everything is still the same. Thankful, Kelenoh sits down on a chair. She looks up at Yufaa, and as he leaves, he gracefully nods to both of them.

On the floor of the room is the fragrance of lavender rising up from the bowls, full of warm water, ready for her to wash with. Kelenoh is just happy to be able to sit down because her body feels weak and she begins to quiver from fatigue. She is so glad that this time it is Kawari who is washing her. Afterwards, when she is lying in bed, Kawari gives her a cup of warm date wine. She only has enough strength to take a few sips before falling fast asleep.

The outside noises awaken her. In the past, she welcomed these same sounds upon waking, but now they are frightening to her. It is as if all those sounds from outside were inside of her room, inside of her body. She begins shaking as before, but with the power of her thoughts she is able to put those sounds back outside where they belong.

Now, feeling totally refreshed, she gets up. Her body isn't shaking anymore and she is standing strong, calm and happy. Spontaneously, a prayer of thanks to the gods wells up within her. She raises her hands high and starts singing. Then, all of a sudden mid-song she stops singing. Her singing sounds different. The echo is gone! She laughs and continues singing with a new cheerfulness in her voice until Kawari comes in to attend to her. After she has been washed and dressed, she goes outside.

Kelenoh squints her eyes against the bright sunlight. She drapes a cloth around her head and forehead, shielding her eyes from the sun, simultaneously enjoying its warmth touching her body.

She walks over to the harbor and goes and sits down in the warm sand under the shade of a sphinx. Everything she is seeing and feeling, she is experiencing with such intensity the likes of which she had never seen or felt before. In silence she absorbs all of it and becomes used to the light, the colors, and the smells. She closes her eyes and notices the sounds aren't overwhelming her anymore because now they are where they belong.

A shadow falls upon her and when she opens her eyes, she sees Yufaa standing before her. He sits himself down in front of her and they both look at each other in silence. She gets the feeling that she disappears in Yufaa's eyes, and that Yufaa disappears in her eyes.

Gently, he takes her hand and says, "Kelenoh, your lessons are over. For a time, you will stay in Karnak to fortify yourself in all you have learned. I will stay around in case you have any questions. Take your time to get back to the here and now completely, and also do your daily meditations. You can go outside the temple complex as long as you take Kawari with you, but please wait a while longer before you do so. I will let you know when you are ready to return to Samos."

He keeps silent for a moment giving Kelenoh the opportunity to absorb the instruction he has given her. When he gets up, he says, "In a short time I will have a surprise for you." Then he leaves.

The days are strung together quietly and evenly. Often Kelenoh will go and sit silently by the holy pond of the Temple of Mut. There at the pond, she is able to return to the here and now.

She will visit the banks of the Nile River on a regular basis, where she and Kawari will stay for the whole day. There Kawari tells Kelenoh about how things had been during the past year, and how she had worked in the kitchen helping prepare food for the people in the temple.

From listening to Kawari's stories Kelenoh can tell that she had a good time. She already knew she liked being in the kitchen, because after getting water from there, she would always come back with many wonderful stories. Yufaa must have noticed that too and that is why he placed her there.

After a day of picnicking at the Nile and when they get back to the temple one evening, Yufaa meets them. "Kelenoh, I have to talk to you."

Kelenoh hands her bag to Kawari and joins Yufaa who takes her back to the harbor. "A ship arrived today in Karnak from Memphis. Remember when I told you I would have a surprise for you?"

Kelenoh's eyes and body start beaming, anxious with expectation. "Of course I remember. Are you going to tell me?"

"Yes. Somebody has come to Karnak who would love to see you." Yufaa says.

When they arrive at the harbor, Kelenoh looks around to see if she recognizes anyone. Tears well up in her eyes when she sees him there in the distance, a tall, broad man, walking toward her, and for a moment Kelenoh has the old urge to start running.

When they stand opposite each other, they stretch out their hands clasping them together. Immediately, the energies of their beings blend together. For a time they just look at each other and Kelenoh can feel his joy and emotion. She sees that he is aged. Visible are the grey hairs on his black curls, and lines have appeared on his face. Kelenoh is the one to say something first, "Pythagoras, I am so happy to see you!"

Her throat feels thick and sore when she speaks. He too has trouble speaking, and with a big smile on his face, Pythagoras nods at her. Kelenoh can see tears welling up in his brown eyes. Yufaa, who had been looking on from a distance, now comes closer.

"Come," he says. "Kelenoh, go to your home to refresh yourself and eat. I will take Pythagoras and bring him to his room. He needs a little time to recover from the journey. Tonight you will see each other again."

The threesome walk back to the temple complex. Kelenoh turns to the left, while Yufaa and Pythagoras continue straight on their path until they both disappear under the large pylon.

Afterwards, she is sitting in front of her house, tense, while waiting for the arrival of Pythagoras. When she does see him coming, she gets up and walks toward him. "I am taking you to the desert," Pythagoras says. "I want to show and to let you hear something there."

When they have gone far enough into the desert, they sit down opposite each other and Pythagoras takes both her hands in his.

"Kelenoh, I hear from Yufaa, and I can also see for myself how well and fast you have completed your training here. I am proud of you."

Kelenoh hears something in his voice. It is the same something she heard before in Yufaa's voice. And just like Yufaa, he uses short sentences, speaks clearly in a deep and calm tone. She realizes that Pythagoras, like Yufaa, had lived in solitude for five years.

A deep respect, and great love for him wells up within her. Having her hands in his, gives her a feeling of oneness that she hasn't felt before. She discerns that Pythagoras is feeling the same way about her. There is no need for words.

Their love is pure, wholesome and all-encompassing. In silence, they enjoy this moment of solidarity. It is getting dark around them, for night is falling.

"Look up," Pythagoras says. Kelenoh bends her head back and sees a blue-black sky with thousands of stars and planets.

"Look and listen." he says.

Kelenoh continues looking up for a long while, becoming one with the universe. She is the sky. She is the wind. She is the stars. She closes her eyes and listens to all of nature's sounds and is delighted. The harmony is grand. She has never heard anything like this before. The first time, when she had heard the sounds of the Nile, she was so moved, but it was nothing quite like this! Tears roll down her cheeks and she has the strong desire to just stay there.

A sudden squeeze to her hands, and Pythagoras brings her back to the here and now. Opening her eyes, she can see that Pythagoras had heard it as well for he too has tears flowing down his cheeks.

"This is what I wanted you to hear and experience. Our earth and cosmos are united as one perfect and complete whole. Only a few people can hear and feel what we were able to experience a few moments ago. The harmony of the cosmos has its reverberation on the earth. Remember that there is a connection in everything. All is one!"

"I will stay in Karnak for a little while longer, and then I will depart to the city of Babylon in Persia. I intend to study relationships within the sciences of nature while I am there."

They remain sitting together in silence with this great energy flowing between them. It is as if they supply each other with this energy. When the first rays of the sun start to shine, they get up and walk back to the temple complex.

In the days that follow they meet often and sit together by the holy pond of Mut. It is a quiet place where they can talk undisturbed about the things which they have experienced and done in the last few years.

Once in a while Yufaa will join them and their discussions usually consist of the cosmos, the gods, and all that is important in life. These conversations always supply them with a great energy, and Kelenoh enjoys these talks immensely.

One day Yufaa asks whether she and Pythagoras would like to go and visit the Valley of the Kings. Kelenoh gasps, it had been a longstanding and silent wish of hers to visit the Valley of the Kings.

The following day, with a number of servants accompanying them, they take a boat from the small harbor of Karnak to the other side of the Nile. The water is like a mirror and the boat effortlessly glides to the other side. From there, they have a great view of both the temple complex of Karnak, and of the temple complex of Luxor. Wide-eyed Kelenoh takes it all in. She sees how the two large Colossi of Memnon look like they are lying in the water because of the Nile flooding, Yufaa is right! It is as if the two statues are floating on top of the water. She holds her breath when she sees the large Memorial Temple that lies beyond.

They disembark on the other side, and Kelenoh sees that there are horses and carriages ready to take them to the valley. At the valley, they get out and walk over to the artist's village of Deir el-Medina. On the long road that leads to the abandoned village, one can still see the checkpoints that were once manned by soldiers, because no one was allowed to freely go in or out of the village, but now they are desolated and in disrepair.

In the past, the greatest artists of the land lived in Deir el-Medina. The stonemasons, who cut graves in the rocks and who sculpted splendid statues. The carpenters, who built the grand sarcophaguses, and the painters who painted them and who also painted the walls of the burial chambers beautifully. These artists lived their whole lives with their families in this village. It was an honor to be chosen to live in there.

Kelenoh walks through the small streets and because of her own love for the arts, she feels a strong connection with the artists. The whole village still has a simplicity of beauty.

They walk back, get in their carriages and continue onward to the tombs. They decide to visit two tombs, those of Ramses III and of Thutmose III. Kelenoh is excited about going to the tomb of Ramses III, because she had wanted to know more about the pharaoh ever since having spent so many hours at the holy pond of Mut with a view of the Temple of Ramses III.

They stop for a moment to eat and to drink something before entering the tombs.

With great respect they enter the first tomb. Yufaa leads the way with a torch, Kelenoh follows, then Pythagoras, who is also carrying a torch. The tombs were carved out of the rock. They walk down the stairs, and then enter a long hallway which has storage rooms on either side, and there is also a treasury. They continue on until they reach the burial chamber.

It is cold inside. The walls are covered with a myriad of colors and inscriptions. Kelenoh marvels at the paintings with scenes of the underworld and the quotations from the Book of the Death. She reads the regal names, titles, and the names of the protecting gods. She feels a great admiration for the builders of this tomb. It is empty now after having been plundered long ago. Kelenoh heard from Yufaa that priests from the past had removed the regal mummies from the graves and hid them in a safe place, unknown to anyone.

When they leave the tomb, they are all silent, still in reverence by what they have just seen. They return to the carriages and continue on to the tomb of Thutmose III. This tomb is larger and farther away from the other tombs.

Kelenoh is elated to be there, knowing that the vaults where she had spent a year at, were situated under the Temple of Thutmose III in Karnak. They descend several flights of stairs going deeper and deeper into the rocks. She feels as if there is no end to it. When they finally come to the straight hallway, they see that here are also many storage and treasure rooms and at the end of the hallway lies the large burial chamber.

Yufaa raises his torch while Pythagoras lowers his somewhat, and in this way, they all can better view the splendid paintings. All three walk slowly along the four walls. Kelenoh is mesmerized by it all. Afterwards, in a silent procession, they walk back and up the stairs.

When they arrive above ground, they are pleased to see the food prepared and laid out by the servants. Still impressed by what they have seen, silently they eat their meal as the sun warms their chilled bodies. After they are done, Yufaa gets up and start singing a song of thanks to life and for the food they have just eaten. Pythagoras and Kelenoh also get up and join in.

The carriages bring them back to the boat and the boat takes them back to Karnak.

Chapter 5

For a while there have been rumors going around that Pharaoh Amasis will be visiting Karnak. Kelenoh is keenly aware of this because of all the activity that is going on everywhere in the complex. Everything is being swept and cleaned, and there is a constant hustle and bustle in the kitchen.

One evening, while walking back to their quarters, Kelenoh and Pythagoras see Yufaa approaching. He stops near them, "Tomorrow the pharaoh will arrive by the large harbor," he says, "and you both are expected to attend."

Kelenoh says farewell to both Pythagoras and Yufaa, and walks back home. This will be the first time that she will see the pharaoh. The first year that she was here, the pharaoh had come to implore the blessings of the gods, but she was not yet allowed to attend. The second year, she had spent in the vaults out of sight, and now finally she has a chance to see the pharaoh for real.

Kawari is busy preparing Kelenoh's festival clothing. Her pleated coat is taken from the wardrobe and laid over a chair. The splendid necklace with turquoise, amethyst, lapis lazuli and cornelian stones, is carefully placed on top of it. Kelenoh's golden star-shaped diadem, which is worn on her forehead, is laid on the table along with her golden bracelets and earrings. Finally, she takes out the silver ring with a turquoise scarab. Underneath the scarab is an inscription with the name Nefer (meaning good, beautiful), a name that is supposed to bring Kelenoh good fortune. Everything is ready for the big day tomorrow.

Kawari's cheeks turn red which is hard to see against her dark brown skin. Her eyes are beaming as she looks toward Kelenoh. She claps her hands excitedly and starts rattling on, "Oh, Kelenoh, I'm allowed to join you at the harbor. We are to be dressed in our most beautiful clothes. I'm so nervous, that I'm not able to eat. I wonder if I'll even be able to sleep at all tonight."

Kelenoh goes and embraces the nervous Kawari who is trembling in her arms. She keeps holding her until she relaxes and becomes more at peace. Then says, "Kawari, please go and get my food. I am hungry." Kawari obeys.

In the meantime, Kelenoh admires and then caresses her beautiful pleated coat, made of fine linen. She takes her small box of makeup from the dresser and sits down at the table with it. This is the first time it will be used because she has never needed all this finery before. She does use kohl daily as an eyeliner because it somewhat diminishes the brilliance of the sunlight, and then nightly her skin is rubbed with oil by Kawari. But that is all she ever uses. She opens the little chest and looks at the beautiful, small alabaster bottles containing delicious smelling oils, and at the small containers which have the ground up pigments for her eyes.

Tomorrow morning, Kawari will first get herself ready, then come to dress Kelenoh and to do her makeup. Next, she will have to work on Kelenoh's wild curls with hair irons so her hair will lie down neatly and flat on her head. It is understandable why Kawari is so nervous. In the entrance of her room, Kelenoh sees a pair of new reed sandals sitting on the floor. No detail has been missed.

When she wakes on the following morning, Kawari is already bustling about her room. She smiles at Kelenoh and says, "Good morning Kelenoh. I have already picked up breakfast from the kitchen. It's best that you eat first before I wash and dress you."

Astonished, Kelenoh looks at the splendidly dressed Kawari. She is wearing a new linen dress draped around her left shoulder and held together with a silver pin. A colorful shawl is draped around her head covering her hair, and she is wearing new leather sandals made from strips of oxen leather. Like all priests and priestesses of the temple, Kelenoh is not allowed to wear leather shoes, "You are looking wonderful, Kawari."

Kawari blushes and bends down to put the bowl of water carefully in the room. "Please eat your breakfast now," she says.

Kelenoh jumps out of bed and starts her morning prayers, thanking the gods for this new day. She eats her meal at a leisurely pace, making Kawari grow impatient from waiting. Once she is done, she rises. Kawari sighs out loud; finally she is able to start.

Carefully, Kelenoh is bathed and dressed. She can't help but laugh silently to herself at the unusual seriousness of Kawari taking care of her today. After she puts on her long straight dress, Kawari fastens it over her right shoulder with a golden pin. "Please sit down now so I can put makeup your face."

Gently, she rubs cream on Kelenoh's face, then opens up the small box with green, ground malachite to color her eyes. The green color is a sign of Kelenoh's fertility. On her eyelids, she paints a black rim of kohl. Her cheeks are colored with ochers that are made of iron oxide and fat.

When Kawari is finished, she takes the bronze polished mirror and holds it up in front of Kelenoh. Kelenoh gazes at the strange face that is looking back at her. Her face feels tight. Kelenoh, feeling the tense expectation coming from Kawari, says, "Splendid."

Next, Kawari takes the tongs and starts straightening out Kelenoh's hair. Then, she takes the diadem, centering the star on Kelenoh's forehead. Once Kelenoh has all her jewelry on, Kawari takes a step back and starts clapping her hands. "Kelenoh, you look so beautiful!"

Kawari walks around her, picks up the mirror again and has Kelenoh take another look at herself. With amazement, Kelenoh looks at the woman she sees in the mirror, but isn't quite sure she likes what she sees. Kawari takes the cloak from the chair and drapes it around Kelenoh's shoulders and replies, "We are ready to go."

As they step outside, they see many people walking in the direction of the harbor. The temple grounds have been decorated. Everywhere hang long, red-green colored pennants on high flag poles that are attached to the sides of the pylons. Kelenoh smells many different scents floating in the air. She looks around and sees that everyone is made up and that their bodies have been rubbed with fragrant oils, so many different scents that she begins to feel a little overwhelmed and slightly sick to her stomach.

The priests look splendid! They are all wearing pleated skirts with a broad golden belt around their hips. Their breastplates reflect the splendid colors of the sun. The young priests, who have not yet been initiated, have at the top of their shaved heads a shining black strand of hair that has been rubbed with oil, which hangs down on the right side of their face. Some of them also have beards as a sign of their youth.

Nearby a group of priestesses is approaching. They are singing and dancing and making music by striking the sistrums with their right hands. Kelenoh tries to keep her distance from the large group, because all of the sounds, the colors and smells are still too much for her to deal with.

Kelenoh's senses are being assaulted by the various energies hovering above the large group of people. They are a combination of mixed feelings, high expectations, jealousies, and fears, but also positive feelings like happiness. They are so strong, that she feels as if she is being thrown down. Using her power of thought, she tries to separate her energy from the masses by focusing on herself. She takes Kawari's hand and looks at her for a moment. Kawari is beaming and brimming over with feelings of happiness. This touches Kelenoh and makes her realize that she still needs a lot of practice to be able to hold her own forcefield steady and intact.

She stretches tall to see if she can spot Yufaa and Pythagoras. Far off, she sees them walking, their tall figures are at the head of the group. Feeling proud of them, she instinctively begins to walk more upright, full of confidence as she continues toward them. As she walks on, the people move out of the way, and soon thereafter, she is standing eye to eye with Yufaa. He looks at her, understanding how she is feeling. "Come stand over here Kelenoh, from here you can see everything."

He shows her a spot where she can be apart from the groups of people. She then looks over to Pythagoras and although he does know it is customary for the reception of a pharaoh, she can see in his eyes that he is not at all pleased about her being all made up. She smiles at him. He bows and laughs in reply. They understand each other without words.

Kawari and Kelenoh walk to the spot Yufaa had shown them. They stand against the front left side of the building wall. This is the building where important guests are received so that they may recover from their travels in a quiet space and enjoy refreshments and snacks. To the left and to the right of the building, people are streaming toward the harbor in an orderly procession, though Kelenoh does discern that some of the people feel that they should have been the ones up in front.

Yufaa and Pythagoras stand along the waters' edge waiting for the boat. Kelenoh is happy to see that Pythagoras is allowed to stand beside Yufaa, it shows how important Pythagoras is deemed here in Egypt.

Suddenly, a trumpet call comes from the area near the large pylon, heralding the arrival of the pharaoh's boat! Kelenoh looks in the direction of the pylon and for a moment enjoys the splendid painting displayed upon it, which tells the story of Pharaoh Ramses II's victorious battle of Kadesh. Like other temple walls, these colors have also faded away, but the red, and the intense blue and white are all still very visible.

All around her loud shouts erupt. Her gaze is instantly redirected back to the Nile River, where she now sees the pharaoh's boat within sight. And from the boat comes the blare of a trumpet, resounding from across the water, answering the trumpet call from the pylons.

The pharaoh stands under a canopy with his entourage around him. Kelenoh is astonished to see how small he is. She expected a large, statuesque man, but instead sees a short, lean young man with no energy at all radiating from him. This is Pharaoh Amasis?

He is wearing a red crown on his head with a high cap that bends backwards into a point. Secured around his head is a wide golden band with a snakehead at the front. In his left hand, he holds a shepherd's crook and in his right hand a flail. He holds them crossed in front of his chest. The crook symbolizes leadership and the flail symbolizes life, death and fertility.

Since he is holding his arms crossed in front of his chest, Kelenoh knows that this symbolizes death. And as such, it is a sign that he has come to implore the gods for new life for the country, its inhabitants, and for himself.

The pharaoh is not married and so he travels alone. Kelenoh knows that he has many lovers, but can hardly imagine that on seeing him for the first time as he is so small of stature. Suddenly, she is startled by a loud voice within that says, "What right do you have to judge?"

She bows her head in shame. Kawari looks at her puzzled. She shakes her head and says, "I am ashamed of myself because I judged someone in my thoughts."

The boat drops anchor in the harbor and Pharaoh Amasis is helped ashore by his servants. Kelenoh looks around and sees that everyone bows when he gets off the boat. She feels ashamed again, because it didn't dawn on her to do the same. She sees Yufaa and Pythagoras greet the pharaoh and then they disappear into the building at the harbor.

Pharaoh Amasis comes from a rich family of generals from Assyria. The Assyrians conquered Egypt about one hundred years ago, and have been the rulers ever since. Pharaoh Amasis has enriched Egypt from trade with other nations and also from collecting treasures of art. He was so infatuated with the Greeks, that he even gave them their own city in the Nile Valley named Naucratis, making it an outpost for trade. Yufaa said that city of Naucratis is now one of the largest trade centers in Egypt.

The large group of people leaves the harbor and returns back to the temple complex to resume their work duties. Kelenoh, still feeling somewhat nauseous, slowly walks back home with Kawari. She is not exactly sure how to regain the equilibrium that she had when she first emerged from the vaults.

Yufaa had said that she needed to continue strengthening her thoughts and feelings, and because of this, would have to remain in Karnak a little longer. He is right, after this episode, she can clearly see that she is not at all ready to return to Samos.

At home, Kawari pours a cup of warm wine for Kelenoh. Kawari is silently staring at her, not understanding Kelenoh's sorrow, or why she is as white as a sheet under her makeup. She hands the cup of wine to Kelenoh and softly admonishes her, "Drink." Then, she removes the cloak from Kelenoh's shoulders, places it on a chair, and goes off to her own room to rest.

Kelenoh slowly drinks from her cup and begins to feel the color returning to her cheeks. She would much prefer to crawl into her bed right away, but knows she will soon have go to the temple and participate in the procession that will bring Pharaoh Amasis to the inner chamber of the temple.

A shadow falls in the room. Kelenoh turns around and sees Yufaa standing in the opening of the door. He sits down on her bed and looks deep into her eyes. She closes them out of shame and starts crying. Yufaa consoles her, "Don't be so hard on yourself. You have just returned from a year of solitude and the emotions of all those people bring you into an out of balance state. You will be required to deal with this more often. Every time you go out, you will learn how to stay better centered within yourself."

He lays his hand on her forehead and she feels the energy streaming back into her body. Only now does she realize just how exhausted she was. "Remember this Kelenoh, you never will be able to protect yourself a hundred percent, but your harmony of thought and feeling will become stronger and stronger. Have faith, Kelenoh."

Yufaa gets up and as he walks to the entrance, reminds her before leaving, "Kawari will come to pick you up soon to bring you to the temple square."

When he is gone, Kelenoh takes her mirror and looks intently at her face. Her eyes are clear again, but the kohl around her eyes has run. It looks hilarious and Kelenoh starts laughing out loud. Kawari comes storming into her room not understanding why Kelenoh is laughing so hard, that is until she sees Kelenoh's face and the black tracks running down over her colored cheeks, and starts laughing too.

She pushes Kelenoh onto a chair and says, "Come, I will clean your face and make it up again. Please sit still, we have to hurry. You have to go soon. She wipes Kelenoh's face clean. Kelenoh has trouble keeping her face still. She feels like bursting out in laughter again and again!

After Kawari is finished, she again places the cloak on Kelenoh's shoulders. Kelenoh suddenly shrinks back, fearful and uncertain. She is dreading going back to the Temple Square and joining the group in the procession. What if it happens again? She sits down on her bed for a minute and starts meditating. With her thoughts she asks for help. Kawari gets impatient knowing that they should have been at the Temple Square by now. As soon as Kelenoh opens her eyes, Kawari commands, "Hurry! We have to go."

When they arrive at the Temple Square, Kelenoh sees Yufaa looking around, searching for her. Finding her, he nods at her with an approving smile. He is standing at the front of the group with Pythagoras and with Pharaoh Amasis. Kelenoh sends Kawari home and joins the parade by herself.

Kelenoh arrives just as the priestesses strike up a song. The procession starts moving. Her fear disappears, and a feeling of serenity and reverence take over making her feel quiet and peaceful inside.

Calm, she joins the walk until they arrive at the holy chamber. The procession comes to a standstill and Yufaa starts to sing a song of praise. It sounds splendid in the large space. The vibrations from Yufaa's voice moves through her whole being. When the song of praise is finished, Yufaa and Pharaoh Amasis kneel down in front of the doors. Yufaa continues singing, asking the gods to grant the pharaoh permission to honor them, and to offer them gifts.

When Yufaa finishes the song, it is followed by a deep quiet. Everyone is silent. All who are present in the temple fall to their knees. In the back of the temple, somebody sounds a gong. After three strokes, Yufaa stands up. He and Pharaoh Amasis enter the sanctuary. On his arm Yufaa carries a situla, an ornate bronze water urn with a pointed bottom, filled with water from the holy pond. Pharaoh Amasis enters the sanctuary carrying a basket containing flowers and grains from the nearby fields. The doors are closed behind them.

The priestesses begin singing. No one is allowed to hear what is happening inside. They sit in a meditative posture, facing the doors of the sanctuary, while the remaining participants in the procession kneel in a forward bend with their hands outstretched before them on the ground.

Kelenoh, however, can hear what is happening inside. She looks up to Pythagoras for a moment and knows that he too can hear what is going on. She hears the voice of Pharaoh Amasis saying, "O Isis, you who grants me the might and success that belong to this kingship, I give you praise!" After a short interlude of silence he continues, "I offer you every victory I have won. I offer you all of life and stability."

The priestesses continue singing louder. Kelenoh looks over her shoulder and sees that everyone is still prostrated, waiting for the moment when Yufaa and the Pharaoh Amasis will leave the sanctuary. She can smell the incense and hear the words, "The king presents this offering to the gods. May he receive life in return."

The priestesses stop their singing and it becomes silent in the temple. The gong sounds and on the third strike, the doors of the sanctuary open once more. Yufaa and Pharaoh Amasis exit through the large doors.

Curious, Kelenoh looks up to catch a glimpse of the pharaoh's face. Expecting to see a glow or happiness about him, full with the anticipation of a new life, nothing of this shows on his face. Pharaoh Amasis hasn't changed at all since before entering and Kelenoh feels a slight disappointment. "Don't judge," she tells herself.

Everyone rises. They place their hands together in front of their chests, and then make a deep bow for the pharaoh with their heads almost touching the floor. Yufaa stands, faces the people in the temple and starts singing a song of gratitude. The priestesses join in, repeating in chorus what he sings. When Yufaa and the priestesses are finished singing, the priests on one side and priestesses on the other side, align themselves forming a path that is open in the middle. Pharaoh Amasis, Yufaa and Pythagoras walk through at the head of the procession, and then the rest follows as all leave the temple. Egypt has been renewed and purified for another year. This evening Pharaoh Amasis will leave Karnak with his entourage.

Kelenoh stands once again at the harbor with the other people from the temple. The whole departure ritual is the reverse of the pharaoh's arrival. The only difference now is that the pharaoh carries the crook, the flail and his scepter crossed in front of his abdomen. This is symbolic of the resurrection. The trumpets on the boat sound the signal of departure, and then a trumpet from the pylon echoes this announcement.

The setting sun radiates across the Nile, giving the water a red glow. Kelenoh shivers as she stares into the sparkling water. Then all of a sudden it is as if she sinks down into the water and time stands still. The sounds around her fade away, and the red colored water changes into blood. She hears shouting and sees men battling. She sees the women and children running, and feels the panic of the people as she hears their shrieks and screams of pain. She covers her ears with her hands. Then, a large Pharaoh Amasis appears before her. He is older, he has visible wrinkles on his face. He is driving a chariot, and is hit by an arrow. He falls down. The horse bolts up, and the pharaoh is thrown from the chariot. He lies on the ground, the sand absorbing the blood of his wound. He is dead. She hears an enormous roar thundering through her. Egypt has been conquered. This is the end of Egypt, and the end of the pharaohs.

Somebody pulls her arm. It is a frightened Kawari staring at her. Kelenoh looks up to see the Nile with the pharaoh's boat gliding calmly over the sunset-colored red water. The people are cheering all around her.

She takes a deep breath, looks and sees Yufaa feeling her eyes with his, and then smiles at her. But the smile disappears when he looks at her face. He gives her a little nod, assuring her that he will come to see her after it is all over.

When the boat disappears out of sight, although she feels totally confused, Kelenoh heaves a sigh of relief. The disappointment she felt when Pharaoh Amasis exited the sanctuary resurfaces. The yearly ritual is now over and she notices that everyone is relieved and happy. Egypt is once again safe for another year. The mass of people no longer bothers her, for she took care to remain apart from the group.

To put Kawari at ease, she forces a little smile on her face. Kawari, feeling reassured, proceeds to happily tell Kelenoh everybody she has seen and had spoken to. How she had spent the whole day in the kitchen helping prepare the meal for the pharaoh. There is no sign of disappointment in her, she has enjoyed the hustle and bustle, and all of the finery and the important visitors that came to the temple.

Back home, Kawari cleans Kelenoh's face, takes off her festive clothing, then proceeds to wash and prepare her for the night. Kelenoh instructs Kawari to put her in her white linen dress again, because she expects Yufaa to come. Now that she is back wearing her usual daily clothes, she is feeling refreshed and satisfied. She goes outside, sits down on a chair and waits for Yufaa.

Walking faster than his usual quiet step, she sees him approach. They both go inside the house and Yufaa, with a tense expression on his face, sits down across from her. He takes her hand and says, "Talk."

Kelenoh tells him what she had seen at the Nile and when she finishes, Yufaa silently looks at her for a little. Then he says, "I know this will be so. You have seen it well. The end of Egypt is near. Your ability to see into the future is growing. It is not always a blessing to see things from the future. I am happy to hear that it is revealing itself to you. You have received this talent to prepare you for the things that are to come, to be able to help people who are ignorant. Remember that even with all your talents, you are not better or worse than anyone else. Be careful not to place yourself above or under someone else. The talents you have received at birth are meant to help others. This requires you to be very responsible in order to handle it well. That is it. Nothing more and nothing less!"

They stay seated together in silence for a short while, as Kelenoh reflects on what she has just heard. Then she says, "I have to tell you something else." She tells Yufaa about her disappointment when seeing Pharaoh Amasis leave the sanctuary with no change in him. She also tells Yufaa how she felt ashamed for having judged him.

It takes a long time before Yufaa answers. Finally he replies, "This will be your weak spot in the future. Make sure to always stay close to yourself, that will keep you in balance. If you fail to do so, you will be out of balance and you will become lonely and unhappy."

Again, they sit together in silence for a short time. Then Yufaa gets up, blesses her and leaves.

When Kawari enters to get her ready for the night, Kelenoh sends her away, she wants to be alone and think about all that Yufaa had told her. Kawari puts a cup of warm date wine on the table and retreats to her room.

Kelenoh remains sitting for a little while longer. Feeling the importance of Yufaa's words, she gets the sudden impulse to run away; away from Karnak, away from all of her responsibilities! She stays put and forces herself to get undressed, then sits down on the bed. In her mind, she goes to the pond of Mut because at that pond, when her thoughts are all over the place, she is always able to find equanimity within herself. She concentrates on her breathing and notices Yufaa sitting beside her. She is not alone. In meditation she can always ask for help, the people that can help her are present there. Tears flow down her cheeks and she thanks the gods for their assistance.

Her fear for the heavy tasks at hand disappears, along with her feeling of loneliness. She spreads her arms and says, "Here I am. Use me the way you intended." She is touched by an intense white light, so bright, she shuts her eyes tight because she cannot look into it. She experiences a deep, all-enfolding peace and power. With this feeling, she falls asleep.

Chapter 6

Kelenoh wakes up well-rested and full of joy. She notices how, when Kawari enters in, she does so carefully and with uncertainty. Kelenoh also notices how Kawari doesn't know how to approach her anymore because her changing moods make her feel nervous. Kawari does start chatting like her usual self, but her story telling is incoherent.

Kelenoh gets up, goes and gives Kawari a hug and says, "Kawari, be at ease. I understand that you're getting confused because of me. I sometimes don't even understand myself where those feelings come from, and I'm somewhat absent-minded until I understand them. I do see and hear you though."

Kelenoh feels Kawari calming down in her arms but then notices that she is crying. She keeps embracing her until she is done sobbing. Kawari then looks at Kelenoh rather ashamed. Kelenoh wipes the tears from Kawari's face and says: "Come, I am going to eat now, shall we go to the Nile afterward?"

Kawari smiles broadly at Kelenoh and then promptly begins to prepare everything for her. Afterward she leaves to go and fetch all the things they will need for a day at the Nile. That whole day Kelenoh is attentive to Kawari and by the end of the day, she is back to being her usual high-spirited, full of energy self.

When they arrive back home, Pythagoras is there waiting. He asks Kelenoh to join him to go to the pond of Mut. She hands her bag to Kawari and goes off walking with Pythagoras. Once in a while she looks at his face, it looks serious. Kelenoh starts getting the feeling that what she will hear in a moment will bring a great change to her life. They arrive at the pond and go and sit down at the water's edge under the palm trees. Pythagoras stares over the water while Kelenoh patiently waits for him to start talking.

"I have received a message from Samos today," he starts out, still staring over the water. Kelenoh feels her body stiffening, and with close attention she waits for Pythagoras to continue. She looks at the setting sun, then closes her eyes trying to calm the unrest in her body and mind by focusing on the sounds about her.

Then Pythagoras looks at her, grabs both her hands in his and says: "You have to go back to Samos. Hestia has passed away."

He looks deep into her eyes and sees the fright this message has caused. Pythagoras was prepared for this reaction and, while gently caressing her hands, he says: "I have talked to Yufaa. He told me that you had a vision of Egypt. You now have acquired the gift of seeing. You are ready for the task. I realize that your weak point can be detrimental but Yufaa also thinks that you are ready. He will discuss this with you in person."

Kelenoh feels as if her throat is closed. She doesn't know what to say as all kinds of feelings are going through her. Anguish and sorrow, because she won't be able to see Hestia again, and joy at the same time because she is going home. She looks over at Pythagoras with eyes that express all of this.

Pythagoras lays his hand on her forehead and she feels the quiet energy flowing through her. "Kelenoh, breathe those emotions in deeply and speak." She closes her eyes and takes in a few deep breaths.

"Pythagoras," she stammers, and then she starts crying. It is too much to name all what she feels and thinks. When she is done crying, Kelenoh realizes that the anguish she felt first, is the feeling that predominates. "Pythagoras, I am afraid. Afraid that I will not be able to handle the great responsibility."

"Listen Kelenoh, there is a ship on its way to pick you up. You will have some time to assimilate this message and prepare for your departure. Yufaa and I will do everything to help you. I will delay my journey to Persia and stay with you until your departure."

They sit together a little longer in silence; all the while Pythagoras holds her hands. Now and then he gives her an encouraging little squeeze when he notices that her doubt and fear are striking again. When her breathing has quieted down, he gets up and says: "Come, let's get you home to your bed. We will talk more tomorrow."

That night Kelenoh is not able to sleep. The message that she has to return to Samos and that Hestia is no longer there, brings up many emotions. She gets up and pours herself a cup of date wine. It has become lukewarm. She slowly drinks from the cup until it is empty.

She hasn't told anything to Kawari yet, she just couldn't get herself to say it, even when she got home and Kawari was looking at her so entreatingly. She sits down on the bed and positions herself in a meditative posture and asks the gods for help and strength. "Wherever you go, Kelenoh, we will be with you."

She feels the vigor coming from the answer which gives her a sense of consolation. She then notices that she is no longer alone, that Hestia is sitting there beside her, smiling. Looking at her she says, "It is all good Kelenoh, it was my time."

Kelenoh looks at Hestia's lovely face and feels the need, as she used to as a child, to crawl into her lap and for a moment feel the protection and safety in Hestia's arms again. "Don't be afraid of the task that is awaiting you Kelenoh. You have given proof here in Egypt that you are the person they are waiting for on Samos. They need you."

Then Kelenoh sees the Temple of Hera and the people in desperation, sitting there together in the large dining hall. She sees Cassandra, Theano and Selene sitting at the large table looking still and defeated. Cassandra raises her head and is again the first one that feels Kelenoh's presence. Kelenoh has the feeling that she is embracing all the people sitting there in the large hall. There is so much love surging through her for them, that she is able to reach all of them with her love. She sees smiles appearing on their faces and says out loud, "I am coming." She opens her eyes and feels at one with herself once again. Quietly she falls asleep.

Kelenoh is already awake when Kawari enters in and she greets her with a smile. Kawari, reassured by this greeting, immediately starts chattering as usual until Kelenoh interrupts her.

"Please sit down for a moment Kawari." Because of this unusual request, Kawari becomes uncomfortable; she sits down and looks intensely at Kelenoh. "I am going back to Samos. The ship that is coming to get me is already on its way."

Kawari opens her mouth to react but then Kelenoh sits across from her, takes her hands and says, "Hestia has passed away. I have to go back, they need me. I'd rather stay a little longer with you, but it is impossible. I thank you for all your good care and friendship. Because of you I have felt less lonely here."

Kawari starts crying quietly, she looks at Kelenoh with despair in her eyes. "I cannot miss you yet, Kelenoh."

Kelenoh embraces her and says, "I'm still with you a while longer, and I will need your help to get ready for my departure." Kawari jumps up and darts out of the room to go fetch warm water and food. She is happy to have something to do so she can deal with the news of the impending departure by keeping busy. In the kitchen, she shares her story with the others and is consoled by the girls that work there.

When she returns, she is already calmer and without saying a word, attends to Kelenoh, then washes and dresses her. When she is done she leaves, retreating to her own room.

Kelenoh is still eating when Yufaa enters. He takes a seat across from her and looks her straight in the eyes. "You already have accepted it. I am proud of you." He waits until Kelenoh has finished eating before he continues.

"Kelenoh, I know that it is too early for you to leave. I trust that you will be able to manage. The coming weeks, until the boat arrives, we will be working on your power to stay united with your feeling and thinking. We will be working on your weakness as well, judging people, so that it will not be detrimental to you when you are on Samos. Through the lessons you have learned, you have acquired the power to heal people mentally and physically."

"You can see the future and your telepathic powers have been developed. You can travel in your thoughts, you are able to influence the weather, and you have received the power over life and death. I will explain now how those last two gifts work. When you become one with nature and your environment, you can ask for instance for it to rain on the island. By becoming one with the cosmos, you can ask to have someone's life taken. I hope you will never have to use this. That choice is yours. Be fully aware that your power is great. I repeat it one more time, this does not mean that you are anything more or anything less than other people."

Yufaa gets up, and as he is leaving the room, turns around and says: "Go now to the pond of Mut. Think about what I have just told you. Tomorrow I will bring you to the vaults. You can spend another week there to strengthen the unity of your feelings and your mind." Yufaa looks at her with a stern face and leaves the room.

Kelenoh's sense of being one with herself, which she had found the previous evening, has all but disappeared. Now, feelings of fear inundate her all over again. It is as if the responsibility itself that she will have to bear, is choking her. Her throat tightens. She forces herself to get up. She goes about the house, gathering the things she will need for a day at the pond of Mut.

Slowly she walks in the direction of the pond. When she arrives at the Lane of the Sphinxes, she stops, sits down on the pedestal of one of the sphinxes, and takes a deep breath. The sun is shining brightly but she hardly feels its warmth. She is cold and feeling nauseous. Nobody is walking about in the Lane of the Sphinxes and a sense of loneliness surrounds her. She falls down on her knees and starts sobbing and cries out to the gods: "I cannot do it. Is there nobody else that can take over?"

A deep silence descends upon her and that feeling of loneliness gets even more intense. Have the gods abandoned her as well? When Kelenoh stops crying, she gets up and laboriously walks toward the pylon of the Precinct of Mut. Still nauseous, she continues walking. When she smells the water of the pond, she inhales deeply and can breathe easier again.

She walks to her familiar spot on the banks of the pond, and starts to cry again. In between the tears, she stares over the water with an empty gaze. There is no bird to be seen, even the reed is soundless. The silence presses down on her more heavily and she has the feeling that everyone and everything has left her.

Gone is her confidence, her love for everything. She feels as if she is dying. Kelenoh prostrates her whole body over the sand, closes her eyes and surrenders herself to die. She begins to feel all of life flowing out of her.

Then the cast of a shadow falls over her. With difficulty she attempts to open her eyes. When she finally does, standing there is Pythagoras, looking down at her with a stern face but full of love. She doesn't even have the strength to sit up. Pythagoras grabs a hold of her, and sits her upright. He then offers her a cup with warm water. "Drink, Kelenoh. Feel the water flowing through your body. Water gives life."

Pythagoras puts the cup against her lips and with difficulty she takes a drink. She feels the water gliding down her esophagus and then her whole body starts trembling. "Good," says Pythagoras, "You are starting to come alive again."

She drinks from the cup till it is empty, and begins to breathe more quietly. "In the same way you empty this cup, you must drink in life as well. Life includes everything within and around you."

Kelenoh looks at his face and steadily looks him in the eye. "I can't do it. Everything is gone. The gods have abandoned me."

"The gods have not abandoned you Kelenoh. You have abandoned the gods by not trusting in yourself any longer. The gods will always be there. It is we, the people, who abandon them. This is a lesson you had to learn. You had to 'die' to the old life first in order to be reborn into the new life that is awaiting you on Samos."

Kelenoh looks at Pythagoras and he sees in her eyes that she doesn't understand it at all. He grabs Kelenoh under her armpits, walks her over under the shade of the palm tree and sits her down with her back against the trunk. Then he takes her hands and Kelenoh feels his energy streaming through her body. In silence they sit together for a little while.

Then Pythagoras starts talking and begins telling about her birth, how he found her, and how her life has been so far. Slowly, Kelenoh returns to the here and now. "Why did I have to die now?"

"First of all, that was your own choice, but it is also the beginning of a new life. With the knowledge you have acquired, you will do great things for the people with your life. Secondly, you had to be convinced within the deepest part of your being that the gods will never leave you. It was because of your own doubts that you didn't believe in yourself any longer, and because of this, you lost your trust in the gods."

A smile appears on Kelenoh's face. She understands. She gets up, walks to the pond and enters the water. Refreshed she emerges a little later, feeling literary reborn. She then goes and sits down beside Pythagoras and asks, "Will I still be Kelenoh or will I receive a different name?"

Pythagoras bursts out roaring with laughter until tears run begin to run down his cheeks. "You are Kelenoh. That name is predetermined by the gods and until your body dies, you will be Kelenoh. Your body didn't die in reality. You have said farewell to your childhood in an accelerated way. You have grown up. It is required for the tasks that are awaiting you."

Quietly they remain seated together, enjoying each other's company and the silence all about them until the sun sets.

The next day, Yufaa comes to pick her up to take her to the vaults. She is prepared. Together they walk to the Temple of Thutmose III. When they stand at the top of the stairs leading to the vaults, Yufaa looks at her and says, "Kelenoh, this time it will be different than the year you spent here. This week you will have to fast. It will be dark. That is the same as you have already experienced before. It is up to you what else will happen during this week. Strengthen your feelings and your mind to be in unison. That is what I ask of you. The gods will assist you with this."

Together they walk down the stairs, Yufaa again guiding her to the room at the core of the vaults. Kelenoh enters but Yufaa remains at the doorway. She turns to him and says: "It is good Yufaa, I am ready." Yufaa says farewell with a little nod of the head. He leaves. She looks on as the illumination from the fire of his torch disappears.

In the dark, she feels her way to the bed and stands in front of it. Kelenoh spreads her arms and begins to thank the gods through song. When she has finished singing, she sits down on the bed and positions herself in a meditative posture. She begins her meditation by asking the gods for help. She feels their presence. A great surge of gratitude and joy fills her soul. She lets these feelings penetrate through her deeply until she has the sense that she is radiating light from all sides of her being. She opens her eyes and sees that it is no longer dark in the room and that the light that she is radiating has lit up the room. In full harmony, she continues enjoying herself and her environment a little while longer.

When she feels the fullness of harmony, she closes her eyes and ends her meditation, but keeps her eyes closed and stays seated a little longer. When she finally opens her eyes, the room is dark again.

She gets up and feels her way toward the table where she had just seen a bottle of water and a cup. She pours the water in the cup, then very consciously drinks the water. Kelenoh hears in her mind the voice of Pythagoras, "Drink and feel the water going through your body because water gives life."

Pythagoras! He arrived here in Karnak at the right time and she is happy that he will be staying till she departs.

She sits down on a chair. The fact is that she doesn't know what else to do or what to expect. The harmony that she has felt and just experienced has settled in so deep inside of her that she starts doubting Yufaa's decision about her staying here for one whole week.

She says out loud, "What do I have to do now?"

She has to get used to the echo again, and she hears, "Nothing."

"What do you mean, nothing?"

"Everything is present inside of yourself."

"But why do I have to be here?"

"To unify your feelings and mind, so they will stay unified in the future." Her future is Samos.

For the first time since hearing that she has to return to Samos, a wave of happiness washes through her. She sees the green island with its dense forests. She sees the mountains, the splendid valleys with flowers and the blooming shrubs. She sees the birds, the olive tree groves, and the people that live there. She smells the scents of the island washing over her.

Again she feels that homesickness which bothered her so much during her first year here. She is going back. She is ready. Excited, she gets up and walks to the opening. She wants out; she wants to go to Samos now. She stands straight as an arrow before the opening and demands that the gods to let her out now!

A great gust of wind throws her down to the floor. Dazed she stays down for a little while. Then she hears, "No!"

She gets back up on her feet and says, "I am ready, I want to go home."

"Kelenoh, your strong will, your pride to think that you are ready, and the feeling that you have the right to judge people will be detrimental to you if you don't continue working on the harmony between your feelings and your mind. Use the time that you are still here and do the meditation as you did when you arrived here, every day, and as long as you live."

Defeated she lies down on the bed and falls into a restless sleep. Upon awaking, she doesn't know where she is. But then remembers the voices who told her yesterday that she had to meditate every day. Getting up, she goes and walks to the air shaft, looks up, but it is also dark there. It is night. She refreshes herself and drinks a cup of water.

Is her will so strong? Is it that bad to have negative thoughts about people? She notices that by thinking about those thoughts, her mind prevails over her feelings. But what is so bad about that? Unexpected the voices sound out, "Kelenoh, if you want to help people optimally and want to heal them, as was determined before your birth, you have to be in harmony with yourself and your environment. You will always keep your gifts, so you will always be able to help and heal, but these merits depend on your unity within."

During the days that follow, she teaches herself to accelerate the process of unity so it will benefit her in the future. She realizes that her tasks will be difficult and that the gods are right, that it is necessary to be in harmony with yourself, otherwise she will not be able to fulfill her tasks properly. She loses track of time and has the feeling of having been in the vaults for a very long while.

She then confronts the problem that make her restless and which has occupied her senses from the very first day. The gods call her haughty and they say she has a strong will. When she is finished with her meditation and the room is dark again, she asks the gods, "What is wrong with pride?"

"Kelenoh, once again, nothing that you think or feel is wrong. Pride is not wrong. You can be proud of yourself, or a friend, or loved one and their accomplishments. But pride that puts itself above others as better or more than they are, is unbecoming and detrimental to both yourself and another. It is pride without balance and right perspective. Just remember that, Kelenoh!"

"And my strong will?"

"That strong will has been given to you in order to fulfill your tasks and only for that reason, not because you are more or less than anyone else. Because of your combination of pride and a strong will, it is easier for you to be tempted into thinking that you are better than all that lives, and because of this, you will be quicker to judge other people. Always be aware of this!"

The voices become quiet. The deep silence that follows presses down on Kelenoh. She lies down prostrated on the bed, closes her eyes and lets the words of the gods penetrate her deeply. The love and unity she feels, coming out of her meditation, help her. Slowly, she becomes conscious of what the gods really meant, and to what she must be alert to from that day on, and from every day thereon.

She whispers softly and it sounds as music because of the echo. "Thank you very much."

Her words are answered by the soft laughing of the gods accompanied by the little bells of the sistrum that Kelenoh hears.

The pressure on her body diminishes and with a satisfied smile, Kelenoh falls asleep. She is awakened by the feeling of a warm, flickering light on her face. She opens her eyes and looks straight into the eyes of Yufaa who is standing there beside her bed with a torch in hand.

"Kelenoh, I am here to get you."

She gets up and follows, walking behind Yufaa through the small corridors. And like the last time, Yufaa turns around at the bottom of the stairs that lead to the main floor. He looks at her, nods his head, and then slowly walks up the stairs.

This time Kelenoh is prepared to confront the first sounds and light. At the top of the stairs, she squints her eyes and places her hands over her ears. They walk through the temple which is lit by torches and filled with the sounds from the singing of the priestesses whose voices reverberate loud inside her head. She remembers how last time she had to put the sounds back where they belong. She notices that this time, she was able to do it more quickly than before.

Relieved, she follows Yufaa until they are both standing outside in the courtyard. The sudden shock of the light, even the evening light, makes her swoon and she leans back against the temple wall for support. Yufaa smiles at her and he waits before continuing on. Eagerly she breathes in the outside air. They walk through the six pylons that belong to the complex, and before long, they are standing outside at the main harbor.

Kawari is waiting there with a blanket which she promptly wraps around Kelenoh's shoulders. The scents, the colors and all the sounds of the harbor, thunderously enter Kelenoh's being. She immediately closes her eyes tight until it again becomes quieter around her.

Now back at the house, when she enters her room, the smell of food waiting for her on the table makes her feel nauseous and her stomach is in pain. Yufaa takes his leave with a little nod of the head and says, "I will come back tomorrow morning so we can talk."

With effort, she is able to put a little smile on her face and nods back to him, signaling that she has heard what he said and understands. She goes and sits down at the table. Kawari, who has not yet spoken a word, pours her a cup of warm date wine. Kawari's face is radiating. Slowly, Kelenoh drinks the warm wine until the cup is empty, then she starts eating. When Kelenoh is finished eating, Kawari leads her to the warm bath she has prepared for her. In silence Kawari undresses and washes Kelenoh who almost collapses from exhaustion. After all is done and she has put on a fresh garment, Kelenoh slides into her familiar bed and immediately falls into a deep sleep.

Chapter 7

The following morning Kelenoh sits outside on a chair, patiently waiting for Yufaa. On purpose, she had dragged the chair outside so that she was better able to listen to and hear the sounds around her, and to more quickly place their origin. She hears the sound of Yufaa's footsteps and of someone else. She looks up and sees him and Pythagoras approaching.

Kelenoh looks directly at the two men in the distance, measuring her ability to focus by the sound of their footsteps, thus gaging their distance from her more easily. As they draw near, Kelenoh beholds the faces of the two men she loves and admires the most.

They both send forth a smile to her. Inside of her, a feeling of happiness arises. She gets up and carries the chair back inside and together they walk in. Pythagoras sits down on another chair, Yufaa takes a spot on the bed, and Kelenoh seats herself in between them both.

They quietly sit there together for a while. Then Yufaa breaks the silence. "Kelenoh, it is time that you return to Samos. We know what happened in the vaults, but we would like you to tell us, in your own words what happened there. What did you think about it? What did you feel when it happened?"

Kelenoh begins to tell them, and as she does, she notices that the meaning of her experience was penetrating into her more deeply. Yufaa and Pythagoras listen attentively. When she has finished, they both reply together, "Good."

Suddenly, Kelenoh fills the room with a burst of roaring laughter. Not having laughed like that for a long time, the old desire to start running resurges. Although she is feeling high spirited, she forces herself to stay seated.

Yufaa, recognizing this, says, "Go outside and run. Take Kawari with you. Go sit down at the banks of the Nile and enjoy the day. We will be back tonight." Kelenoh looks at them and, without saying goodbye, gets up, runs out the room, immediately colliding with Kawari. Excitedly she proclaims, "Get our stuff Kawari, we're going to the Nile!"

A short time later both girls are off and running. At the harbor, they stop a moment to catch their breath. Then without pause, they run all the way to the banks of the Nile. Kelenoh gets there first. Kawari, who is slowed down by the heavy bag she carries, finally catches up and panting, stands beside Kelenoh. They both plop down, and prostrate their out-stretched bodies over the sand, their laughter dissipating above them.

When their laughter subsides and they finally catch their breath, they sit upright, enjoying each other's company in silence; that is until Kelenoh gently speaks, "Kawari, this is the last time that we will be here together."

She turns to look at her friend and sees big tears rolling down Kawari's cheeks. Kelenoh wraps her arm around Kawari and she too starts crying. Both are painfully aware of the impending farewell that is approaching. Eventually, they regain their strength to say their good-byes to each other, and to that very spot they are sitting at by the Nile. When evening sets in, they get up and walk slowly back in a shared silence, knowing that this is the last time they will walk this path together.

After having refreshed herself and after finishing her meal, Kelenoh goes outside to sit down. In her thoughts she goes back to when she first arrived in Karnak, musing just how childish and naive she really was then. Now she is grown up, her training is finished, and in a short time, she will be responsible for the temple complex of Hera on the Island of Samos. She thinks about the great responsibility which awaits her. As feelings of doubt and fear try to resurface, she says out loud: "Kelenoh, trust the gods and yourself!"

Startled, she jerks in her seat at hearing Yufaa's voice say, "Say what you have just said out loud every day when you have doubts or fears. It is exactly the right sentence for you to remember."

She looks up, straight into Yufaa's eyes, and sees only love and trust in them. Her doubts and fears disappear, only to be replaced with a stinging pain in her stomach at the thought that in a short while, she won't see him anymore.

She then looks over at Pythagoras, who now is standing beside Yufaa. In his eyes she can also see the warmth and love he has for her. Still remaining silent, she responds to his gaze, sending her heart's love, thanking him that he had stayed with her these past weeks.

It then dawns on her that when she departs for Samos, she will no longer see him. She also realizes that this next phase of her life must be done on her own and only with the help of the gods. The intense connection the three have, one to the other, is so powerful, that all of that combined energy seems to expand the very room itself.

Pythagoras goes and takes both of Kelenoh's hands in his and says, "Kelenoh, we will separate soon, but remember, we will see each other again. I will be there at the moment you need me the most."

Yufaa stands up. Kelenoh does the same and positions herself in front of him. He puts his left hand on her forehead, and with his right hand holds her left hand and says, "Kelenoh, I bless you. We will not see each other again in this life."

A white energy, the same energy she experienced in the vaults, fills her and the surrounding space. The power emitting from this energy imparts to her an indestructible feeling that she can deal with anything. As Yufaa lets go of her, the light slowly dissipates until only the glow from the fire in the bowls lights the room. There is nothing else to say. All that can be said, has been said.

Kelenoh goes and pours cups with warm date wine, which they drink together in silence. After a short while, both Yufaa and Pythagoras get up, and before they leave the room Yufaa says, "Tomorrow the ship from Samos will arrive. Be ready to depart, Kelenoh."

After the men have left, Kawari enters, carrying a large bag and sets about packing Kelenoh's belongings to be taken to Samos. Kelenoh sits in her chair and watches. The message from Yufaa comes unexpectedly. It dawns on her that tomorrow she will be leaving. She looks around the room, saying good-bye to everything that has become dear to her over the last three years.

Then she looks over at Kawari who is almost done packing, her face is at peace even as she works diligently. When finished, Kawari lays out a new linen dress and puts the golden pin to fasten the dress on the dresser. She looks at Kelenoh, their eyes meeting for a moment. It is good they have already said their good-byes. Kawari's eyes are reflecting the relief in that finally there will be an end to the waiting. "I will get you some water," says Kawari as she walks out of the room.

Kelenoh, though feeling happy, has a nervous feeling come over her. She is going home. Soon she will see Cassandra, Theano and Selene again. She stands up to release the nervousness from her body, stretches her arms upwards, and starts singing a song of gratitude. At first, her voice is somewhat hesitant, but before long, she is singing at the top of her lungs and starts dancing.

When she finished the song of gratitude, she then starts singing a song of victory for the voyage, and what awaits her and her people.

At the close of her song and dance, she sees Kawari standing patiently in the doorway, waiting until she was finished. A warm love for Kawari wells up within her. She walks toward her dearest friend and embraces her.

That night, Kelenoh's head is too full to sleep. Through the opening in the room she sees the sun rise and is glad the new day has arrived. Having eaten, she puts on her new dress, and then walks to the harbor. Yufaa and Pythagoras are already there. In great anticipation they look toward the end of the canal that merges into the Nile.

It isn't long before a large ship comes into the canal. Its large square sail is being lowered as the ship slowly glides toward them. Kelenoh recognizes the large bird's head of the gryphon on the forward deck. The gryphon is the symbol of protection that makes it known that the ship belongs to the Temple of Hera. At the stern, because the sail has been lowered, she can now see the large head of a bent snake.

As the ship draws ever closer, she looks again toward the bow. Squinting her eyes, she tries to make out who is the small figure of a woman standing there. Cassandra? It is Cassandra! A pure joy wells up in her heart at getting to see her dear friend again.

When the ship has moored, Cassandra is the first to come on shore. She spreads her arms wide. Kelenoh runs to her until they collide. For the first time in three years she can smell and feel Cassandra. Cassandra grabs Kelenoh's upper arms pushing her away to get a better look. "You have grown." She says it so matter-of-factly, that they both burst out laughing.

After silence finally settles over them, they continue looking at each other until Yufaa intercedes and says, "Cassandra, welcome to Karnak. Food and drinks are ready for you and the crew in the dining hall." Cassandra thanks Yufaa by putting her hands together, then bowing her head.

She sees Pythagoras, and smiling walks toward him in greeting. "Pythagoras, how wonderful to see you here."

Pythagoras and Cassandra begin talking as they walk together toward the dining hall. Kelenoh following close by, catches bits and pieces of their conversation. Pythagoras wants to know everything about what has happened at the Temple of Hera since he left. All Kelenoh hears is the name of Hestia mentioned.

She turns back around and looks toward the ship as the gifts for Karnak are being unloaded. There are barrels full of olive oil, barrels full of wine, blocs of marble, and a large Kouros statue is being unloaded. Astonished, she stares at the crew. Suddenly, she recognizes the men. They are soldiers of the Temple of Hera. Soldiers who with their great strength are able to get this large statue of a young Greek man onto the quay with perfect ease. At first, it hangs in the air with ropes, then they slowly lower it on the left side of the harbor onto the spot cleared for it. Kelenoh gazes at the statue with pride. Something from Samos will stay here forever.

Then she turns around and continues following the others. At the Lane of the Sphinxes, Yufaa is waiting for her. Silently they walk together to the large dining hall. At the entrance she sees that Cassandra and Pythagoras are still talking.

When Yufaa and Kelenoh enter, everyone stands up and bows to them. Yufaa spreads his arms, thanks everybody, then he signals that they may sit down. The food is brought in. Pythagoras stands up and goes and sits beside Yufaa. When the food is on the tables, he and Yufaa begin singing a song of victory. Kelenoh feels tears of emotion welling up in her eyes and streaming down her cheeks. Her throat tightens and she is unable to sing the verses meant to be sung by everyone.

As the song finishes and the voices die down, she takes a seat beside Cassandra, who in turn takes her hand, giving it a little squeeze as a sign of understanding. Not much is said during the meal, they will have plenty of time to talk during the journey back. After the meal is finished and the song of gratitude has concluded, both women walk to Kelenoh's home where Kawari is waiting. When they come in, she offers each a cup of date wine.

Kelenoh sees that everything has been packed and now the empty room doesn't feel like her home anymore. When they have finished the wine, they leave and walk together through the complex to the Temple of Mut. Kelenoh wants to show Cassandra the pond where she so frequently sat, and where so much happened to her. In this way, Cassandra will know the spot she speaks of when she shares her experiences. During their walk, Kelenoh is silently saying goodbye to everything around her.

Back at the harbor, she notices that all the necessities for the return journey have been loaded on the ship and that it is ready for departure. In the interim, the crew, having already eaten, is sitting on the edge of the quay, resting and awaiting the signal to set sail.

Suddenly, Kelenoh sees a faithful friend from her early childhood years. Stephanos! The small, yet broad and big young man (at least in her memories he was big), with a dark, wild head of hair. The young man who was always able to make her laugh. He is now at the head of the soldiers! She swiftly walks toward him and goes to greet him. She can tell that he doesn't exactly know how to address her. Bashful, he looks down until Kelenoh says, "Stephanos, I am so happy to see you."

His face changes into one big smile. He bows his head and says, "Woman of Hera, I am happy to see you." For a moment Kelenoh is taken by surprise. He is the first one to call her by the title that she will bear from now on.

Kelenoh smiles, pauses a moment and then asks, "Are you the person who is in command of the ship?"

"Yes," he says, "and I will make sure that you arrive safely in Samos." She thanks him and walks back to Cassandra.

Together they wait, watching the ship that will be their home for the next few weeks. Kelenoh hears the footsteps of Yufaa and Pythagoras behind her. She turns around and sees both men approaching. Yufaa is carrying a ceramic pot with small round openings in his arms. "Come," he says to Kelenoh. Together they walk to the shade of the sphinx and sit down across from each other.

"I want to give you something so you will always have a part of me with you when you are on Samos." Kelenoh hears a soft little noise coming from the pot, and that little noise reverberates inside of her. Through the opening in the pot she sees something moving and waits eagerly until Yufaa takes the lid off the pot.

"I will tell you something about it first. It is a young bird, a cockatiel. A small part of my spirit is in it. The sound it makes will resonate within you and you will be able to hear my voice and know that I am with you."

Carefully, he opens the pot and Kelenoh beholds a small bird. It has a little yellow head with a little yellow tuft, and on each side of its face are two round, rose-red spots. The body of the little bird is perfectly proportioned to the little head. The light grey feathers are spotted with a touch of blue and black. It has a long yellow tail and tiny rose colored legs.

The little bird looks at her with black, clear, quiet eyes, opens its little beak, and releases a sound that touches her deeply, so deeply that tears well up in her eyes. She takes the little bird in her hands and looks at Yufaa with a grateful glance. She doesn't have anything to say. With care she puts the little bird back in the pot and wipes the tears from her cheeks.

"Kelenoh, this bird will go wherever you are. It will grow and become an adult bird as big as a pintail duck." Yufaa picks up the pot and gives it to Kelenoh who takes the pot carefully in her arms. "Take the pot to the ship and find a quiet spot where the bird will be able to stand the journey comfortably, and then return to me."

As she walks to the ship, she sees Pythagoras and Cassandra sitting down by the last sphinx before the harbor. Pythagoras sits on the pedestal and Cassandra sits at his feet. Cautious, she walks up the gangway. The smell of cedar wood that the ship is made of, is faint upon the air. She can feel the soft rolling of the ship.

At the back-end of the ship, under the head of the serpent, are the quarters which have been prepared for her and Cassandra.

She walks between the oars which gently move up and down with the surge of the water, and proceeds to the back. She opens the door to the small room where the cedar wood smell is stronger. She takes a deep breath, inhaling its delightful sweet scent. The two beds flank the hold. The beds are built from lygos wood, the holy tree of Hera.

Kelenoh, sensing the love with which the room had been prepared for her and Cassandra, is unable to hold back the tears. It is dark in the room. The only light comes from two openings on either side of the hold. Against the back wall lie her things in two large carrying bags. Carefully, she positions the pot with the bird in between them. Softly she talks to the bird who is restlessly flapping back and forth in the jar until it calms down.

On her way back to Yufaa, she thinks about a name for the bird. Yufas! She will call the bird Yufas. It is the Greek name for Yufaa. Excited by this appropriate name, she runs the last stretch to Yufaa. When she reaches him, she plops down in the sand and breathlessly says, "Yufas. I will call him Yufas."

Seeing the disapproval in Yufaa's eyes she has often seen before, she bows her head down and makes up her mind to from now on never to run again and henceforth, behave as a mature, stately woman. She looks up and graciously takes the cup of warm water that Yufaa holds out for her. Slowly and calmly she empties the cup.

Yufaa breaks out in laughter and explains, "Kelenoh, never betray yourself. You know who you are and that is good. The disapproval you have sensed in me over the years and sense now has nothing to do with you, but everything to do with myself. This high-spiritedness of yours," he pauses, "I don't have it. May you cherish that love of life and know how to use it for yourself."

They sit together in silence watching the sunset until Yufaa rises, "It is time. Your departure is nigh. You, Kelenoh, are the last one I will ever train for high priestess."

Kelenoh looks at him in terror, suddenly seeing and feeling the vision she had when Pharaoh Amasis had visited the temple. That vision signified the end of the pharaohs of Egypt. What will happen to Yufaa? Looking at him, she can tell he knows what she is thinking. She nods to him, understanding his quiet repose. In her thoughts she lets go of the vision and any fear for him. All is well.

They get up and walk together toward Pythagoras and Cassandra. She sees Kawari waiting for her at the harbor. Pythagoras, seeing that they are approaching, stands up from the pedestal and walks to greet them. "Come," he says, stretching out a hand to Kelenoh, who can't help but smile at the way he talks to her, in the same way Yufaa does.

They walk away from the others and go sit down on the sand opposite one another. Pythagoras takes both her hands in his and says, "Kelenoh, your time has come. We have to say our good-byes, but we will see each other again. Remember what I have taught you." He puts both his hands on her head. She feels his energy going through her and the deep solidarity which connects them. "Go now. And don't look back."

Kelenoh rises up and with tears in her eyes, walks toward the harbor. When she arrives at the harbor, she is again in control of herself and walks straight up to Cassandra and Kawari. Yufaa and Pythagoras are gone!

She embraces Kawari who is weeping uncontrollably. Kelenoh puts her hands on her head, and looks one more time at the beautiful, dark brown face, and into those loving brown eyes before her, "Kawari, thank you so much for your love and friendship." She slowly pulls herself away and then together with Cassandra walks up the gangway and onto the ship.

The ship starts moving forward, and then the bow turns in the direction of the Nile. Kelenoh and Cassandra walk to the front. Cassandra wraps her arm around Kelenoh. Together they look forward, where in the distance the end of the canal joins up with the Nile River. As they get closer to the Nile River, the large square sail is raised. When they reach the end of the canal, Kelenoh turns around, and for a moment, glances back to the place where she had spent so much time with Kawari. Then she looks ahead just as the ship turns to the left and merges with the Nile. Kelenoh doesn't look back anymore. She is on her way home.

Chapter 8

Cassandra and Kelenoh walk the middle lane in between the sweating oarsmen sitting at the oars and continue on to their area on the afterdeck. They arrange the space in such a way that, for as long as the voyage may take, they each will have a small area for themselves. They decide to remain on the afterdeck for a short while to enjoy looking at how the small lights of the houses dot the shore.

Thebes will soon appear on their left side, and Kelenoh regrets that she won't be able to see the city by daylight. They stare over the water in silence, straining their eyes to make out the dark contours of the temples and the houses. The ship now bows to the right as it follows the course of the river.

Cassandra and Kelenoh decide to enter their quarters for the night and go to sleep. It had been a long and emotional day for both of them.

The next day, while leaning against the railing, they enjoy a view of fertile green fields, punctuated by bushes and the occasional palm tree. Beyond the fields, in the distance, they admire the yellow-gray mountains which vary in design and formation. Some of the mountains have dark, straight, cliff-like layers, while others are more rounded, their slopes merging with the fields. It is a splendid site to behold, and Kelenoh can feel the tranquility which the mountains exude. The left-hand side of the river is colored by a green strip of fertile soil, bordered by the golden-yellow desert beyond it. Dispersed along the middle of the

Nile River are small green islands which they pass as they continue on their journey home to Samos.

Kelenoh is astonished at the impressive landscape. Though Cassandra had seen all of it before on her voyage into Karnak, she again enjoys the surroundings along with Kelenoh. Once in a while, the ship rocks sideways from a hippopotamus ramming against it. On occasion, Kelenoh catches a closer glimpse of these large, gray mammals with their huge open mouth. Her eyes blink widely in amazement at the enormous size of their rose-colored jaws and their large, canine-like tusks.

The morning passes by quickly. Satisfied with enough "sightseeing," they go and sit down on the chairs in front of their quarters. Cassandra is the first to speak, "Kelenoh, would you like to tell me now about Karnak?"

Kelenoh nods. She starts from the beginning when she had first arrived in Karnak and had taken her first step on its land. Cassandra listens, now and then nodding to make known that she is keeping up with what Kelenoh is sharing.

As she tells her story, Kelenoh detects within her a longing for the deep listening of Yufaa and Pythagoras. Both of these men were able to listen to her with great attentiveness and the ability to perceive the deeper meaning of all things. She had become accustomed to communicating like that. Suddenly Kelenoh feels very lonely as she realizes that from now on she is alone, even though Cassandra seems to be someone who can listen well.

After Kelenoh had finished her story, both women remain silent for a while. The singing of the oarsmen, the clapping of the wind in the sails, the babbling of the water under the ship that play in the background, are likened unto a musical medley. They both close their eyes and slowly doze off, eased by the sounds they hear and the warmth of the sun, that is until a shadow falls over them. Stephanos stands before them with a pitcher of water and a bowl of food. Thankful, they drink the water, but save the food for later.

Both women are filled with what one had just recited, while the other listened in silence. They glance toward the oarsmen and see that they are going to be switched, indicating that four hours have gone by again. The group that has been relieved makes its way to the forecastle where they have places to sleep and an area to eat.

Stephanos tells her it will take seven days until they reach the sea and that along the way, they will anchor in a number of places to stock up on drinking water and food. He also tells them which route they will take in Upper-Egypt and in the Nile Delta. The reason is because the Nile branches off into two main rivers with several smaller tributaries. The women learn that they will take the main river to the left which ends at the city of Rosetta. There, they will stock up on the final amount of fresh supplies which will be needed while crossing the sea to Samos.

Kelenoh realizes that she doesn't remember anything from the initial voyage when she was first brought to Karnak. She was too sad at that time and confined herself to her room, but now she is enjoying the trip thoroughly.

The large sail billows as a sultry wind blows in from the south. Pleased, the oarsmen relax a bit and use less force while rowing.

Kelenoh stands up on the afterdeck, spreads her arms, closes her eyes and lifts her face desirous to feel one with the wind. She asks the wind to blow a little harder and to keep following the ship when it changes course on the Nile, so that the ship and her people will arrive as soon as possible on Samos.

Kelenoh, feeling one with the wind, is unaware that Cassandra, who is standing in the forecastle, is looking at her smiling and thinking: good times are ahead in the Temple of Hera!

As the gusts of wind become more intense, the ship increases its speed and their surroundings begin to rush by. Stephanos comes on deck to see what is happening and a big grin appears on his face at the sight of Kelenoh standing on the afterdeck, hair blowing straight back in the wind, tall thin body, arms spread wide, standing out against the deep azure blue sky. If they keep sailing like this, they will be in Rosetta earlier by one day, maybe even two. Stephanos feels her greatness, but with it the cost of loneliness. In that moment he determines to always be there for her, and protect her with all his might.

Kelenoh lowers her arms and turns around, looking directly at him with a smile on her face. Startled, Stephanos wonders, did she feel what I just thought? His respect for her grows.

Kelenoh turns back toward the water, spreads her arms again, and thanks the gods. A feeling of self-confidence washes over her and she starts to roar with laughter. How was it ever possible to doubt herself? The fear of her great responsibilities has vanished.

The ship turns left following the natural course of the Nile, its large sail still billowing in the wind.

Kelenoh, feeling hungry, walks to the forecastle where food and drinks are waiting, and starts eating. The oarsmen, Stephanos, and Cassandra look silently at Kelenoh, who is now sitting quietly, preoccupied with the eating of her breakfast. Once finished, she stands up and says, "Let's sing a song. It is time to thank the gods for the elements. Without their help this journey would take much longer."

Kelenoh starts singing a song of gratitude and as she does so, it is as if the ship heaves a deep sigh. Everyone joins in singing at the top of their voice. As soon as the song ends, Kelenoh goes to her quarters to spend a little time with Yufas. The little bird greets her with a deep trill. She takes Yufas out of the pot and holds him in her hands.

Full of pride she says, "Yufas, I was successful in becoming one with the cosmos."

The little bird looks at her and it is as if she was looking into the approving eyes of Yufaa. She puts the little bird on her left shoulder and speaks softly to him, "I will take you on the deck, so you can see where we are."

When Kelenoh comes outside, silence falls over the whole ship as everyone stops what they are doing. They all stare at her with open mouths, gaping at the tall woman before them wearing a floor-length white dress, accessorized with a colored bird on her shoulder.

Kelenoh looks at the blank faces and explains, "I am the Woman of Hera, and I am here for all of you. The bird on my shoulder is named Yufas. It is a gift from Yufaa, high priest of Karnak. A piece of his spirit inhabits this bird and will help me with the tasks that await me. That is all, no more, no less." Everyone starts talking at the same time and Kelenoh notices that the tension has left them.

The ship bows again to the right and from now on the course that they follow on the Nile is fickle. They approach the city of Akhetaton where they will anchor to stock up on fresh drinking water and food. By evening, when the ship docks, Cassandra and Kelenoh, along with Yufas on her shoulder, go ashore, escorted by four soldiers.

On the quay there stands a small group of people—men, women, and children. Some of the women are carrying babies in their arms. Taken aback, Kelenoh stands looking at the small group, but especially at the women with their babies. It is the first time in her life that she has even seen a baby.

Why is this small group standing there? Why are they looking at her as though full of expectation? The answers are known the instant the questions come to mind "They have been waiting for you and want you to help them."

She looks at Cassandra and asks how was it that these people knew that she would be coming here. Cassandra answers, "On our way down from Samos we docked here too, and told the inhabitants that we were going to get you in Karnak."

Concentrating on the people, Kelenoh walks toward the small group. She sees various colors around them and can feel what they want from her. A woman comes forward who lays her baby in Kelenoh's arms. Kelenoh looks at the baby, then takes him out of the cloth he is wrapped up in in order to be able to better examine him. Full of admiration, she scans the naked body, looking at the little toes and the little fingers. She seizes the baby's hand and looks at the collapsed abdomen. The baby has diarrhea and is almost dried out, it doesn't even have any strength left to cry.

Kelenoh focuses her attention on the abdomen for a few moments and then gives the baby back to its mother. "Give the baby a drink. It is healed."

The mother walks away full of joy. Then Kelenoh re-directs her attention to the whole group, and one by one inspects all the people. The seemingly quiet group suddenly becomes a cheering multitude. The people walk back to their homes only to return a short time later bearing gifts. Kelenoh accepts none for herself but blesses the gifts, mainly consisting of food, and returns them to the people.

"Eat of it and go in peace with yourselves and others."

Turning around, she signals to Cassandra and the soldiers that she wishes to go for a walk. They walk through the narrow streets and Kelenoh can't help but stare. It is new for her walking through a city. She abhors the smells and the rubbish they encounter on their way, and can hardly believe that people actually live in such dilapidated houses. They soon reach the outskirts of the city and begin to climb a hill. When they are high enough, Kelenoh turns around, admiring a splendid view of the city and harbor.

Cassandra and Kelenoh sit down beside each other, and the soldiers go and sit down a little distance behind them. Up until now, no one has spoken a word, all being impressed by what they have just seen.

Kelenoh is suddenly aware of the tension which seems to fill the space between her, Cassandra, and the soldiers. Slowly she rises up, turns around and looks directly at the soldiers. She sees a flash of panic in their eyes, as though they are truly afraid of her. Are they afraid because they fear she will read their thoughts? It is entirely possible for her to read their thoughts, but she doesn't feel the urge to do so. Instead, she studies everyone and through the power of her discernment senses that their fear stems from the fact that they don't understand her, and don't know what to expect at any given time.

She transfers the tranquility she has inside of herself, and before too long, the small group is busy talking, the tension gone. She again sits down beside Cassandra and asks, "Are you afraid of me too?" Even though she knows the answer, she wants to hear it from Cassandra.

"Kelenoh, I knew you as a child, and I knew your gifts then, but the Kelenoh you have become, I still have to get used to. I am not afraid of you because I love you and I always will. "Kelenoh wraps her arms around Cassandra and they remain sitting together in the silence looking at the city and the harbor before them.

It is beginning to get dark so they decide to return to the ship, only this time they take a different path. When they arrive, everything has been loaded onto the ship for the continuation of their journey. Kelenoh and Cassandra head off toward their quarters. Kelenoh puts Yufas safely back in his pot, and then readies herself for bed. She can hear the excited voices of the soldiers as they tell to the others the story of what happened on the quay. She falls asleep with a smile on her face.

The following morning the ship is already well on its way to the city of Memphis. From the left-hand side of the ship, one is still able to see the high mountains and, on the right hand-side, the desert.

Kelenoh stands against the ship's railing looking out at the desert, where she can see in the far distance a long line of heavily loaded camels, walking toward Memphis, in the same direction as they are sailing. She enjoys seeing that camels are carrying the commercial goods of the land, because in Karnak, all that is needed is brought in by boat. The hard wind, that is still blowing full force on the sails, causes the caravan to quickly disappear out of sight.

Stephanos comes on deck rubbing his hands. He is happy with this favorable journey. He approaches Kelenoh and says, "Thank you very much, Woman. With your help we will surely arrive in Rosetta two days sooner." Kelenoh looks at him.

"Don't thank me, but thank the gods," she says quietly.

A blush of embarrassment appears on his cheeks and Stephanos bows his head. She lays her hand on his arm and says, "Look at me, Stephanos." He lifts his head and Kelenoh is happy to see that there is no fear in his eyes. "I want to thank you for your heart. I know you will always be there for me and you want to protect me."

Her saying this proves to Stephanos that she indeed had read his mind on the day she asked the wind to keep following the ship.

"Woman," he says, bowing before her, "You can always count on me."

He pauses and as he rises, he looks deeply into her eyes as though to reinforce his promise. For a short time, they remain fixed in each other's gaze, then Stephanos lets go and goes off to work. Kelenoh lingers by the railing a bit longer. For the first time, she is truly conscious of a spark within that stems from her desire to start her work at the Temple of Hera.

She roams about looking for Cassandra. When Kelenoh finds her, she asks "Could you tell me what has happened at the temple during my absence?"

They make way to their quarters and sit down on their beds. Kelenoh takes Yufas out of the pot and puts him on a board so she can have a good look at him.

"After you left," Cassandra begins, "we were very sad and it took a while before we again regained a daily rhythm. Theano was assigned to a leadership position overseeing the kitchen and clothing warehouse. At present she works alongside Selene, who was assigned to some duties in the weaving building where they fabricate our clothing. Selene manages all of the flower and herb gardens, and is also receiving training in the art of their healing powers. I myself became the caretaker of Hestia."

The memory of Hestia brings tears to Cassandra's eyes and she pauses midway in her story. Kelenoh waits quietly until Cassandra is able to continue, her sadness is tangible. She too feels sad knowing she will not see Hestia again in this life.

"Hestia selected me to work with her in order to equip me with what I would need to help you with in the future, she literally said that to me. I am convinced that she knew her time of death was not far off, but to all of us it came unexpectedly. One morning when I went to her room to wake her up as usual, I noticed that she had passed away in her sleep."

"There she lay, so peacefully, with a smile on her face. In silent shock, I sat motionless with her for a while until I was in control of myself again. Shortly after that, I went on to inform the others of her death. That was a very hectic day. Everyone on the island had to be informed and some lygos trees had to be felled. She was cremated on the beach while lying on a bed of lygos branches and we returned her ashes to the sea."

"Everyone was weeping and we had trouble singing the lamentations and songs of gratitude. Without delay a messenger was sent to Karnak to tell you that Hestia had passed away and that you had to return to us. Since Hestia has been gone, things have been very chaotic at the temple complex." Cassandra falls silent and both women quietly sit together, each immersed in their own thoughts.

From the board he is perched on, Yufas blinks at Kelenoh. He opens his little beak and the joyful trill that escapes from him causes the women to immediately look up. Suddenly, there is a light in the small room and Kelenoh detects Yufaa is with them. She hears him say, "Kelenoh, Hestia greets you. She is very happy that you are on your way to Samos. She will be with you now, and then in the future as is necessary. For now, you may know that where she is, she is taking time for herself."

The light disappears and Kelenoh tells Cassandra what she heard. The women embrace each other, feeling consoled by Yufaa's words. Kelenoh then grabs Yufas from the board, puts him on her shoulder, and together the women go on deck to deeply inhale the fresh, outside air.

They look at their surroundings and see that the desert now stretches along both sides of the Nile for, they have left the mountains behind. Now, the green agricultural fields contrast strongly against the golden glow of the desert.

The ship continues on, sailing at a constant speed across the water. The oarsmen sing their song, and everyone and everything about them breathes peace. Stephanos comes to join Kelenoh and Cassandra to tell them that within a few hours they will pass Sakkara, and that shortly thereafter they will reach Memphis.

As evening begins to set in, they can see in the not too far distance the city of Memphis, being bathed in the red light of the setting sun. The red sheen, emanating off the houses, gives the whole city a golden-red glow throughout. It is a grand and warm scene.

Kelenoh holds her breath, for there are many people walking along the harbor. As the ship safely docks, she stares at the many people walking to and fro, seemingly without direction or purpose. But, upon closer observation, she realizes that the people know exactly what they are doing. The many ships along the harbor are being loaded and unloaded; it appears chaotic, but there is a precise system at work.

As she scans the bustle of people, her attention is caught by a small group huddled together. Right away she knows that this small group is waiting for her. She glances to her side at Yufas who blinks his little eyes, as if to say, "Please go there, they need you."

The gangway is laid out and Stephanos orders four soldiers to accompany her and Cassandra into Memphis. Two of the soldiers cross the gangway first, Kelenoh and Cassandra follow, and then the other two soldiers close up the line from behind. Yufas sits silently on Kelenoh's shoulder.

As they approach the small group that is there, she sees the children staring open-mouthed at the bird. Kelenoh starts laughing at such a sight. Open and friendly, she greets the small group by saying, "Thank you very much for waiting for me so long."

She puts her attention on each person individually. Just as it was in Akhetaton, she senses a measure of fear in the people. Soon, however, as she continues to engage with them, faces and bodies relax, the tension replaced with calmness. As was the case before in Akhetaton, the people run back to their homes and then return with presents; except for one woman who falls on her knees before Kelenoh, reaching to kiss her feet. Startled, Kelenoh grabs the woman's shoulders and commands, "Woman, get up. Don't honor me, but honor the gods."

She looks straight at the woman, and understanding an inner dilemma, says to her, "Go presently to your sister, she needs you."

The woman pulls back, with fear in her countenance, and aggression in her eyes. "I am not going there," she snaps.

Silently, Kelenoh looks at the woman until she casts down her eyes and relents. "I will go."

"By going, you will not only honor the gods, but you will also honor yourself," says Kelenoh.

Softness has now replaced the fear and aggression that was so palpable but moments before, and the woman collects herself and leaves.

The first people she met when landing, return with food and place it on the ground in front of Kelenoh. She blesses the food and gives it back to the people with the words, "Eat of it, love yourself and others."

As the people of the small group return to their homes, Kelenoh, Cassandra and the soldiers walk further through the streets of Memphis. They arrive at a bustling square, men are shouting back and forth as they contend with dismantling their market stalls. Kelenoh shudders at the stench that hangs over the market square and the filth that lies on the ground. At one corner of the square, a small group of camels rests, quietly ruminating, free from their baggage. Their large broad jaws, with drips of slime on their chins, move slowly to and fro. The odor is strong as she walks up to the camels. She stops at one camel, the color of its coat differing from the others. She stands hovering over the animal and then gently bends to touch it; the hairs on its back feel greasy under her hands. The camel lets out a satisfied grumble, turns its head and looks at her with splendid, large dark-brown eyes.

The wind that suddenly explodes out of the body of the camel is so loud that all in the marketplace comes to a standstill and look in their direction. The stench is unbearable. Kelenoh puts the shawl wrapped around her shoulders against her nose, and quickly walks away from the camel. With enough distance between them, she glances back and sees that now they are all radiating the same color.

Continuing their walk, they arrive at a small temple complex with a high surrounding wall and a closed door. Not very inviting. Nevertheless, Kelenoh bangs on the door, she feels the need to thank the gods and be in a familiar environment.

The door opens slightly and a priest, clearly displeased by being disturbed this late, glares at them. Kelenoh feels a subtle anger rise up in her, thinking temples should be open to anyone and at all times.

She introduces herself and the others, explaining their intentions. The priest opens the door wider allowing them to enter. Along the wall of the forecourt there are bowls of water for visitors and travelers to wash their hands, faces and feet. Thankful, they use it freely because after their visit to the market place, they feel dusty and soiled.

The priest leads the way and shortly thereafter they enter the temple. It is very dark and Kelenoh feels an animosity that she cannot explain. She asks Cassandra and the soldiers to wait for a minute and she walks through the temple to the rear, where a large statue of Horus stands. The statue is illuminated on both sides by torches.

Yufas lets out a trill when he sees the large falcon on the head of the statue. Kelenoh takes a torch, and starts to sing a song of gratitude to, "Him who is in heaven."

Finished with the song, she sits down on her knees. She lays the torch down beside her, bows her head, and feels Yufas sitting down on the middle of her back. Giving thanks to the gods for the prosperous journey so far, she asks for a blessing of the days they will remain at sea, and for a safe arrival at Samos.

The priest hides in a corner, peering at her. Kelenoh feels the almost disdainful look of the priest and looks back at him. She takes the torch and approaches him, her anger growing, as she comes closer, she can clearly see the disdain in his eyes. When she stands in front of him, she is taller than the priest.

She looks at him straight on and with angry, flickering eyes says, "How dare you treat people who want to honor the gods like this. The temple doors should be open to everyone and the fear I sense in these halls shouldn't be here! You do not have the right to place yourself above others."

The priest tries to maintain his haughtiness, but shrinks under her penetrating eyes and angry tone of voice. Before he gets a chance to say anything, Kelenoh turns around and walks back to Cassandra and the soldiers. For her there is no value in remaining any longer in the presence of this priest.

Outside once again, she takes a deep breath. A flash of intuition passes through her and she feels once more the nearness and end of the dynasty of Pharaoh Amasis. She misses the serenity of the Temple of Karnak. Yufas lets out a comforting little sound, causing the last of Kelenoh's anger to disappear. Thankful, she looks at the little bird, her love for the people resurfaces, and she radiates this love over the city of Memphis.

They walk back to the ship that is ready to go. When all are aboard, Stephanos gives the command for departure. By early morning, they are approaching the city of Letopolis. Not too long after they pass Letopolis, they will come to where the two main rivers meet and split off from the Nile into the Nile Delta.

By the time Kelenoh comes up on deck, they have already passed Letopolis, and she can smell the sweet scent of marsh grounds, characteristic to the Nile Delta. Soon thereafter, the pressure of the humidity in the atmosphere causes her to be wet all over. She shivers when the wind blows, and wraps the cloth she is wearing more securely about her shoulders.

The ship bears left on the river with its many curves as it becomes unpredictable once again. The view has changed. They seem to have left the desert behind. Green vegetation now appears on both sides of the river.

Kelenoh wonders how people can live in this unhealthy environment. For the first time she sees large crocodiles who, affected by the waves of the ship, hurriedly swim to the shore. Shuddering, she flees to her abode where Cassandra and Yufas have meanwhile awakened. She feeds the little bird and a servant brings breakfast for her and Cassandra. She will be happy when they arrive in Rosetta.

After breakfast, she walks to the stern and stretches her arms out to be as one with the wind again. She asks if it could blow a little harder and to keep following the ship.

The oarsmen take their oars in; it has suddenly become impossible and dangerous to row. Stephanos has difficulty correcting the ship. Sweat runs from his face as he calls over a soldier to aide him. Together they struggle to keep the ship under control.

Toward the evening, they reach the town of Sais and Stephanos utters a sigh of relief. Yet, he looks about and there are no people to be seen, the threat of the windstorm forced them to seek shelter inside their homes. Kelenoh stands at the stern again, but this time to entreat the wind to blow a little less. Stephanos walks up to her, "Woman," he says, "I am grateful for this day, but the ship, crew, and her precious cargo, cannot handle another day like this."

Kelenoh listens and says, "Be not afraid, Stephanos, for the ship and her crew. The gods are protecting us, but from now on the wind will be tempered as it was before."

The windstorm abates and the people leave their homes to see the ship, but Cassandra and Kelenoh do not go ashore this time. The plan is to continue their journey on to Rosetta after a short break. This is the last part of the Nile and everyone is eager to see the sea. After only a few hours on shore, they are on their way once more. The boat glides quietly away in the night and before long, dawn is breaking as they reach Rosetta.

Kelenoh is enticed by the scent of the sea and comes out on the deck. A loud cheer of the crew rings out as soon as they see her but Kelenoh quickly stretches out her arms and says, "Don't thank me, but thank the gods."

Cassandra maneuvers about to stand beside Kelenoh, and together they sing a song of gratitude. It isn't too long before everyone on the ship has joined them in happy chorus. People begin flocking in from all directions of the harbor toward this strange ship with the loud crew. Some join in the singing and spontaneously begin to dance.

When Kelenoh and Cassandra have finished the song, Kelenoh walks to the bow, places her hands on the railing, and takes a deep breath. She welcomes the fresh sea wind, allowing it to blow through her hair and brush against her body. She enjoys the wind and the aroma of the sea that is carried upon it.

The crew gets busy scrubbing the ship clean and a number of them go ashore. This is the last time it will be possible to buy food and fresh drinking water before reaching Samos.

Kelenoh walks down the gangway to go ashore. She is accompanied by Cassandra and four soldiers. There are a lot of people who have gathered at the harbor when suddenly a group of people starts running toward her. Frightened, she takes a few steps back and immediately, the soldiers rush to stand in front of her, protecting her against the multitude. Arms stretch out toward her as they attempt to get through the barricade of soldiers. The people are clamoring, shouting, pushing, and pulling from all sides. For a moment Kelenoh doesn't know what to do. She takes a deep breath, puts her arms straight up in the air and commands, "Be quiet. The gods want to help you, but they cannot do it like this."

A sudden hush falls over the multitude. Now only the tinkering sounds of laborers working along the harbor, and the surge of the sea can be heard. Kelenoh lowers her arms and looks at the people. Just as in the other cities in which they docked, she observes each one, noticing colors and energy changing about them. The people let out glad cries and shouts of joy, and then begin to walk away. It is clear that they go to get gifts of food from their homes. The scene has become all too familiar to Kelenoh. After she blesses the food and instructs, "Eat of it, love yourself and others," the people leave.

Kelenoh, Cassandra, and their four accompanying soldiers walk to the beach and for the first time in years, she dips her toes in her beloved sea. They all sit in the sand, sharing the silence, reveling in the sea's vast beauty. Only Yufas utters some squabbling sounds! He is not too fond of the water. With a calm voice Kelenoh talks to him for he will have to learn to get used to the sea.

As they walk back to the ship, they see that the sail has already been raised. Ship and crew are ready to cross the great sea. Stephanos stands at the gangway waiting for her and says, "Come aboard, we all want to go home."

Kelenoh smiles, looks him straight in the eyes and says, "Stephanos, take us home."

The gangway is hoisted up onboard and the ship starts moving away from the shore. As they sail out of the harbor, Kelenoh walks to the stern and watches as the land, where she had lived these past years, slowly disappears. In a moment of silence, she says good-bye to Egypt.

Chapter 9

Crossing the sea was prosperous and quick, after only a very few days they reached the waters of Samos. Yufas refused to sit on Kelenoh's shoulder during that time, and chose instead to sleep in her room.

As the island comes into view, Yufas suddenly wakes up and with a cheerful trill, makes it clear that he wants to participate as the ship reaches its final destination: Samos. Kelenoh, now with Yufas comfortably perched on her shoulder, and Cassandra go and stand on the forecastle at the head of the gryphon, looking at the approaching island.

Though it is yet still some distance away, they can see two large standing kouroi. Kelenoh holds her breath. Those welcoming male statues sparkle. Their golden hair reflects the rays of the sun and the warm, red color of their marble bodies make for a splendid contrast in the light.

Suddenly Kelenoh hears the screams of peacocks as their sound carries far over the water. Even though she has hated this sound, its familiarity makes her feel welcomed.

The large temple complex is set in a backdrop of mountains. As the ship steers closer to the island, she can now make out the many colored statues along the Sacred Road. Behind the statues are gray-white buildings and the dark wooden temples amidst green trees in-between.

Kelenoh feels tears rolling down her cheeks. How much she had missed the temple complex. Finally, she is home again! Yufas hops on her shoulder and utters a cry of happiness, touching Kelenoh deep inside. She bursts into laughter and says to the little bird, "You are surely happy to see land."

She hears him respond, correcting her, "No, Kelenoh. I am happy to be home."

As the ship is docking in the harbor, Cassandra takes Kelenoh's hand and holds it tight. The place is black with all the many people waiting there to welcome them. When the ship moors at the quay, cheering breaks out.

For a moment, Kelenoh is gripped with panic and doubt. She takes a deep breath and looks into Yufas' assuring little eyes. Receiving strength from them, she becomes straight as an arrow, and walks down the gangway.

The first people in the crowd she recognizes are Theano and Selene. Selene is holding a lygos branch in her hand, the token of the Woman of Hera, and presents it to Kelenoh. The three women fall into each other's arms and let their tears of happiness flow freely. The crowd's loud cheering begins to swell.

Kelenoh lets go of the women and goes back to take her place beside Cassandra, who is still standing near the gangway. She walks the short distance back up the gangway to be above the multitude, raises her right arm up as a sign she wants to speak. Again, Kelenoh feels a slight panic tug at her emotions. There are so many people that she is now responsible for.

The fierce stinging pain in her left shoulder from Yufas' little claws, fastened into her skin, brings her back to the present, reminding her where she is and what her purpose for being is. As the panic subsides, all fear and doubt is forgotten.

Kelenoh drops her right hand and says, "I am the Woman of Hera and I thank you all for welcoming me to Samos. This is Yufas." She grabs the little bird from her shoulder, puts it on her hand and holds it up.

"He is a gift from my teacher, High Priest Yufaa of Karnak, and a part of Yufaa's spirit resides in him to help me serve you."

Loud shouts and applause break out, but Kelenoh indicates that they have to be silent for she hasn't yet finished.

She continues, "I promise with all that is in me, and with the help of the gods, to faithfully serve the temple and all who grace her doors. From now on, this shall be a day of celebration. I proclaim this day a holiday! Now, go back to your homes, prepare a feast, sing, dance and enjoy each other." The multitude leaves buzzing with chatter and laughter.

Kelenoh descends the gangway and is suddenly alert to the presence of someone whose attention is fixed upon her. She glances in the direction of a pair of beady eyes, and sees a small group of men. Her eyes rest on the shortest person of the group, dressed up in bright, pretentious clothing and looking at her with a watchful gaze.

"Who is that?" She whispers softly to Cassandra.

"That is Polykrates."

As they speak amongst themselves, the man starts moving toward her. He has a stately walk with a large abdomen positioned forward in the direction of Kelenoh. He is followed close behind by a small group of four men. Not quite realizing it yet, she stands eye to eye with the ruler of Samos. In silence they examine each other. Kelenoh can almost smell the fear his ego tries to hide. His fierce, penetrating eyes look at her. He has to bend his head backwards in order to match her gaze. Kelenoh can tell he doesn't like it.

He places his hands on his hips, elbows facing outward, and says, "I am Polykrates. These are the men who help me govern the island." He points behind him where the men stand looking back at her with stern faces. Kelenoh looks at the men and feels that they too are as afraid as is Polykrates. She instinctively knows they are not helping him to govern the island, but are there to protect him. She turns back to Polykrates and waits until he speaks again.

"I welcome you to Samos and hope that together we will perform great works for the island. I have big plans that I would like to discuss with you."

Kelenoh puts the palms of her hands together and makes a little bow toward Polykrates, resulting in a triumphant smirk from Polykrates.

She responds, "Polykrates, Ruler of Samos, I thank you for your welcome and greetings, and of course I would like to discuss the plans you have for the island. Everything that may benefit the people of the island is very important. Let us talk about this in a few days. For now I would like to go to the temple. I will need some time to examine the temple complex and make the necessary adjustments for it to function well again for the people. I will send a messenger to let you know when I am ready and able to receive you."

She nods to him and his men, and turns and begins to walk away even before he can respond. Polykrates' anger strikes her from behind. Kelenoh is keenly aware he cannot tolerate it when he doesn't know what to expect of people. She laughs inwardly, but at the same time realizes she will have great trouble with this man.

Cassandra, Theano and Selene had been waiting on the sidelines so they can all walk together to the temple complex. They take the Sacred Road with the life-size marble statues, painted in a variety of splendid colors, positioned along the road that runs by the sea. Their red bodies are accented by white, yellow and blue cloaks; the hair on their heads is covered with brilliant gold.

When they reach the two kouroi that stand as though guards in front of the temple, Kelenoh halts for a moment. The statues tower high above her. Kelenoh tilts her head back, blinking against the sunlight that is bouncing off their golden hair. She scans them from head to toe. Around each left arm is tied a golden ribbon, and the blue of lapis lazuli on their chests shimmers. As she is close enough to touch them, she reaches out a hand and reverently caresses the marble statues. Tears of joy roll down her flushed cheeks, hot from the sun. She is home! It is the moment she has been dreaming of for many years!

They walk in-between both the kouroi to enter into the temple complex grounds. The Sacred Road continues on until it meets the Temple of Hera. All along the way statues, standing tall, flank both sides of the road. On the right side there is a small building where gifts and offerings are kept; past it is the Temple of Artemis and Apollo, with a small temple dedicated to Hermes. Beside the small Temple of Hermes is the dilapidated Temple of Aphrodite. All of the temples look in disarray, especially the Temple of Aphrodite. Kelenoh is shocked, it looks as though it is about to collapse!

On the left side of the road is housing for the priestesses, and in-between the houses grow many lemon trees. They arrive at the main altar, erected in front of the holy lygos tree. Kelenoh walks to the altar and after a single glance, she instantly determines to build a new and larger altar. With quiet adoration, she touches it for a moment, then turns around and sees the entrance to the Temple of Hera.

Her mouth drops open. Everything looks so neglected. She looks at Cassandra, whose head is turned down to the ground in shame. Since Cassandra had been absent for the last few weeks, she looks quizzically to Theano and Selene, the next in line of responsibility. Both women also look down, hanging their heads in shame.

Since Hestia's passing the Temple of Hera has not been used.

Kelenoh leaves the temple to be alone with her own thoughts. She turns left and continues along on the road leading to the river Imbrasos.

At the banks of the river she sits down under a lygos tree. These trees grow in abundance along both sides of the Imbrasos. She rests her back against the tree, closes her eyes, and attunes to become one with the gods. She asks for strength and advice. Immediately, before her eyes, appears a temple from Karnak, and she hears the directive, "Build this temple here. Believe in us and in yourself."

A feeling of peace and confidence floods her whole being. She rises and without delay walks back to the women. Kelenoh's face is aglow. The women stare at each other in disbelief. Who is this young woman that they all once knew so well?

"Come," says Kelenoh, "I want to thank the gods in the Temple of Hera, and then retire for the rest of the evening."

For the first time in a long time, the following morning a thanksgiving feast is held to celebrate new cycles at the temple complex. From now on Kelenoh will tend to the statue of Hera instead of Hestia. As part of the Holy Ceremony, she first uses lygos branches and holy oils to sprinkle on the statue. Next, she dresses the statue in fresh clothes. As she lays down fresh flowers and food at the statue's feet, Kelenoh asks Hera to protect everyone and to bless the new day. Priestesses, their faces peaceful and happy, sing songs of gratitude at the top of their voices.

Kelenoh appoints Cassandra and a few other priestesses to the task of cleaning the temple. With the others she goes to the dining hall and distributes the workload for the day. Now with everyone having been assigned to their duties, she lingers in the dining hall a little longer. She takes a walk around the hall and then goes and sits down on the chair of Hestia, and notices that the chair is too small for her.

There are so many things that need to be done at the complex. Where do I begin? She decides to make the rounds visiting every part of the complex in order to take stock of what needs to be done first. Before she embarks on her rounds, she walks back to her house to pick up Yufas who had been in a deep sleep that morning. She walks the Procession Road that runs parallel to the Sacred Road, straight through the middle of the temple complex.

The kitchen and the large dining hall are situated to the left of this road and can be seen from the Temple of Hera. To the right of the road she eyes a large workshop. She decides to go there after a stroll through the gardens in order to have a new chair constructed for her. Across from the workshop is the residence of Nearchos, its supervisor and master craftsman. Beside his workshop is her residence, and that of Cassandra, Theano and Selene.

Adjacent to her house sleeps her friend and protector, Stephanos. And just a few meters, across the road, is the weaving mill and clothing warehouse. Honeysuckle adorns every one of the building and residence structures, its delicious fragrance wafting throughout the grounds of the temple complex.

As soon as she enters through the small kitchen of her home, she hears Yufas. He is sitting, bobbing up and down on her office table, and by the sounds he is making, she knows he feels offended. With soothing little whispers, she picks him up and puts him on her shoulder.

"Sorry Yufas, you were so comfortably asleep this morning after our long journey. You certainly need your rest, you are still growing."

The little bird answers with a cheerful trill, and Kelenoh walks outside with him. First she heads to the vegetable gardens, they being the most important contributor to the daily sustenance of the people. The garden beds are located at the right side of the temple behind the kitchen building. The beds are divided into large sections and are growing amongst other things: onions, leeks, carrots, beans, lettuce, squash, cucumbers, melons and garlic plants. Kelenoh tramples on a carpet of weeds, noting that it is obvious that not much work has been done in the gardens.

She pulls up her skirt and sits down cross-legged, closes her eyes and becomes one with the earth. Kelenoh feels the rumblings of the earth and hears the harmonic bass tones that it sends out. Its animated life makes it almost impossible to sit still.

The earth is in balance. Realizing this, she opens her eyes, and looks straight into the curious faces of the priestesses at work around her. Rising from her earthen seat she says, "Be thankful to the earth, she takes good care of us. We will not suffer hunger this year."

Then she orders the women to first weed the fields that contain the vegetables which are almost ready to be harvested. The women start working, singing all the while. Singing during work is a much-loved habit at the complex.

She continues walking through the vegetable garden until reaching the area behind her house where the smaller flower and herb gardens are located. The gardens are well taken care of by Selene. The strong fragrances of the flowers and herbs meet her head on.

Selene sees her approaching and goes to greet her. Together they begin to walk through the gardens, starting with the rose garden, dedicated entirely to roses. The other flowers and herbs co-mingle in a lively and colorful feast for the eyes and nose. Bushes of oleander and yellow broom border the gardens.

They continue on to a swampy part of the garden with a small lake, the grassy path turns into a marsh. Kelenoh sees a few flamingos in the water feasting on fish. There are reeds growing along the border of the little lake, and springing up in-between the reeds are yellow flags and blue irises.

Just as is the vegetable garden, the herb garden is also divided into square plots where there grow a variety of sage, thyme, chives, rosemary, mint, and dill. There is a larger square just for lemon balm. In the midst of the lemon balm, under a small shelter, are several large beehives. The bees love the lemon balm flowers. Kelenoh can still taste the delicious honey she had tried for the first time that morning. She absorbs the tranquility issuing from the gardens.

Not long before Kelenoh had arrived back at Samos, Selene had completed her studies on the healing power of flowers, plants and herbs. As they walk about, Selene points out her favorites and tells Kelenoh about their medicinal qualities. Kelenoh is impressed by her knowledge and the love it reveals for men and nature. As Selene continues talking, Kelenoh looks on, admiring her slender and straight figure, with long, curling hair cascading down her back. When she shares herself, her beautiful face lights up and her splendid brown eyes sparkle brightly. She is the personification of Aphrodite!

"Selene, I wish to appoint you as Priestess of Aphrodite." She says, interrupting her for a moment, "You will take care of her temple. I know that this temple is dilapidated at present, but I have plans to build a new one near the open parcel beside the Temple of Hera."

Selene gasps and falls into Kelenoh's arms, "Kelenoh, I am so happy. I had already had it in mind to talk to you about this. I feel deeply connected to Aphrodite. How did you know?"

The women stay embraced for a little longer, Kelenoh lays her hands on Selene's head and kisses her on the forehead and then leaves. She continues on from the gardens and makes her way to the olive grove where men are busy removing weeds and rocks from the earth around the young trees, so that they will grow strong, unencumbered, and free.

Stephanos is likewise busy beside his men. When he catches a glimpse of her, he gives her an enthusiastic wave. Kelenoh is pleased. All looks well here too. To the left of the olive grove there are stables sheltering the livestock, and an open field where they can graze. She pops her head into one of the stables. There are donkeys, goats, and even two giant pigs grubbing the earth with their snouts, also chickens roaming free and puttering about.

Kelenoh halts for a moment, the fields behind the gardens and the stables are piquing her interest. They are considerably larger because this is where the barley, wheat, flax and hemp are grown. Behind the fields, there are three large barns where the crops are stored. The barns are set against the heavenly blue skies in sharp contrast to the green mountains.

She decides to have a closer look at the barns and stables tomorrow. All looks good at first glance. The crops are sorted and well stacked. She continues walking through the grove and sees the mountains far away, and she lingers for a moment to enjoy the view. The green mountains, how much she has missed them! She squints, to make out movement that suddenly catches her attention. Small figures appear busy on the mountain across from the complex. A long row of small figures, from the top of the mountain to the foot of it appear to be cutting a strip of the forest!

It looks like something is going to be built there. Kelenoh determines to ask Polykrates what is going on as soon as she meets with him to discuss his plans for the island.

Kelenoh walks back along the Procession Road admiring the splendid statues. Along this road are the accommodations for the men as well as guest rooms for travelers visiting the temple. Sizable orange trees grow amongst these buildings.

Now, her next destination is the workshop. She will leave the weaving mill and the clothing warehouse for tomorrow as well. A delicious sea breeze sweeps in over her body. She stops a moment, spreads out her arms to savor the cool air and the briny smell of the sea. Yufas spreads his little wings and hops on her arm, back and forth, back and forth.

"Are you enjoying the sea wind as well?" she asks Yufas. He lowers his little wings, nests on her shoulder again and roguishly looks at her.

When she enters the workshop, the scent of wood fills her nostrils. Nearchos, the supervisor and master craftsman, approaches her.

"Woman, welcome to my domain. How can I help you?" She explains that she needs a new chair for the dining hall. Nearchos calls over one of his men and instructs him to take Kelenoh's measurements. The man brings a piece of rope and measures the length of her back, arms, bottom, thighs and legs. He marks the measurements on a large clay tablet lying on the table.

Nearchos promises Kelenoh that the chair will be finished as soon as possible and that he still has enough logos wood to build the chair. She nods in acceptance and leaves.

Once outside, she crosses the road at an angle, heading toward the kitchen building. Singing mingles with the aroma of food being prepared. Kelenoh stops for a moment, lingering outside the door, listening. She hears the voice of Theano above everyone else's leading the Victory songs. Kelenoh relishes in the harmony of their voices and the peace it brings her, as Yufas skips on her shoulder.

When she enters the kitchen, the singing and work suddenly stop. All is quiet and still as a mouse. Startled by the reaction, Kelenoh glances back and forth at the priestesses, looking in the eyes of one to the other, and for the first time since arriving at the complex, she detects fear in the priestesses. Confused, Kelenoh wonders, where does this fear come from?

Beaming, Theano comes toward her without any sign of fear, only happiness. They embrace each other and start off for the dining hall.

"Please don't pay attention to them," says Theano, "they have heard stories from the crew and are a little confused about who you are."

Kelenoh nods and asks if everything is according to their wishes in the kitchen, and whether or not there is enough food for everyone.

"We have enough," says Theano, "but I would like to ask you a question." She turns and takes Kelenoh's hands. "Could you find someone to take over my kitchen duties? With the care of the kitchen and clothing I have my hands full. I would like to spend more time worshipping in the Temple of Apollo, and lose myself in the art of music. I feel very drawn to Apollo." Surprised by Theano's choice, Kelenoh feels her deep love for the god of the sun.

"Of course Theano, from now on you are a Priestess of Apollo and will be the head of his temple. I will appoint someone else to your tasks in the kitchen."

She turns back around, re-enters the kitchen, and scans the women in the room, choosing the one that looks her straight in the eyes.

"Roxanne," she announces, "from now on, I place you in charge of the kitchen." A blush of joy flashes on the face of the woman.

"Woman of Hera, I will devote myself to the task you deem me worthy of."

"I believe in you," says Kelenoh, and walks back through the kitchen where Theano is still standing, waiting for her.

"Theano, I ask that you go now to the Temple of Apollo and clean it. When I passed by yesterday, I took note of its neglect."

Tears roll down over Theano's cheeks and Kelenoh is touched by the deep love they feel for each other.

"Thank you, thank you," says Theano, backing out of the dining hall and heading to her new post.

Kelenoh strolls along the Procession Road with screaming peacocks ambling about and between the buildings. She puts her hands over her ears. They still give her such an unpleasant feeling. Soon she reaches the spring at the end of the road where it bubbles over and flows into the River Imbrasos. The Temple of Hera is directly across from where she is standing. Left of the temple is another spring and also a large plot of untouched land. Behind her is the Sacred Road.

She sits down on the low wall by the spring and playfully moves her hand through the water. She turns around admiring the beautiful statues, and savors the scent of citrus coming from the lemon trees.

Suddenly, she sees Theano, red faced, exiting the Temple of Apollo. She holds a broom in her hand and dust blows in all directions. Kelenoh smiles and looks at Yufas. "We will make something good and beautiful of this," she says out loud. Yufas doesn't answer; he just blinks at her, and tilts his little head as though in a query.

Gathering her skirt about her, she gets up and begins walking along the Spring Road toward the Imbrasos River. This road, smaller than the other two, is plain, absent the guardian presence of statues. To the left on the road, between the lemon trees, are the accommodations of the priestesses.

At the end of the Spring Road she turns right and follows a path running along the Imbrasos River which leads her right up to the site where laundry for the complex is taken care of. Here, clothes are washed in the river and then hung to dry on long ropes that stretch between poles set up in the field behind the laundry.

As Kelenoh approaches, she can see women sitting on their knees, bent over by the waterside, washing clothes. Further down the line, a small group is rinsing the clothes. They all chat and giggle amongst themselves with the occasional burst of roaring laughter wafting from the crowd.

Watching the scene, Kelenoh can't help but feel a moment of loneliness. She misses Kawari and the life she had in Karnak, free of worry. Yufas suddenly utters a sound that reminds her she is no longer the girl in Karnak, but the Woman of Hera. She straightens her back, and walks toward the women.

The women immediately stand up and look at her candidly. Kelenoh realizes the group before her has yet to have contact with any of the crew of the ship and thus have yet to hear any stories about her. Laughing, she walks toward the women and compliments them on a job well done, acknowledging how everything looks well taken care of. Yet, even as she does this, she has already come up with a plan in her head to ease the workload.

A hefty woman approaches and greets her, "I am Leatis, the head of laundry. Shall I walk you through so you can examine everything?"

Kelenoh nods and the woman leads the way to an oblong shaped lean-to where laundry is being gathered. To the left, under the shelter, a fire burns. Above it hangs a large stone pot, containing a bundle of laundry which later will be rinsed by the priestesses at the river. To the right of the fire are long tables with piles of sorted laundry. Outside, behind the small building, is the large open field where clean clothes are hung to dry in the wind and the sunlight.

"Leatis, I see that you are doing a good job. I would like to talk with you soon to discuss some possible adjustments that may make your work easier." Leatis nods to Kelenoh, puts the palms of her hands together and bows her head.

Kelenoh is still not accustomed to being acknowledged in this way and thinks back to the first time she was addressed in this manner. She had been swimming nude in the pond by the Temple of Mut when the old priest, who took care of the Temple of Ramses III, came outside. A blush of embarrassment returns to her cheeks as she remembers. She suddenly starts giggling and Leatis stares at her, surprised. Kelenoh can tell she is wondering if she did something wrong. Seeing the confusion, Kelenoh assures her, "Leatis, I am not laughing at you. I was just remembering something that happened to me a while ago."

Kelenoh takes her time, walking back to the temple where Cassandra and the other priestesses are still busily cleaning. Almost finished, she is pleased with the work that has been accomplished thus far. The temple sparkles and aroma from the herbs that have been added to the cleaning water, makes everything smell clean and fresh.

Cassandra approaches Kelenoh who speaks to her, "When you are finished here, please come to the dining hall. I would love to share with you my conclusions regarding the complex and its needs."

Cassandra nods and wipes the hairs from her flushed warm face. Both women look at each other smiling, relishing in the happiness that they feel being together again.

Chapter 10

Early the next morning, following the service in the temple, Kelenoh joins Cassandra. They walk together on the path leading to the large grain barns. They keep on walking until reaching the temple. Behind the temple is a fence with an open gate. They walk through and into the grain fields which stretch before them.

Kelenoh, with Yufas perched on her shoulder, leads the way. The sun feels warm on their backs. The golden stocks of grain sway slowly in the light sea breeze. The fields are interspersed with bold spots of color from the red poppies and dark blue cornflowers growing all about. Kelenoh runs her fingers through the grains; they are of the finest quality. Everything is just as it was the day before.

There is no reason for them to starve during the upcoming winter months. It even looks as though there may be enough grain to share with the islands' inhabitants who may not have had such a good harvest this year because of the dry, barren mountain slopes. From her point of view and where she stands, she glances over her shoulder and looks upon the hundreds of priestesses and soldiers hard at work. They look like tiny figures on the very large fields.

The complex is very large, she thinks to herself, which for that brief moment invites doubt. How can she oversee it all? But just as quickly, the thoughts disappear. Yufas, softly pecking at her ear and the women singing in the nearby gardens silence the doubts and bring her back to her sense of self.

They arrive at the barn where the barley and the spelt are stored. There are men about working and cleaning the barn, readying it for the harvest. Fortunately, the wood of the barn and its roof are in good condition. There are no breaks or leaks to be seen, and the foundation is dry. The structures are built against the sloping mountain, which prevents the wood from rotting and keeps the grain dry.

Kelenoh greets the men and walks further on to the next barn. The field of flax has almost the same color as the sea, which she can see in the distance.

Suddenly, a vision of Kelenoh's youth flashes before her. She and Selene are running through the flax fields. Kelenoh pauses for a moment, watching the memory of the two girls screaming with laughter as they run through the fields. It seems so long ago. She was so free and careless then. Though only fifteen, it already feels like a whole lifetime has passed between then and now.

Yufas brings her back into the present by blowing a high trill in her ear. Kelenoh wakes out of her vision. Straightening her shoulders, she takes Cassandra by the arm and together they walk to the flax barn for inspection. Nothing needs to be done to this barn either. However, Kelenoh notes that the tables that are used for processing the flax will need to be replaced.

The flax seeds, which contain much slime, are processed here as a remedy for wounds. The presses, used to extract the oil from the flax, are in good shape, and there are enough pots to catch the oil. The flax fibers have another purpose. They are prepared for spinning yarn, used to make linen clothing in the weaving shop. She will call upon Nearchos to replace the tables.

Over by the hemp barn, men are busy cleaning for the harvest. A vague sweet smell from last year's harvest still hangs in the air. This barn looks good, just as the other two. Kelenoh is happy that nothing has to be fixed. The tables in this barn are in good shape and the wooden spin construction for the fabrication of ropes is new.

One of the men approaches them with a small bottle of water and two cups. Thankful, both women drink the water and rest for a moment on a low wall. As Kelenoh drinks, she hears the voice of Pythagoras saying, "Drink and feel the water flowing through your body, because water gives life."

She wonders where he might be. She directs her attention on him and sees him sitting, bent over large parchment rolls. She feels his enthusiasm about what he reads. He is happy! It makes her happy and she sees him suddenly glance up from his rolls and look straight ahead as though right at her. A smile appears on his face and he raises his hand. Tears of joy stream down her cheeks. He has felt her!

Suddenly, there is a pair of arms locked around her and she looks into the concerned, loving eyes of Cassandra. "What did you see?" she asks.

"I saw Pythagoras. He is happy and I received a greeting from him." Kelenoh wipes her tears away and the women remain in a warm embrace a little longer. "Come," Kelenoh says, "we have to move on."

They leave the cups on the low wall and continue to the stables. As they draw closer, Kelenoh sees what she hadn't seen yesterday. The stables, unlike the barns, are in utter disrepair, the wood is rotten and the stench is unbearable. It is clear they haven't been mucked out in a long time and will need to be replaced. Kelenoh decides to immediately address this matter with Stephanos and Nearchos.

Comfortable enough, the animals approach her. She strokes each of their heads and says, "This afternoon your houses will be cleaned. I don't want you to sleep one more night in these dirty stables."

She turns to face the olive groves, knowing Stephanos and his men are hard at work there. With Cassandra at her side, she walks over and instructs him to ask a few men to clean the stables. Furthermore, she instructs him and his men to tear down the stables as soon as possible, to make way for the building of new stables with the help of Nearchos' skillful hands.

Right away the men start to carry out Kelenoh's orders. Pleased, she lingers for a while watching and monitoring their progress. Before taking her leave, she turns to Stephanos with one more request, "Stephanos, please find Polykrates for me. Invite him to come to the complex tomorrow. I would like to talk to him."

The only other places left I have to look at are the weaving building and the clothing warehouse. When Cassandra and Kelenoh enter the weaving building, they are met with a vision of Selene sitting behind a loom singing softly, busy at work weaving a splendid intricate fabric. She is so absorbed in her weaving, that she doesn't even notice when Cassandra and Kelenoh approach and are standing behind her.

Kelenoh scans the room. Everything is fine. The looms are in immaculate condition and the space is large and clean. Then, tip toeing back to the door, they leave Selene to her weaving and make their way to the clothing warehouse. The warehouse is also in desperate need of new tables. The compartments against the wall are stocked full of clothing and seem to be holding up fine. Kelenoh heaves a sigh of relief; Theano has done her job well.

All and all, she concludes, there aren't too many adjustments to make at the complex, and for the most part it is running smoothly.

When they return to the weaving building, Kelenoh walks up to Selene, lays her hand on her shoulder for a moment and says, "Selene, what splendid fabric you are weaving!"

Selene smiles up at her, "Thank you Kelenoh. I really do enjoy doing this work. It helps me relax and challenges me to create new patterns all the time."

The women say their farewells and Cassandra and Kelenoh set off for the workshop of Nearchos. Kelenoh first instructs him to replace some tables in the flax barn and in the clothing warehouse. Then she mentions that tomorrow the stables are to be torn down and rebuilt. Also in the very near future, she wishes to speak with him about some ideas she has to improve the laundry where the women wash and hang the clothes to dry. She wishes to make it easier for them to wash the clothes. Nearchos takes note of her requests and tells her that her chair is finished and has been brought to the dining hall. She thanks him.

When Kelenoh, with Yufas on her shoulder, exits the temple the next morning, she sees Polykrates approaching. He is closely followed by his four men. Now, on either side, walking in tandem with him are two men she hasn't seen before. One of them is somewhat older, and the other is a younger one.

She can see them well from her point of view at the top of the temple stairs. Once they reach the foot of the temple, remembering how Polykrates doesn't like to be looked down upon, Kelenoh descends.

"Woman of Hera, you would like to talk about my plans?"

Kelenoh gives him and the men a little nod and says, "Come, I will take you to the dining hall, where we can sit undisturbed."

As they pass by the kitchen, the songs of the priestesses preparing food echo through the hall. They enter and sit down at a long table. The four men linger at the entrance. Kelenoh sits in her new chair at the head of the table. Polykrates sits down at her right, and the two unfamiliar gentlemen sit down at her left.

Silence befalls them and Kelenoh looks in the direction of Polykrates, waiting for him to begin

"Woman, I would like to introduce you to these two men that have joined us today. This is Rhoikos." He points to the somewhat older man. "And this is his son Theodoros. They are architects that I have hired to build a new temple."

Kelenoh looks at both men and is unable to hide the joy she feels inside for this plan. She introduces herself and Yufas to Rhoikos and Theodoros and looks back at Polykrates quizzically, desirous to know more about his plans before she shares her own ideas for the new Temple of Hera.

Polykrates stands up and with stately gestures explains his plans for the building of the temple. It has to be the largest temple in Greece, so everyone in the country and all those far and wide will talk about it.

Kelenoh listens to him patiently as he continues on and on. Through his extensive pontificating she can discern his true intentions. Polykrates is using the 'erecting of new temple,' not for the honor of Hera, but for the honor of himself. Finally finished, he looks at Kelenoh, chin and chest puffed up expecting high praise.

Her only comment is, "It is good." Silently to herself she adds, 'You can pay for it, but I will make the decisions about the building of the temple.'

She immediately directs her attention to Rhoikos and Theodoros and asks the men for their input on the new temple and what kind of materials they think should be used. She also wants to know how they intend to solve the problem of the foundation. The ground the temple sits on at present is marshy; the foundation will have to be solid to hold the weight of such a grand, new temple.

There follows an intense discussion, and it is clear to Kelenoh that both men know what they are talking about. She listens with rapt attention and occasionally interjects her own ideas.

Rhoikos reacts enthusiastically to her plans. The older man is as tall as Kelenoh. A mop of curling dark hair with gray streaks and a gray beard frame his kindly face. His soft, dark-brown eyes reflect his intelligence. He has a lively manner of speech, which Kelenoh listens to with pleasure. She is certain. With this man in charge, the temple will be built.

Theodoros is a handsome young man. Taller than his father, he has splendid long, blonde, curling hair that drapes over his shoulders. He is somewhat more reserved in his demeanor and pauses to think before he speaks.

Kelenoh conceals the sense of confusion that arises when she looks at him. He is not easy to read. His dreamy, dark-brown eyes look straight at her, radiating honesty. This is the first time a man triggers feelings in her body that she does not recognize. It makes her restless and unsure. She glances sideways to Yufas for a moment. It is as if he is smirking, having some kind of insight to information she has not been made aware of yet. Kelenoh rolls her eyes. Yufas isn't helping much either.

She directs her attention to Rhoikos again and listens to his explanation on the choice of materials suggested for use. He proposes Theodoros make a few drawings of the new temple. He talks quietly and clearly but with few words. Kelenoh likes this way of talking.

An impatient Polykrates, still standing near the table, joins the conversation. Kelenoh had forgotten all about him. She starts to get annoyed, being drained by his ample explanation about what he thinks the temple should look like.

An awkward silence falls over the hall and Kelenoh decides to continue deliberations later. She rises. "Polykrates, thank you very much for your plans on the building of the temple. I would like to discuss these plans further at another time, for instance, when Theodoros has finished his designs. I will let you know."

The two men get up and say goodbye to Kelenoh in a way fitting to honor a high priestess. Polykrates, on the other hand, was already near the exit whispering to his men. Poised, Kelenoh walks toward him and without hesitation says, "One more thing

Polykrates," she pauses, "I have seen that there are men at work in the mountains. Can you tell me what are they doing there?"

Disturbed, he looks at Kelenoh as if to say, 'Mind your own business!'

"I want to build a wall that will protect the city against the attacks of our enemies."

Kelenoh looks at him quietly and asks, "What of the other people of the island who don't live in the city, don't they need protection?"

"When an attack takes place, they will be warned and can come to the city where they will be received," he answers and continues, "We can feed them with food from the temple complex."

Kelenoh nods. Food was going to be the next matter she would bring up, and then she quickly asks, "And what about the water supply for all of those people?"

"I am currently in discussions with Eupalinos of Megara about the prospect of digging a tunnel through the mountain to supply the city with water. This man has experience in this area and will accept the commission upon solidifying the plans."

Kelenoh is astonished by the man who stands before her. To hear his short and clear responses in comparison to the long-winded, vainglorious talk from just a bit ago is surprising. He has clearly thought long and hard about this problem and she has to admit she admires his plans.

"Polykrates," she says, "I admire your ideas. They are good." With a short nod Polykrates takes his leave of her and walks away with his men.

Kelenoh hangs behind for a moment in the opening of the dining hall, listening to the songs of the priestesses in the kitchen.

Unrest still pulls at her emotions. Is it because she was irritated by Polykrates or is it because of her reaction to Theodoros? She closes her eyes and asks for help from the gods, "Forgive my feelings toward Polykrates. Teach me to see him as he truly is that I may associate with him in harmony."

She hears the little bells of the sistrum and a soft laughing. The strange feelings of unrest have not disappeared. She needs to be alone with Yufas, to empty her head by the sea.

She halts a moment between the two kouroi, and then walks to the kouros on her right, wraps her arm around his left leg and rests her head against it. She stares out over the sea, feeling even more peaceful as she is taken in by the sound of the waves.

The face of Theodoros unexpectedly appears in front of her. She sees his brown eyes and again gets a strange feeling in her body. She has a desire to nestle against his body and hold him.

Confused, she shakes her head and looks at Yufas who is hopping in the sand close to her. She plops down, placing her hands in her lap. Yufas hops toward her and crouches in front of her. He turns his little head back and forth blinking up at her. "Yufas," she asks him, "What kind of feeling is this? I have never felt this before."

She hears, "Kelenoh, you are so wise and so naïve at the same time. You may be the Woman of Hera, but you are still just a woman! You are experiencing love!"

Stupefied, she looks at Yufas. She realizes he is right. So that is what she feels. She has the urge to rise and look for Theodoros in order to discuss this with him, but controls herself and remains seated, turns her head toward the sun, and closes her eyes.

Would Theodoros feel the same? Does she even have to talk to him about this? What would happen if he didn't feel the same toward her? She doesn't know what to do until Yufas utters a sound. She is reminded of something she once said out loud to herself when alone in the vaults. 'Kelenoh, trust the gods and yourself.'

She sits down in a meditative posture and presents her confusion and uncertainty to the gods. An answer from the gods comes fast, "Let it go Kelenoh. When the time arrives, you will know just what to say. Focus on your tasks in the temple."

She opens her eyes. The unrest in her body has disappeared. She stands up, spreads her arms and thanks the gods.

With her attention back on the complex, she remembers that she still needs to talk to Nearchos about her plans for the laundry. Her mind searches for him and she sees him occupied at the stables.

Luckily, the strange feeling in her body is gone and she is free to direct all her attention to the practical affairs that must be dealt with.

By the time she arrives at the stables, they are almost completely dismantled. There are temporary shelters made to protect the animals from the roasting sun. She calls out to

Nearchos and together they sit down on a low wall. Nearchos carries a small stone bottle and cups. He washes his hands and face first before pouring water in the cups for her and for himself. They pass a little time in silence as they watch the men working at the stables. She gives him compliments regarding the progress they have already made.

A few men are occupied tying the old wood onto the backs of donkeys. It will then be transported to the kitchen where the wood will be used for the cooking fires.

"I wanted to tell you about my plans to improve the laundry," Kelenoh starts, "When I made my visit, I saw the women washing clothes at the banks of the Imbrasos. Now my question to you is, is it possible to build a plank-bridge that can float on the Imbrasos, supplied with ropes and pulleys so that one can attach a plank-bridge to the banks of the river when the water is high?"

With a stick she draws a design in the earth to show him what she means. Nearchos nods and Kelenoh continues, "The purpose of this is to make it easier for the women to rinse the laundry. There is more water in the middle of the river and it flows much faster. Additionally, they will have an even surface that is easier to sit on."

Nearchos looks at Kelenoh and says, "Woman, that is a good idea. I will draw up designs for its construction. When they are finished, I will show them to you and when you approve, I will build it for you."

"Of course, first I want you to finish the stables," Kelenoh says, "and replace the tables in the barns. We will harvest the grain pretty soon. I am sure you will find time to make the designs in-between. I will wait for them."

Kelenoh stands up, returns the cup to Nearchos, thanks him and walks on into the afternoon sun.

Chapter 11

A few months have gone by since Kelenoh returned to Samos. The temple complex is functioning as in the time of Hestia. The tables in the barns have been replaced; the new stables and the improvements for the laundry have been finished. Kelenoh has instructed Selene to henceforth take care of the animals due to her great love for them. Leatis and the priestesses of the laundry are excited about the plank-bridge in the river.

The temples are clean, except for the Temple of Aphrodite and the small Temple of Hermes; they were too dilapidated to be used any longer. Kelenoh spoke with Rhoikos and asked him to make additional drawings for one new temple dedicated to both Aphrodite and Hermes that would be built on an open plot adjacent to the Temple of Hera.

Theodoros is almost done with the drawings of the new Temple of Hera and plans for the building of a new altar have also been discussed.

She walked through the old Temples of Aphrodite and Hermes with Nearchos and it was determined that the small Temple of Hermes must be totally demolished, while parts of the Temple of Aphrodite are still in good condition and will be recycled and used to build a treasury. The remaining parts will be removed.

Over the course of the last few months Kelenoh has talked to Theodoros twice. By directing her attention to matters regarding the complex, she has been able to suppress her feelings for him.

Yufas has grown up, he is almost an adult bird now, and he no longer sits on her shoulder that often anymore. What he does is hop and flutter beside or around her.

She doesn't see Polykrates anymore. From a distance she has watched the progress of the building of the wall in the mountains, and from various sources she had heard that Eupalinos had begun digging a tunnel to adequately supply water to the city. Eupalinos has devised a plan to speed up the process. One team of his men hack away at the rock from one side of the mountain, while another team is hacking from the other side.

In her mind, Kelenoh visualizes the tunnel inside of the mountain, and Eupalinos calculations are correct. The men, who are hacking the tunnel, will meet in the middle of the mountain with a variance of about one meter. She can see the sweaty bodies of the men mustering every ounce of their strength, hammering and chiseling away at the rock. When she feels that one is about to drop, she sends them a dose of energy. She cannot avoid the fact that many will die under the pressure of the work, and from the lack of oxygen.

She admires Eupalinos' ability to calculate effectively, and how he has chosen to carry out this risky plan. She hopes to meet him tomorrow during the celebration of the Harvest Festival.

The barley and spelt have been harvested, and the barn is filled to the brim with grain. The flax and hemp have also been abundant this year. Everyone at the temple complex is grateful for such rich harvests.

Kelenoh makes her way home to inspect her festival dress for tomorrow. She will wear the pleated cloak that was brought from Egypt. The Harvest Festival! She has great expectations for what tomorrow will bring.

Cassandra had explained to her how the rituals of this festival are to be executed and what the people expect of her. Cassandra also told her the story of the wooden statue of Hera that a long time ago was stolen from the temple by pirates, who wanted to possess the same fortune as the inhabitants of Samos. The robbery was successful, but the boat was not able to depart. It was stuck in the sand! The pirates became frightened, and the next day, they left and threw the statue overboard on their way out. The statue of Hera belonged on Samos! Every year during the Harvest Festival this ritual is re-enacted.

A smile appears on Kelenoh's face; grateful to the gods that they are so well-disposed toward the island.

Upon entering the house, Cassandra is already busy laying out her clothes on the bed. She greets Kelenoh with a warm smile, saying, "Kelenoh, I am happy you are here. Your beautiful coat is ready; nothing needed to be done to it. Oh, and I instructed Stephanos to cut one lygos branch for you and to also collect lygos branches for our wreaths and those of the priestesses. He will be here anytime to present you with the branch. The other branches will be taken to the dining hall, so the priestesses can make wreaths from them. Now I am going to polish your head decoration."

Cassandra picks up the thick, round silver headband, and walks with it to Kelenoh's office. She sits down at the table and begins to polish it. Kelenoh picks Yufas up, puts him on the table, and sits down by Cassandra.

Kelenoh feels happiness and pride as she looks at the head decoration. It is a thick, round silver snake that warps around her head. The upright head and tail join in the middle of her forehead. It is the symbol of the Woman of Hera.

Stephanos enters with the lygos branch in his hand, and presents it to Kelenoh. "Woman, here is your branch. I brought the other branches to the dining hall, and the priestesses are already busy making wreaths from them."

Kelenoh takes the lygos branch and holds her left hand above the branch for a moment. "Thank you, Stephanos, you have chosen a good branch."

The lygos branch is a symbol of a high priestess and she will hold it during the procession. "Do you have enough branches to make wreaths for all the priestesses?" She asks.

"Yes, Woman, there are enough." replies Stephanos.

Kelenoh gets up and says to Cassandra, "I am going to the dining hall to see how much progress the priestesses have made and to bless the wreaths."

When Kelenoh steps outside, she raises her face to the sun, enjoying the warmth that surrounds her. She ignores the screaming of the peacocks that she has gotten used to by now. Everywhere in the complex people are busy preparing for the festivities and the participants that will come the following day. The whole island shares in the joys of the Harvest Festival.

Drawing near to the dining hall, she pauses for a moment before the altar. It is ready for the offering that will take place tomorrow. It is clean and tidy, yet Kelenoh is still bothered by this old altar.

Until now, she hasn't thought much of her other duties as high priestess; such as tending to the people, giving them hope and healing, addressing the problems that, according to them, make their lives difficult. Getting the temple complex to function normally again has taken most of her time and attention. She determines that after tomorrow, she will begin to seriously address the needs of the people. It will be a good day because the people of the island will be able to make their acquaintance with her on the holiday tomorrow.

In the dining hall, the priestesses are weaving wreaths all the while singing songs of gratitude for the abundant harvest. When Kelenoh enters in, they stop singing and look at her with big smiles on their faces. A great feeling of happiness streams through her. In a short time, she has been able to make the complex function well and restore happiness.

She sits down in her chair to admire the wreaths which she blesses. Together, with the priestesses she sings another song of gratitude. She closes her eyes and directs her attention inward, searching out where Theano and Selene are. She finds Theano in the Temple of Apollo and Selene at the beach. She leaves.

First, she makes her way to Theano who is busy preparing the temple for those who will visit tomorrow. Kelenoh hangs back in the vestibule to observe her. Theano hasn't changed much over the years; she is still the short, lively woman she remembers from her childhood. Her dark curls roll on her back as she hurries toward the statue of Apollo to arrange the flowers. Feeling someone is watching her, Theano turns around. Her smiling eyes meet Kelenoh's and she runs toward her. The women embrace. They go and sit on the stairs of the temple and discuss what else needs to be done.

When Kelenoh goes to see Selene, she finds her sitting in the sand playing her zither. Kelenoh stops some distance away and quietly listens. The pure chords belong to Selene's aloneness. She has noticed often how Selene seeks solitude, and for a time, sequestering herself away from others. It is as if only then can she be perfectly happy. Kelenoh comes up slowly behind Selene, then sits down in the sand beside her. Selene stops playing, and together they listen to the surf.

"Are you happy?" Kelenoh asks Selene.

"Yes," answers Selene.

She looks at Kelenoh, "Since your return, I have been able to concentrate more on myself and that makes me happy."

"And your happiness touches others and makes them happy in turn," remarks Kelenoh, grateful for her friend's natural gift.

In the last few weeks, fall storms have blasted the seas and raged over the island, and as Kelenoh walks back home, she senses that another storm is approaching. She turns her face toward the wind rippling over the sea. Dark clouds have gathered above her and the first drops of water wet her face. She tightens the shawl around her, grateful for the rain. The dry earth needs the rain. She picks up her pace, and walks swiftly back home to where Cassandra is cooking a meal in their small kitchen.

Today all four of them refrain from eating in the dining hall so that they can quietly prepare for tomorrow. Hungrily, she sniffs the delicious smell that rises from the pots. Soon, Theano enters and begins to set the table. Kelenoh decides to retire to her room for a while. As she listens to the sounds of the kitchen, she goes and sits down on her bed and closes her eyes. She begins her daily meditation practice which she learned in the vaults in Egypt. This helps her return to the sense of unity in her mind and feelings.

Suddenly, she is back in the vaults. She hears the voices that once answered a question of hers, "What is wrong with pride and strong will?"

"Kelenoh, nothing you think or feel is wrong. All of life is one, and each one affects the other. It is when you in your pride put yourself above others, and willfulness without discretion is exercised that life may be affected. The strong will that you possess has been given to you in order that you might fulfill your tasks. It is only for this reason that you have any divine quality, not because you are more or better than anyone else."

Upon opening her eyes she is confused for a moment. She is not in the vaults, but in her room on Samos. She realizes that she is sitting on the large, wide, soft bed and is staring into the flickering light coming from the fire-burning bowls situated on both sides of her bed. The pleasant scent coming from the bowls co-mingle with the smell of food wafting in from the kitchen. Ah, yes, she is home in her familiar room.

Why is it now, that she is being reminded of her questions and answers from her time spent in the vaults? Yufas sits on her abdomen and it is as if he laughs inwardly.

Then she hears a voice say, "Because tomorrow you will be meeting the people you will heal and help." She closes her eyes, the joy and gratitude streaming through her is immeasurable.

Selene enters the room to tell her that the food is ready. She notices how she did not hear when Selene came home.

"I am coming," she says.

The storm rages outside around the house, but inside, in the small room behind the kitchen, it is warm and cozy. The four women chat about tomorrow's festivities. Everything is ready for the big reception for the people of the island.

The following morning Kelenoh gets up early. Strong gale-force winds and heavy rain are still beating at the house. Regardless of the weather, she makes her way to the beach to commune and unite with nature. She goes and sits down in the sand by the kouros on her left.

She closes her eyes and when she feels herself one with the wind and the rain, she quiets her whole being. As she does this, the wind calms and the rain stops. She thanks the gods and stays seated until the warmth of the sun fills her completely. She lets this warmth stream from within her to all around, and not very long after, the whole island is bathed in the sun.

Today is a day the sun must shine! With a bounce in her step, she walks back home, enjoying the many fresh scents that entice her along her way.

When she arrives, Cassandra is already standing by, ready to dress her for the day. Cassandra looks splendid! Her snow-white dress glistens in the light of the fire. The dress is held together by silver pins on her shoulders. The lygos branch wreath is secured on her head and contrasts beautifully against her white dress.

Under her breasts there is a golden band that accentuates her slender figure.

Theano and Selene enter, wearing the same dress as Cassandra. Kelenoh will also be wearing a similar white dress with one difference, as the high priestess, Kelenoh's dress will be held together with golden pins. As Cassandra places her pleated coat on her, it falls down over her dress and the snake band is then placed on her head. Immediately Kelenoh feels the energy emitting from it. She picks up the lygos branch that Stephanos cut for her, and places Yufas on her shoulder.

Then the women step outside, they walk through the complex to the dining hall to gather the other priestesses so that they all can proceed to the Temple of Hera for the morning service.

During the service, as the priestesses begin to sing, Kelenoh retreats to the room where the statue of Hera stands and lovingly removes the summer dress it is wearing. In silence, she thanks the gods and asks their blessings for the festival day.

At the end of the service, they move outside to see the first people from the island walking on the Procession Road. Kelenoh remains at the top of the stairs so she can easily see the people, and they in turn have a good view of her. Cassandra, Theano and Selene stand close behind her.

The other priestesses go down to the road to greet and welcome the people. They provide them with drinks, and show them spots along the road where they can sit down until the procession begins.

The soldiers, assigned to protect the priestesses, also live on temple grounds. Now they are standing erect and ready, their long spears in hand, positioned in rows in front of the temple. To the far left, in front of the line, stands Stephanos. All the soldiers are in formation and they look marvelous as a barrier between the people of the island and the inhabitants of the temple complex.

With a beaming smile, Kelenoh gives Stephanos a nod of approval. He bows his head, as he acknowledges her nod, and remains in a posture that radiates a certain pride.

Kelenoh redirects her attention to the road and the people that are approaching. It is a cheerful sight. The men, women and children wear colorful clothing; talking and laughter echoes in the temple complex.

The women bring flowers, and the fresh produce of the land is carried in bundles or in baskets in their arms. A part of what they bring will be placed on the altar, the rest will be offered to the sea.

Kelenoh looks at all the people with a wide brimming smile appearing on her face. Her gaze rests upon a woman approaching with two little girls holding onto each of her hands, one girl is a little taller than the other. The woman is tall, with a large, square, hard face, and black hair. She is wearing a very beautiful but simple colorful dress.

She comes across as confident, but Kelenoh feels her secret sorrow and is drawn to this woman. She had determined not to look inside people today, but she cannot avoid it with this woman. She turns to Cassandra and asks, "Who is that woman?"

"That is Hefaisteon, the wife of Polykrates," Cassandra answers.

Kelenoh directs her attention again to the woman. She can sense a silent battle that persists between her and Polykrates. Though an intelligent woman, Hefaisteon cannot match him verbally and struggles with an inability to resist her husband. The woman feels her gaze and looks straight at Kelenoh. There is a very profound moment between the two women as they gaze deeply into each other's eyes. It is the beginning moment of a deep and lasting friendship between the two of them.

Hefaisteon nods to Kelenoh and Kelenoh answers with a smile. Slowly, a smile appears on Hefaisteon's face, softening the hard lines around her eyes. Suddenly, the deep exchange between them is disturbed by a group of men walking noisily up on the Procession Road.

Kelenoh recognizes Polykrates who leads the group, and has to suppress a feeling of antipathy toward him. The other people move aside as he passes, and the busy cheerful atmosphere disappears. Polykrates looks up with pride and nods to her affably. Kelenoh returns his greeting with a closed mouthed smile, raises her face to the sun, lets the warmth stream into her, and radiates that out to the people. On the instant, the road is filled again with cheerful chatter.

Kelenoh can hear a group of people singing from far off as they approach the road. Kelenoh assumes it is the men of Eupalinos who are digging the water tunnel. She turns to Cassandra who confirms that it is.

Eupalinos appears over the road. She had depicted him taller, but what he lacks in appearance he makes up for in the strength and confidence he exudes. Later, after the ceremony, Kelenoh looks forward to becoming more acquainted with him.

Kelenoh searches the group for Rhoikos and Theodoros. Suddenly, she sees father and son standing near the Temple of Aphrodite. Separate and apart from the others, Kelenoh concludes that Rhoikos and Theodoros must have come to the temple via the beach and the Sacred Road.

When she looks at Theodoros, her heart jumps in her chest. He looks splendid and stately! Both his father and Theodoros himself are dressed in white tunics with golden belts, and wear sandals with leather bands wrapped up around their legs to the knee.

Yufas lets out a trill in her ear that sounds like a burst of laughter. She looks at him, undisturbed.

She nods to both men who place their hands together and bow in response.

'It is time.' Kelenoh heeds the inner prompting and begins to descend the stairs. Cassandra, Theano and Selene follow close behind. Selene is carrying a zither under her arm. The four priestesses walk together, making their way through the long double row of soldiers standing in front of the temple as they walk quietly and with great dignity to the altar.

When they reach the end of the lances, Kelenoh stops in front of Stephanos who is standing with a torch in hand, which he quickly presents to Kelenoh.

A cheer rings out when Kelenoh accepts the torch! She raises it up high with her right hand. Large groups of people now begin to move about so as to position themselves behind the great altar. The women reach into their bundles and baskets, take out their offering for the altar, and in procession, one after the other, gently place their offerings on the sacred altar.

The group near the altar gathers behind Kelenoh at the open space beside the temple. Kelenoh keeps the torch raised the entire time so that everyone can see it. Once all have passed by the altar with their offerings, she switches the torch to her left hand and lights the gifts that have been presented on the altar.

Kelenoh begins singing a song; everyone joins in a rousing chorus. Smoke along with delicious odors billow into the air. After the song, everyone starts cheering at the sight of the smoke, straight as a pillar, rising to the skies. This is seen as a sign that the gods favor them.

Kelenoh stands up straight and motionless in front of the altar. She starts talking to the gods and slowly it becomes silent around her. Not even a sound from the peacocks can be heard. The people stare at the woman with the bird on her shoulder, their mouths wide open in awe.

Kelenoh, put into a trance by the combination of her own prayer and the herbs burning on the altar, is unaware of the people's reaction. Kelenoh is lost to what is going on around her, enveloped in two worlds: the cosmos and the earth. She asks the gods to bless the people, protect them and all that lives. She thanks them for the abundant harvest and all the blessings the island has received during the past months. Quietly, she listens for an answer from the gods, but the gods are silent. It is good as it is. The gods are pleased.

Slowly, she comes out of her trance and hears the crackling of the fire on the altar. Cassandra offers her a cup of water. As she gracefully sips the water, she feels the presence of Pythagoras and Hestia. Hestia appears in front of her. She looks at Kelenoh lovingly and embraces her, after which she places her hands on Kelenoh's head for a moment and then disappears.

Six soldiers in rows of two arrive. They are carrying the statue of Hera high above their heads. Kelenoh comes up from behind them, followed by Cassandra, Selene and Theano. Roxanna, head of the kitchen, follows Selene and Theano with her priestesses. Leatis, head of the laundry, is close behind with her priestesses, followed by the priestesses of the gardens, then the weaving mill, and lastly priestesses who are in training. Two by two they all walk in a long row, protected on either side by the soldiers walking in tandem with them.

The inhabitants of the island trail at the end of the procession. They are busy chattering and laughing. Kelenoh catches bits of conversation here and there and smiles. They walk via the Sacred Road in the direction of the beach. On the beach they spread out along the water, and wait for the next part of the ceremony to commence.

Kelenoh gives a signal to the soldiers carrying the statue to put it in the sea. As the statue floats on the waves, shouts and applause erupt within the crowd. The statue continues bobbing in the same spot. It doesn't leave the beach. That is another good sign. Hera indicates she wishes to stay on Samos and that the coming year will be prosperous.

The women of the island walk to the edge of the water and throw the rest of their offerings into the sea. The sun is high in the clear blue sky and the wind is calm.

Kelenoh raises her arms and asks the sea to accept the offerings. She absorbs into herself the sight of the Hera statue amidst the varied mixture of flowers, plants, herbs, and the stalks of grains all floating about on the sparkling sunlit sea. Suddenly, there emerges a swelling wave above all the offerings. It comes crashing down, swallowing it all up. Shortly thereafter, the only thing that returns from the sea is the statue of Hera.

The cheering is deafening. People are jumping, dancing and clapping their hands. Kelenoh looks at the people and feels happy she was able to perform the ritual well.

Kelenoh raises her right hand to announce that she wants to speak. When all are silent she says, "The gods have returned Hera to our island and have accepted our gifts. We will not suffer hunger this winter."

Kelenoh approaches Cassandra who is standing by, ready with cloths and a splendidly woven new winter dress with gold and silver for the statue of Hera. They walk to the statue lying washed up on the beach, covered with lygos branches. Kelenoh takes the cloths in her hands and orders the soldiers to remove the branches, and then to stand the statue upright. As she dries the statue with the cloths, she sings a song of gratitude. With the statue now almost dry, she signals Cassandra to bring over the new winter dress, and together they both adorn the statue of Hera. When they are finished, Kelenoh beckons the soldiers and she orders them to carry the statue back to the sacred temple.

Kelenoh directs herself once more to the people of the island proclaiming, "Today is a day of celebration and feasting, enjoy yourselves and each other. Before I retire, I wanted to let you all know that starting tomorrow, I will be available to address any sickness or illness you may be dealing with, any problems or other matters oppressing you. Every morning I will be in the Temple of Hera, and you are always welcome there."

Cheers rise again and Kelenoh sees smiling, laughing faces everywhere. She urges them to be silent once more so that she may finish speaking.

Kelenoh raises her arms, palms open to the sky, "In conclusion, I would like to offer a song of gratitude to the gods."

Selene approaches and kneels down in front of Kelenoh and starts playing the introduction on her zither. Kelenoh joins in singing. The sound of the zither and her voice carry far over the sea.

Several people start crying spontaneously, touched by the pure tones of the zither and Kelenoh's voice. When the song has finished, it is still and silent on the beach. The people gather in small groups and look for places to sit down to eat and drink. It isn't long before talking and laughing is echoing all along the beach.

Kelenoh turns around to the priestesses and says, "Come, we will now go to the dining hall and enjoy the food and drink the earth has given us."

Slowly and reverently, they walk back over the Sacred Road. Kelenoh halts when reaching a kouros that stands to her right, and lays her hand on the left leg for a moment before proceeding. The priestesses continue on toward the dining hall.

Kelenoh first goes into the Temple of Hera to place her lygos branch at the feet of the statue of Hera, and to thank the gods in a moment of silence by herself.

Then she enters the dining hall and sees cheerful faces sitting at the long table candidly talking about the oblation festival. A hush falls as she walks to her chair. She reaches her chair, puts Yufas in front of her on the table and says, "I thank you all for the work that you are doing at this complex and for the help you offer the people of the island. Without you, the temple complex could not exist. Each of us is a small link in the large singular chain. Let us be aware that every person has his or her own place and is of importance. Come! Let us sing a song of gratitude before our meal and then enjoy all that the earth has provided."

Everyone stands up and Kelenoh starts singing a song.

After the meal, the dining hall is cleaned up and the priestesses, except for a few, disappear into the complex. They have the rest of the day off and go out to mingle with the population of the island. Cassandra, Theano and Selene remain seated at the table with Kelenoh. Cassandra says proudly, "Kelenoh, today you have proved to everyone on the island that you are the Woman of Hera."

The women sit for a while and then Kelenoh breaks the silence saying, "Theano, I ask that you go to the Temple of Apollo, there will surely be people that need you. Selene, you should go to the Temple of Aphrodite to meet people there. Cassandra and I will stay here to receive anyone that I need to talk to."

Wine and honey cakes are brought in, and laid on the table by Kelenoh and Cassandra. Another priestess brings in fresh flowers and fruit. Kelenoh signals to the priestesses that they are now allowed to leave and enjoy the rest of the day.

Chapter 12

Today is the day for visitations. Kelenoh is sitting in the dining hall at the Temple of Hera awaiting the first visitors. She closes her eyes and concentrates on the conversations to come.

A shadow falls over her; a presence has entered the dining hall. She opens her eyes and sees Polykrates standing at the far end of the table looking straight at her. Close behind him, are his four men.

Kelenoh opens her arms and says, "Welcome, Ruler of Samos, please take a seat. There is wine, there are cookies and fruit for you and your fellow governors, help yourself if you like."

Polykrates thanks her, but raises his eyebrows, curious at the use of the word governors. Kelenoh almost bursts out laughing, discerning his thoughts, 'Is she making fun of me or is she serious?'

He opens his mouth to say something, but stands open-mouthed as he is interrupted by the arrival of new guests. Eupalinos, Rhoikos and Theodoros are standing in the open portico. Irritated, Polykrates sits down.

Eupalinos introduces himself to Kelenoh. The man is short and stalky with a wide body build. His trimmed short, dark hair frames his face. Kelenoh likes his boldness. She invites him to sit down and enjoy the wine and food.

Rhoikos and Theodoros greet her and sit down at the table as well. Upon seeing Theodoros her heart leaps and she notices she is afraid of looking him straight in the eyes.

Polykrates gets up and starts an exhaustive speech about the good course of the festival. Kelenoh suppresses her impatience and listens quietly to his words, concentrating on the cup of wine and the gifts lying on the table. She wants to talk to Eupalinos and discuss the advancements of his tunnel that will guarantee water for the city.

Polykrates notices her disinterest and cuts his speech short with the words, "As a thank you for your good work on the complex, I want to tell you that the design plans for the new Temple of Hera are ready. I would like to go over them with you at the next most convenient time."

Satisfied, Polykrates sits down, knowing that he now has the full attention of Kelenoh. Delighted, Kelenoh looks at Polykrates, and then looks quickly to Theodoros, who sits quietly at the table. He glows with an inner pride about the work he has done.

She directs her attention back to Polykrates and says, "Polykrates, thank you for your praise regarding the festival. I am happy to hear Theodoros has finished the designs for the temple so soon. I invite you, Rhoikos and Theodoros, to look over the designs with me tomorrow afternoon here in the dining hall, and discuss when we can start the construction."

The three men stand up, take a bow and confirm that they will be there tomorrow afternoon. A silence sets in at the table, Kelenoh directs her attention to Eupalinos who is quietly drinking wine and eating a honey cake. She feels the imperturbability of this man. He has a great confidence in his own abilities and has no interest in anything someone else thinks or does.

"Eupalinos, what progress have you made with the water tunnel?"

Eupalinos looks disturbed as he looks up from his cup of wine, and brutishly answers, "The tunnel has been dug out on both sides for a quarter of the mountain." He takes another drink of wine from his cup.

"What do you do with all the rocks that are removed from the mountain?"

"They are used to build the wall around the city and for roads within the city." He grabs another cake from the bowl and takes a generous bite.

Kelenoh is a little disturbed by his disrespectful attitude and replies, "I admire your ability, but I would like that when I talk to you, you stop eating and drinking. I want to be able to look at you, because my interest in your work is genuine."

Red-faced, he puts his cup down and places the cake on the table and looks at her with evident anger in his eyes. Kelenoh feels a ticklish laugh rising in her throat, but it disappears when she sees Polykrates actually enjoying their conversation immensely. She feels anger welling up inside of her because of the contempt shown on the part of both men toward her. It is the same kind of anger she felt for the priest in Memphis, whom she almost had to beg to enter the temple.

She stands up, her growing anger becoming hard to suppress. She doesn't hear the soothing little sounds of Yufas. Trembling she says, "Eupalinos, I want you to leave the complex right now! Next week we will continue this conversation. I will have Stephanos pick you up and accompany you to the temple. I expect at that time we will be able to speak with respect for each other."

Eupalinos looks up to the woman standing before him and for the first time he looks straight at her, his jaw relaxes a bit and his attitude shifts. Kelenoh can see surprise in his eyes. He turns his head sideways to Polykrates. She then realizes that both men have spoken about her, and their opinions of her are not very flattering.

Eupalinos pushes his chair back, and in a huff marches out of the dining hall. Just before he steps through the open doorway, he spins around and says, "I will hear from you." He grunts, and then disappears outside.

Kelenoh's anger instantly diminishes. She slowly lowers herself to the table, sits down, and looks at Yufas in his little eyes, searching for some support and help to restore harmony within her. She puts on the best face and says, "Drink and eat, because this is a day to be grateful. She raises her cup and looks Polykrates straight in the eyes. Polykrates raises his cup, but lowers his eyes, avoiding her gaze. In silence, they continue drinking and eating until Rhoikos and Theodoros stand up and thank her for her hospitality.

Rhoikos nods agreeably, "We will see you tomorrow afternoon."

Bowing respectfully, they leave the dining hall. Theodoros' eyes are fixed in her vision, and for a moment, Kelenoh feels sad. How should she approach him and how can she express her feelings? For a moment, the weight of being the high priestess presses heavy on her shoulders.

Again, there is a silence filled with tension. The only people left in the room are her, Cassandra, and Polykrates and his men. Nervously, Polykrates shuffles back and forth in his chair. He knows Kelenoh understands that he talked to Eupalinos about her, and is unsure of how to react in this moment. Suddenly, he stands up and with a sweeping gesture says, "The Ruler of Samos greets you! I will see you tomorrow at the meeting."

He signals to his men to get up and they all leave.

Quietly, Kelenoh sits in her chair. Cassandra stands up and wraps her arms around Kelenoh. "Kelenoh, you were fantastic. They know now they cannot get away with anything."

Arm in arm they leave the dining hall and take the road home.

After the morning service in the temple, Kelenoh sits, tense with expectation, waiting to see if people will come seeking her help. Yufas sits on the armrest of the chair and gives her a little nudge now and then with his little head as if to say, "I am with you."

She looks at the little bird, her heart is assured and the tension diminishes. Stillness flows in and around her. In the stillness she hears the wind that rages around the temple. The fall storms have resumed. Suddenly, she sees a man and a woman tentatively walking up the stairs. They are clearly nervous, but curious.

Kelenoh stands up, puts Yufas on her shoulder and walks toward them, stretching her hands out welcoming them says, "What can I do for you?"

In truth, she already knows the answer, but wants the people to express themselves and tell her directly. Both fall down on their knees. Kelenoh bends down, takes the woman by her arm and says, "Please stand up, both of you, and tell me what I can do for you."

The woman starts sobbing and the man stands by somewhat helplessly. With a shaky voice the woman says, "Woman of Hera, we have been together five years now, and I still have not been able to have a child. We would like to have children."

The woman looks desperately at her. Kelenoh glances over to the man for a moment also feeling his desperation. She directs her attention on the abdomen of the woman and sees that her fallopian tubes are closed. In her mind she opens the tubes and says to the man and woman, "Go. You will bear a child next year."

Astonished and relieved, they don't know what to say. They turn around and disappear among the people that have gathered in the meantime in front of the steps of the temple. Kelenoh looks at the small group before her as they watch the happy couple exit the temple. Yufas sounds a trill and the small group looks up encouraged, but also slightly afraid.

"Welcome to the Temple of Hera. Please come up to me one at a time, so I can help everyone."

She stretches out her arms lovingly, clearly showing that there is no need to be afraid. With this gesture from Kelenoh, the subtle fears of the people vanish and they ascend the steps one by one.

Kelenoh heals eight people, solves marriage problems and quarrels for twelve others. The people all depart happy and relieved. She knows this group will spread the news of her abilities to the other people of the island.

When the last members of the group fade out on the Procession Road, Kelenoh goes outside, pulling her shawl tightly around her for protection against the heavy wind. She makes her way to the dining hall to dine and prepare for the arrival of Rhoikos, Theodoros and Polykrates.

Just when she is ready for them, the men enter. This time, some unfamiliar men are tagging along behind them. They are carrying clay tablets with designs on them. Under the direction of Theodoros, they lay out the tablets on the table.

Before Kelenoh's eyes, one of the tablets is the very design she had seen in a vision the first day she arrived on Samos. It is one of the temples of Karnak. Beaming, she looks at Theodoros who bashfully turns his head under her gaze. She feels his pride and joy because of her approval. When the men finish laying out the clay tablets, they take a bow and withdraw outside.

All gather around the table admiring the work that has been done. Rhoikos is the first to speak, "Because this temple will be larger than the present one, I propose to build it more toward the West. I know it is very swampy there, but we can use rocks from the mountains of the island, transported in blocks to the complex, to reinforce a strong foundation.

"In front of the temple," he continues, pointing to the tablets, "We will create a large space where people can be received when there are festivities. Extending out from the temple, I want to build a new altar on the same spot where it is at present. Since it will take years to build the temple, I have another proposal."

He pauses, looking to Kelenoh. "You also wanted a new temple for Hermes and Aphrodite beside the large new Temple of Hera. If we build that temple first, we will obviously be finished sooner, because it is smaller. Then, during the demolition of the old temple, which will also take some time, we can place the pedestal with the statue of Hera temporarily in the new Temple of Hermes and Aphrodite. You will still be able to do the work you are doing now in the Temple of Hera, but for the time being, it would simply be in the Temple of Hermes and Aphrodite."

Somewhat surprised, with what he has proposed, Kelenoh looks at Rhoikos.

"What a good idea, Rhoikos! I am in full support of this, and did you..."

Suddenly, she is interrupted by a furious Polykrates who stands up, and bursts out, "Rhoikos, did you not have to consult me about that first? It is I who gave you the instructions for the building of the Temple of Hera."

Kelenoh directs her attention to Polykrates, who she has ignored until now because of what happened with Eupalinos yesterday. She recognizes his deep insecurity, which he often tries to compensate by a display of forced power.

Rhoikos bows to Polykrates and says, "Ruler of Samos, I am aware that you are the appointed authority over this and I am honored that you trusted me with it. But the Woman of Hera is the head of this temple complex, and she and her priestesses will have to work here, so I think it logical to discuss this with her first. That being said, I have brought this up in your presence as well, you are free to interject your thoughts and discuss them with us."

Polykrates' anger diminishes when Rhoikos addresses him with his title. He takes a respectful bow and says more quietly this time, "Yes, you are right. We will discuss this all together."

Polykrates turns back to Kelenoh and asks, "What did you want to say?"

"I wanted to ask Rhoikos if the drawings for the Hermes-Aphrodite Temple and the altar are complete."

Theodoros answers for his father, "Woman, the drawings of the Hermes-Aphrodite Temple are almost finished. I have yet to begin the drawings of the altar. We have spent most of our energy on designing the Temple of Hera, but it didn't take long to realize that the construction of it is going to take a quite a while. That is when the idea of building the smaller temple first came to us. However, we didn't want to do it without deliberation. We will focus on finishing the designs for the Hermes-Aphrodite Temple if this company approves of our idea."

Kelenoh nods, catching him deliberately eyeing her, and at the same time looking to Polykrates. She grins at the tactical play.

She responds, "Again, I like the idea. What do you think?"

She looks Polykrates straight in the eyes and he gives her a short nod. Then he says to Rhoikos and Theodoros, "It seems a good plan to build the Temple of Hermes and Aphrodite first. Finish your designs and then show them to me."

Polykrates, having spoken his mind, abruptly turns around and walks toward the exit of the dining hall followed by his four men. Without another word, he marches out of sight.

Kelenoh continues, "You heard the orders. Please complete the designs and I will see you again when they are finished."

She makes her way around the table to stand beside Theodoros. She cannot help but reach out and touch him. Laying her hand on his arm, she says, "I am very happy with this design. It is exactly the way I imagined it to be."

Theodoros places his hand on top of Kelenoh's. A shiver goes through her body. It is the first physical contact she has had with him. In her lower abdomen something comes alive that she never has felt before. Though a pleasant feeling, she suppresses it and looks freely at Theodoros.

"Woman," says Theodoros, "I am happy you approve of my design. My father and I will make sure there will be a temple the way you like it."

He removes his hand, takes a bow and calls for the men who had been waiting outside, to come gather the clay tablets and bring them back to his home. Rhoikos and Theodoros say farewell to Kelenoh under the agreement that they will let her know when the other designs are ready.

Kelenoh stays behind with a feeling of loneliness. The contact with Theodoros makes her realize how far apart they are. Nevertheless, she can tell he also has feelings for her.

Feeling the pressure of his hand, as though it is still resting on hers, she stands there looking at her hand. She doesn't know what to do with the feelings still raging through her. Her whole body tingles and is alive.

Suddenly, someone touches her and Kelenoh almost utters a cry from fright. She turns around and looks into the face of a slightly concerned Cassandra.

"Where are you with your thoughts?" Cassandra asks. "Do you want to talk about it?"

For a moment Kelenoh is tempted to tell Cassandra about her love for Theodoros, but instead she says, "I feel a little tired. I want to go home and retire for a short time to renew my energy." Kelenoh grabs Yufas from the table and together they walk home in silence.

In the evening, she discusses with the other three women of her household what she has decided to do regarding construction of the new temple. Selene is honored that her temple, as priestess of Aphrodite, will be used for the time being until the Temple of Hera is finished.

A week has gone by since the festival, and every morning, Kelenoh heals and cures people of the island. She enjoys this work, realizing that it is for this purpose that she had been well trained in Egypt.

Having the strong sense of being one with the cosmos and the earth, she walks around the complex beaming. Everyone who sees her is struck with a ray of pure light, and is affected by her radiance.

Kelenoh decides it is time to have another conversation with Eupalinos. She sends Stephanos to get him, and to then escort him to the dining hall where she will be waiting. A short while later, Eupalinos, wearing an old, brown tunic, enters. Kelenoh realizes that this man does not care about what he wears or how he appears to others. It doesn't interest him.

He is closely followed by Polykrates and his men. Polykrates looks like a dolled up peacock in his richly decorated clothing.

Kelenoh suppresses her disgust, and invites everyone to sit down. Polykrates stays standing, and without being asked, starts explaining the reason for his presence with wide hand gestures.

"I was with Eupalinos when Stephanos came to get him and I think, since the tunnel is my idea, that I should be present for this discussion."

Kelenoh nods to him, "Please sit down, Polykrates. It was not my plan to exclude you, but because my questions are related to the work of Eupalinos, I did not think of you."

With an aggrieved face, Polykrates sits down. She looks at Eupalinos. He has a sly grin on his face. Surprised by his reaction, she looks inside this man who, while waiting for her questions, pours himself a cup of wine and starts to take a large bite from a cake.

Kelenoh's inner vision reveals a scientifically minded man, dispassionately involved in life in order to get things done. Occupied with himself and his work, he doesn't tolerate anyone who contradicts him; his vision is the right one. Kelenoh sees he is annoyed by Polykrates, who, in his opinion, uses too many words. Eupalinos is a thinker, a doer. He doesn't like dawdling and whining.

Suddenly, Eupalinos looks up and straight at Kelenoh, "You wanted to ask me something? Ask," he huffs, "there is much work waiting for me."

Kelenoh smiles and says, "I understand. Well first, I would like to know how you got the idea to dig a tunnel through the mountain to provide water for the city."

Eupalinos looks at Kelenoh, disapprovingly. He hadn't expected such a dumb question of her. Kelenoh knows what he is thinking, but wants him to talk.

"The answer is simple. The water is behind the mountain, not in front of it."

Kelenoh finds it difficult not to burst out in laughter. She contains herself and says, "Last time you told me you had progressed through a quarter of the mountain. I think it was an innovative idea to dig the tunnel on both sides of the mountain. How long do you estimate it will take, and what are you doing about the lack of oxygen for the men, especially now that they are deeper into the mountain?"

Stunned, Eupalinos looks at Kelenoh and even puts his cup of wine down.

"I think it will take several years before we make it all the way through the mountain. Concerning the lack of oxygen, I have the men work shorter shifts so they can take breaks outside."

Kelenoh closes her eyes and sees the men busy at work in the mountain come outside sweating and gasping for air.

"How many men will survive?"

"I wouldn't know. There are plenty of men available for this work," Eupalinos answers. Polykrates joins the conversation, "Where are you going with your questions? Do you think my plans are careless?"

Kelenoh looks at Polykrates and doesn't say anything. He lowers his eyes. Kelenoh takes a draught of wine to collect herself, and to drive away the picture of the men in the mountain. She turns her attention back to Eupalinos.

"Do you think your calculations are correct, and you will meet exactly in the middle?" Kelenoh asks, though already knowing the answer. They will get there within about one meter of difference.

"Of course my calculations are correct. Who do you think you are dealing with?"

"Good," says Kelenoh, "Now I have something else I would like to bring up. In regards to the wall you are building, will there be enough gates so that the people of the island, in an emergency situation, will have safe and sufficient passage?"

Eupalinos stands up fuming.

"I don't feel like having this conversation anymore. This is my business. My calculations are correct and twelve gates are enough."

Kelenoh snaps back, "It's true this is your business. But the people of the island are my business." She has to restrain herself, so as not to explode in anger and looks helplessly to Yufas in order to stay in balance. The peace radiating from his little eyes gives her the strength she needs so much.

Kelenoh stands up, bows to Eupalinos and says, "Thank you for this conversation, a lot has been made clear to me."

Confused, Eupalinos blinks at her, then, with a curt nod, spins around and walks out. With a half-hearted smile, Kelenoh follows him with her eyes. The man doesn't know what to think of her. It doesn't matter. She knows he will not spend any time trying to 'figure her out.'

Polykrates looks at Kelenoh somewhat disapprovingly, stands up with his men, ready to leave as well.

"How are your wife and daughters?" asks Kelenoh. "I would like to meet them."

"Thank you for asking, they are well. I will let Hefaisteon know. I am sure you will hear from her."

Grim faced, Polykrates turns around. He and his company leave the dining hall.

Kelenoh sits back down in her chair. She lets out a deep sigh, and then directs her attention to the men in the mountain once more. An image of herself in the vaults flashes before her eyes; she stands under the airshaft inhaling oxygen. She shakes her head and sends energy to the men in the mountain.

Chapter 13

It has been raining a lot the past three days, with harsh winds battering the island. Whenever there was a break from the inclement weather, Kelenoh would quickly make her rounds at the temple complex.

As she is making her way over the Procession Road, a man, unknown to Kelenoh, approaches her. The man bows and says, "I am Cleitus, the servant of Hefaisteon. She invites you to have a little bite to eat this afternoon."

"Thank you for bringing me the invitation. Please tell your mistress that I gladly accept her invitation."

The man takes a bow, turns around and leaves. Kelenoh follows him with her eyes then turns her gaze within to look for Hefaisteon. She sees her walking through her house and Kelenoh senses she is worried about one of her daughters.

With her mind, Kelenoh searches the complex for Stephanos for he will have to accompany her to Polykrates' house this afternoon. She sees him in the grain barn. Immediately she begins walking in that direction, traversing the path between the barren fields. She is very much enjoying the view, and the scent coming from the earth. The wind and rain of the last few days have swept away any fragrance of summer, and now rising into her nostrils is an air that is heavy with the full rich smell of the fertile dampened earth. She inhales deeply and is filled with the life that is contained within the earth beneath her feet.

Stephanos sees her nearing and walks toward her. Kelenoh looks at his friendly, always smiling face, which makes her happy inside.

"Hello Woman, what can I do for you?"

Stephanos, I need you this afternoon. Hefaisteon has invited me to her home. Would you be able to accompany me?"

"Of course Woman, this afternoon after lunch, I will come and get you by the dining hall with two of my men."

When Kelenoh walks back, she takes the road that leads to the flower gardens; she wants to see whether or not they have suffered badly from the storms. Kelenoh sees Selene busy at work in the rose garden. She is removing the overgrown roses, and binding the shrubs that have blown down. A large part of the garden has been flooded by the overflowing pond.

Selene tells Kelenoh that this happens every year in the fall, especially in the marshy part of the garden. Kelenoh thinks about the flooding as she walks to the dining hall.

'Maybe there is a way to catch the water,' she muses, 'or lead it to basins, so it can be used during periods of drought.'

After her meal, she meets Stephanos who is waiting for her outside with two soldiers. Kelenoh is excited and so is Yufas who is uttering happy cries. It is the first time they will leave the complex to visit the city.

They walk over the Sacred Road along the beach. Once they reach the end of the road, they make a right turn, and then walk along the harbor of the temple complex toward the city. Stephanos leads the way, followed by Kelenoh, followed by the two soldiers.

Kelenoh stares at the long straight road that leads to the city. To the left of her there are mountains, and to the right, a flat piece of land stretching out to the sea. As they approach the city, Kelenoh sees houses. The houses look new, but are very small indeed.

Kelenoh cannot imagine whole families living in them. When she passes by, the people stop their work and bow. It is hard for Kelenoh to get accustomed to this. Her feeling of love is so great that she has to suppress the inclination to embrace everyone. Far away, on the right side of a hill, she sees the palace of Polykrates.

The palace sits on a piece of land extending into the sea. Left of the palace is the harbor of the city. Ships, large and small, are floating on the water. The sweet scent of cedar wood fills the air.

The palace looks splendid. Even as the temple complex is, this castle must also be very visible from the sea to the ships sailing into the harbor of Samos.

Stephanos knocks on the door and Cleitus, the man she had seen that morning at the complex, opens the door.

He bows and then opens the door wider to let them in. They enter in, Stephanos and his men say goodbye to Kelenoh, and then leave to wait in the kitchen until she has finished.

Though her face doesn't show it, Hefaisteon greets Kelenoh with wide, open arms, happy to see her. Hefaisteon is clearly worried.

Kelenoh looks around the big room. Large fires burning in high and low bowls illuminate the space. There is a large table filled with bowls of food and fruit. Along the sides of the table are bench seats, and there is a chair pulled up at each end. At the other side of the room are two benches to lie on, each having a small side table decorated with flower pots. Large tapestries made with splendid colors hang on the walls. It is a fine room, filled with color and warmth, yet Kelenoh still detects loneliness and coldness.

Suddenly, she hears giggling and turns in the direction of the sound. There the little daughters of Polykrates sit in a dark corner. The little girls stare at her and the smiles on their faces disappear when they notice someone is looking at them.

Kelenoh invites the little girls to come near. Hesitating for a moment, they stand up and then walk to her. She feels Hefaisteon stiffen up behind her. Already aware that Hefaisteon is worried about one of her children, Kelenoh doesn't say anything, and holds her hands above them.

As she pays attention to the oldest girl, Kelenoh is suddenly seized by sorrow. She scans the little girl that looks back at her with a serious expression. Kelenoh knows that she will pass away in a short time. With all her power and gifts, there is nothing she can do about it. Tears well up in her eyes; a short life for her was predestined, an agreement between herself and the gods before being born.

She strokes the children on their heads and waits until she has her voice under control again. Then she says, "Go on with your play now."

The little children run away giggling. Kelenoh holds still for a moment, then turns around and smiles gently to Hefaisteon who looks at her, fearful. Hefaisteon speaks out, "Kelenoh, I am afraid. There is something wrong with my oldest child. That is why I called for you. I noticed that you saw something."

Kelenoh wished she could take Hefaisteon in her arms, but she understands that Hefaisteon doesn't like to be touched. She stands in front of her and says, "It is good that you called for me, but there is nothing I can do for you. I only can be here for you. The gods and your daughter have made their decision."

The face of Hefaisteon contorts into a grimace. Her mouth opens, but no sound comes out. She grabs her hair with her hands and stares desperately at Kelenoh. Kelenoh hears the primeval scream that soundlessly comes out of her. The sound strikes Kelenoh as though she has been punched in her diaphragm.

Kelenoh wants to grab the hands of Hefaisteon, but she steps back, still without making any sound.

Then the scream comes out. Kelenoh feels Yufas shrink on her shoulder. The sorrow of the woman causes Kelenoh to burst out in tears. Hefaisteon sees the empathetic tears of Kelenoh. She takes her hands out of her hair, hands filled with tufts of hair, stretching them out as a rejection in front of her. Hefaisteon starts screaming, "No, no," and falls on the floor unconscious.

Cleitus hurries in after hearing the screaming of his mistress, and sees her lying on the floor. With a look of reproach toward Kelenoh, he lifts Hefaisteon up and lies her down on one of the benches. Kelenoh walks to the bench and sends Cleitus away.

She kneels beside Hefaisteon and puts her hand on her head, giving her love and peace. Hefaisteon opens her eyes, quietly looks at Kelenoh. The two women sit together for a little while in silence. Then Kelenoh takes Hefaisteon's hand, who allows her to touch her now.

Then the question comes Kelenoh had been expecting, having already read it in the eyes of Hefaisteon, "Why?"

Kelenoh hesitates, not answering immediately, so Hefaisteon whispers once more, "Why?"

"Hefaisteon, as humans, we do not know why children die. I know that before a human soul is born, there is an agreement made between the gods and the soul as to what experiences the soul wants to have on earth, and how long the life of the soul will be."

"Your daughter had already long made the decision in cooperation with the gods that she would not grow old in this life. The time she would spend here would be enough. After this she will go on to have different experiences in other lives, until the time comes when she doesn't have to be born again. First, she will go back to the gods for a while to rest in Love."

Kelenoh looks at Hefaisteon who now lies on the bench quietly, unmoved, eyes closed. Tears are rolling down her cheeks. Kelenoh knows that Hefaisteon is trying to absorb what she just heard.

Suddenly, the silence is disturbed by Polykrates who comes darting in. He has been called by Cleitus. For the first time Kelenoh sees him alone, without his men. Angry, he yells, "What is happening here?"

He first looks to his wife, then to Kelenoh. His shouts are directed only to her, "Is there anyone who can tell me what happened? I thought you wanted to visit my wife and now I hear Hefaisteon has fainted? What did you do?"

Kelenoh stands up, looks straight at Polykrates and says, "Your wife is my friend. I wanted to visit her. However, she also had a question for me when I came, and I have given her the answer."

The face of Polykrates turns red from anger. Kelenoh's calm exterior irritates him, and he shouts in her face, "What kind of question and answer is it, that would cause her to faint?"

"It is up to your wife as to whether or not she tells you," Kelenoh answers.

She places her hand on Hefaisteon's comforting her and saying, "I am going to leave you now, but you may always come to me if you have any questions, or if you want to talk about anything. I will be there for you."

She nods at Polykrates and asks Cleitus to inform Stephanos that she wishes to return to the temple complex.

Once outside, Kelenoh tells Stephanos she would like to go to the harbor for a short time; having the need to be by the sea to bring her thoughts and feelings back in balance.

There are not many boats in the harbor and Kelenoh searches for a spot where she can sit down and watch the sea undisturbed. Stephanos and the two soldiers sit down a little further away, waiting until she is ready to continue on.

Kelenoh closes her eyes and lets the warmth of the sun shine on her face. She feels a sense of oneness with the red-orange sun and takes a deep breath. After a while, she stands up and calls Stephanos. She wants to go home. She has found her equilibrium and walks straight and tall with poise. Buried in thoughts, she hardly notices her surroundings as they make their way back to the security of the temple complex.

Chapter 14

The fall storms and rain had done their job, and now winter announces itself with a calm, even, cold temperature.

At the beginning of fall, Kelenoh ordered Nearchos to dig small canals and build a water basin in the marshy area of the gardens to prevent flooding. The plan was to have the water, via the small canals, stream into and be stored in the basin.

All in all, Kelenoh ordered the construction of three large water basins to be built. One was to be situated behind the kitchen, one beside the vegetable garden, and the last one behind the flower gardens. The basins and small canals were built from the stone rubble that came from the tunnel of Eupalinos.

The wall around the city progressed constantly, although sometimes the work was not possible because of the fall storms. In the months that passed, Kelenoh didn't talk with either Eupalinos or Polykrates.

She had seen and spoken with Rhoikos and Theodoros a few times on the terrain where the new Temple of Hermes and Aphrodite was to be built. The plot of land has been secured and equalized. In a short time construction would begin alongside the demolition of the old Temple of Hera.

Kelenoh has often thought about Hefaisteon, but hasn't heard anything from her. She could have read the thoughts of Hefaisteon, but she didn't. Instead, wished she would one day come to her of her of own free will.

She had, however, used her gift of sight to check on Hefaisteon's daughter and had seen the end was near. Quietly, from her abode at the temple, she sent love and energy to bring comfort to the child and prepare her for an easy passage.

As she predicted, there was enough food for everyone in the complex during the winter months. Only a few people from the island came to ask for food. Yufas was no longer little, but a full-grown adult bird. His head was still proportionally smaller than his body, and would remain so. Yet, his light grey feathers had darkened, so that the blue-black spots dotting his body no longer stood out. His head, still a beautiful yellow color, marked by rosy-red circles on either side, had deepened in tone, just like his yellow crest. He used his long yellow tail as a type of helm when he tried to fly. Now he seldom perched on Kelenoh's shoulder, but instead was always near her.

In the meantime, word about her work as a healer had reached the whole island, and the amount of people that came to ask for help had grown.

She developed a system to handle the waves of people by grouping together those with similar afflictions and healing them at the same time.

She also grouped people looking to solve problems unrelated to any physical condition. There were times when she still helped someone individually when the complaint or problem was too serious.

As the months went on, Kelenoh grew in power and learned to maintain her balance within. The people of the temple complex, and the inhabitants of the island flourished in harmony; a direct result of the harmony Kelenoh herself held within.

With the advent of spring, Kelenoh ordered the temple complex, as well as all of the temples and houses, to be cleaned. The Festival of Fertility would soon arrive, and with it the collective invoking of heaven and earth, Zeus representing heaven and Hera the earth.

One night she awoke suddenly and knew that Hefaisteon's daughter has passed away. Kelenoh sees a furious Polykrates move through the house. Hefaisteon sits in tears beside the little crib. Her despair has made their home a place of still sadness. She had time to get used to the idea she would lose this child. Kelenoh feels her sorrow and sends her loving consolation and energy. She sees Hefaisteon look up and straight at her, as if she felt Kelenoh's presence.

Polykrates has forbidden Hefaisteon to be in contact with Kelenoh. Kelenoh knows this, and it grieves her she cannot be close to Hefaisteon to console her.

The following morning, as she exits the temple, Kelenoh sees Hefaisteon approaching, accompanied by Cleitus. Kelenoh quickens her pace to reach them faster.

"Hefaisteon," Kelenoh calls, stretching both her arms out to the woman. "I am so happy to see you, come here."

Kelenoh embraces her. Hefaisteon has let go of her aversion to touch. She collapses into Kelenoh's arms and starts weeping; the deep sorrow over her daughter, her loneliness, every pent-up feeling was being expressed by her.

Kelenoh holds her tight and when she feels the shocks of her weeping diminish, she takes hold of Hefaisteon's head with both her hands and looks deep into her eyes. "It is good you have come, don't doubt it."

Hefaisteon starts rattling like a waterfall, "No, Kelenoh, I don't doubt any longer. You were right regarding my daughter, despite what Polykrates said about you. He forbade me to get in touch with you, and he blames you for the death of our child. For months I have been in doubt, locked away by myself in that large house. Last night though, you were there, I felt you, and at that moment I was sure it was not your fault. It was as you said, the gods and my daughter had already decided. Even with all your power, it could not be avoided." Hefaisteon takes a deep breath, "But I still don't understand it all. Could you please help me? I told Polykrates this morning that I was going to you because I needed you, and the only thing he did was turn around and walk away."

Kelenoh takes Hefaisteon by the arm and says, "Come, let's go to my house, there we can sit quietly."

When they arrive at the house, Cleitus remains outside. Kelenoh and Hefaisteon sit down at the little table in the small room behind the kitchen. On the table sit two bowls with fire, warming the space and spreading the delicious fragrance of lavender.

Kelenoh pours a cup of wine for Hefaisteon and says, "I am going to bring something to drink to Cleitus. I will be back in a minute. Drink of the wine, and feel it flow through your body. Feel your body and remember that you are strong and that you are a good person, and you are accepted just the way you are."

When Kelenoh returns she reads the query in Hefaisteon's eyes and invites the question, "Go ahead and ask."

Hefaisteon takes a deep breathe, "Why did I get a child that decided not to live long?"

Kelenoh closes her eyes for a moment to seek help from the gods and find the right words. Then she says, "When a soul decides to return to earth, there is deliberation with the gods as to which experiences will be good for him or her. They determine which country, which parents, and which are the best possible circumstances that will create those experiences."

"Every soul is born with free will, which is the greatest gift that an individual possesses. Oftentimes, when one has been born, he or she has forgotten which experiences they chose to have, but nevertheless that life is utilized in its fullest measure for the greatest advancement possible of that soul."

Kelenoh takes the hand of Hefaisteon, wondering if her words have reached her clearly. With a little nod, Hefaisteon confirms she understands, and with full ardor looks at Kelenoh. She wants to know everything.

"Your daughter," Kelenoh continues, "had chosen you and Polykrates as her parents and guardians here on Samos. She was allowed to experience what it means to grow up in wealth and security without worry. She didn't need many years for that. What she shared with you was sufficient for her."

"Thank you, Kelenoh. I understand what you are saying and it gives me peace, but..." her voice chokes, "what does it mean for me? Did I choose this sorrowful experience?"

Still holding Hefaisteon's hand, Kelenoh closes her eyes again. After a brief pause she sighs, "Hefaisteon, I would like to answer your question, but I don't know if now would be the right time. You are tired from needing to care for your child these past months. Your head is full of sorrow because she is no longer with you. The answer to your question is long and may be hard to understand. I am not sure if it will be clear to you. Is it not better to wait a little longer, until you have fully said goodbye to your child, and you are once more aware of the world around you?"

"No, Kelenoh, I want you to give me the answer now, otherwise I won't be at peace and my mind will keep spinning."

"All right then, I will give you your answer."

Kelenoh places her hands on Hefaisteon's head to infuse her with peace and energy, and then takes her by the hand again.

"The experience you have chosen has to do with letting go. This is one of the more difficult experiences. Every person will experience the death of a loved one in his or her life, at some time or another. We all will have to deal with the concept of letting go."

"Losing a child is one of the more difficult ways to have to learn to let go. Letting go or accepting things as they are and come as they may, is experienced by everyone in his or her own way, more or less. For instance, someone may have an accident and needs to learn to deal with a handicap, or a fire breaks out in someone's house and he or she loses all the material things they possess. So every person on earth will have to deal with this."

"How one chooses to handle this is important. You have free will and you decide for yourself how fast you learn the lesson of letting go."

"Sometimes, as in your case, the experience thrusts you into an accelerated lesson, it almost becomes a necessity to let go because the pain of the experience is so great and life must keep moving on. Learning to let go and accept what is, will set the individual free. It gives one peace of mind and the ability to grow in unconditional love for oneself and others that may be involved."

"There isn't anything more we on earth have to do. We should endeavor not to judge another, because we don't know what is right for that one. It seems some people have an easy life, while others go through the worst of experiences."

"We, with a human mind, attempt to understand why this is so often the case. Yet, all we can really do is stand beside it, as I am standing beside you now."

Hefaisteon looks straight at Kelenoh, tears flowing down her cheeks. The silence in the small room is almost audible. Hefaisteon take a little sip of wine, wipes her tears away and tries to sort it all out, "The way you explain it seems simple enough. What I think you are saying is that, in essence, as we live life, experiences of all kinds are inevitable. Accept them as they come, respond with love, and all will ultimately be well."

"Don't underestimate the power of this equation, Hefaisteon. It is simple, yes, when you understand the principle, but the depth of its meaning is as vast as the cosmos. Don't forget that loss, whether material or immaterial, is only one of the many experiences that a person encounters in his or her cycle of lives."

"The loss of something or someone we have attached ourselves to is hard. Therefore, some people call the process of all we have just discussed, detachment. The human being is its own worst enemy when it comes to this. Conflict arises within himself or herself; the mind and feelings battle for control."

"Most blame the gods or other people when something terrible happens. This can make things easier to bear for a time, but a nagging feeling of dissatisfaction often overwhelms them. Humans are easily distracted by things happening around them, consumed with what other people do or do not do. Some covet what another man or woman possesses. They can be preoccupied for many lifetimes before waking up and focusing on themselves."

"When they finally do, a struggle begins, the war within for one's mind and feelings. You often see people that approach life with mind and intellect; others let the way 'they feel,' drive them. When an individual can find a good balance of both, the struggle stops, the war ends, and peace can reign."

"It is not easy, Hefaisteon, but it is important to process what is happening to you now. Cry when you feel you have to cry, talk about it as much as you need to. Experience your sorrow, then you will be able to let it go and be at peace with it."

Kelenoh stands up and embraces Hefaisteon. Then Kelenoh says, "I will let you alone for a short while. I am going to get some food for you, Cleitus and myself. I want you to have something to eat before you go home."

When Kelenoh returns with a bowl of food, Hefaisteon is still sitting in the same spot staring ahead. "Come, Hefaisteon," Kelenoh urges, "eat something. It will make you feel better."

"I am not hungry, but I will try to eat something. I am already full of everything you have told me. I will now have to concentrate on the funeral for my daughter. I think you may have been right. This might have not been the best time to receive your answer. Still, I am grateful that you have given it. I will put your answer to rest for a while. Is it all right that I come back to it later?" Hefaisteon starts sobbing.

Kelenoh takes her in her arms again and says, "Cry, Hefaisteon, concentrate on the things you have to do now and let everything just be. When you are ready to talk about it again, I will know. If you just wish to visit or spend time with me here, that's fine too, we don't have to talk about it at all. I will be there for you."

Once Hefaisteon has stopped crying, Kelenoh sits down and both women eat the food from the bowl in silence. After the meal, Hefaisteon gets up and embraces Kelenoh. It is the first time she does such a thing on her own initiative.

"Thank you Kelenoh, I do feel better and more at peace. Will you please bless me as I go and give me strength for the days ahead?"

Kelenoh lays her hands on Hefaisteon's head and silently asks the gods to be with her and give her strength. Arm and arm they go outside. Cleitus stands, ready to bring Hefaisteon back home. Kelenoh follows them with her eyes. Once they are out of sight, she turns around and walks to the beach. She needs to be alone.

At the kouros, she wraps her right arm around his left leg and rests her head against it. She looks out over the sea and enjoys the calm wash of the waves.

Chapter 15

The cleaning and reorganizing of the temple complex is in full swing. Theano is busy in the weaving mill and with the clothing warehouse, making sure that everyone has sufficient clothing for the warm season. She is also in charge of preparing the clothes for the Spring Festival. The fields have been plowed and tilled, ready to receive new seeds, which will be sown after the Spring Festival.

The Spring Festival celebrates the marriage of Zeus and Hera. All come together to ask the gods to increase fertility in the earth.

Kelenoh looks forward to her first Spring Festival. She walks happily through the temple complex and enjoys the activity of life all around her. The weather is pleasant and warm; the wind gentle and mild. In the gardens, the first flowers and bushes start to blossom and Kelenoh inhales their fragrance as she strolls past. Yufas flutters about and stands beside her, stopping when she stops, and whenever her attention is diverted. As she goes along, Kelenoh shares her thoughts with Yufas, knowing he hears and understands her. It does her good to speak out loud the things that occupy her mind. It gives her peace and clarity.

Kelenoh makes it a point to go to the water basins to check the water levels. The water has gone down. Some of it has evaporated and some has seeped through the cracks into the marshy ground. Still, there is enough water to use for the gardens. Kelenoh sits down at the edge of a basin and Yufas nestles himself against her. Suddenly, her eye catches movement; it is Theodoros approaching from far. Her heart jumps up, he is alone!

She has never met with him by herself, and a nervous tension takes hold of her. "Help me," she whispers to Yufas, who lets out a cheerful trill that almost sounds like laughter.

Soon Theodoros stands in front of her. His face radiates honesty, and Kelenoh feels she is blushing. She doesn't dare look straight at him, because she knows her eyes will convey her feelings for him.

"Woman, I came to tell you that the designs for the Temple of Hermes and Aphrodite and of the new altar are finished. When might you have time to look at them?"

Kelenoh's throat is closed. Yufas gives her a push with his head. She has to say something. She takes a deep breath and says, "Theodoros, it is great that the designs are ready, but I think we have to postpone viewing them because Polykrates will not be able to attend. His little daughter has recently passed. It would be better for you to deliberate with him first, when he has time, then I will hear from you."

Sure of herself once again, she looks straight at him. Silently, they look deep into each other's eyes. Though only a short time, it is as if an eternity has passed between them and Kelenoh knows for sure that their feelings are mutual. Demure, she looks away, and then whispers, "I love you too."

Theodoros takes a step forward, bends his head, and takes Kelenoh by the chin, so she has to look at him again. Her face blushes red when she looks at him. "Kelenoh, I will call you by your name from now on. I used your title to create distance between us, because I wasn't sure you cared about me." He pauses, looking deeper into her eyes, "You must know, from the first moment I saw you, you have never left my thoughts."

Kelenoh thinks back for a moment to the day she first met him. She was totally confused about the new and strange feelings in her body. Then, she sat on the beach, struggling with whether or not to tell him and what she would even say. At that time, the gods had told her not to worry, the words would come when the time was right. Remembering, she now thanks the gods from her heart, and that the simple and all comprehensive words, "I love you," have come forth effortlessly this day. Nothing else needs to be said.

Theodoros takes Kelenoh by the arms and pulls her up. Still fixed upon one another, Kelenoh feels as if she is drowning in Theodoros' eyes. When his lips touch hers, everything in her becomes alive, tingling all over; she is almost not able to stay on her feet. Theodoros feels this and puts his arms tightly around her. Time stands still and they forget everything around them, until they hear a warning trill from Yufas that brings them back to an awareness of their surroundings.

Not far off a small group of people heads toward them. Kelenoh instantly knows it is Polykrates and his men.

She takes a step back and says, "I don't want Polykrates to know that we love each other."

"I understand Kelenoh. If I know Polykrates, then I know that he will surely use our love against you when it suits him. In his presence, and for the time being when in the company of others, I will use your title and keep the usual distance."

Kelenoh closes her eyes to regain equilibrium with her feelings and mind. She now knows love can override everything.

Polykrates and his men are so close now that they are able to see them well. Kelenoh looks inside him, wanting to know why he is coming to her. She is surprised by what she perceives.

When Polykrates is standing before her, he first looks at her, and then at Theodoros. For a moment, Kelenoh fears that he had seen them kissing. She realizes the feeling of love and connection to one person makes her uncertain, which causes her to lose a sense of union within herself and with the gods.

Kelenoh realizes how important it is to be in balance as Yufaa once taught her. She looks at Yufas, who gives her an encouraging nod. Then Kelenoh looks straight at Polykrates and she knows that Polykrates' darting eyes, from her to Theodoros has nothing to do with 'the kiss', but rather his own suspicions related to the affairs of the temple complex; afraid that something is happening behind his back.

Calm now, she waits for Polykrates to explain why he has come. With scrutinizing eyes, he first addresses Theodoros, "Would you tell me what you are doing here?"

"I came to inform the Woman of Hera, that the designs for the Temple of Hermes and Aphrodite are finished. She has told me that we will have to postpone the meeting to discuss them, due to the loss of your daughter, referring me to you to make the decision as to when would be the best time."

A smile appears on the face of Polykrates. Kelenoh is surprised to see how transparent he is.

Polykrates turns to address Kelenoh. "Woman, at the end of the day, when the sun sets, we will say goodbye to my daughter. Hefaisteon wants you to be present."

His last sentence is spoken with great emphasis, and Kelenoh feels how strong Hefaisteon has become, daring to go against the will of Polykrates. Polykrates has been tamed.

"I will be there," she says, wanting to invite him and his men to the dining hall for something to drink, but Polykrates quickly turns around and walks away. Theodoros and Kelenoh follow the men with their eyes until they are out of sight. With love in her eyes, Kelenoh asks Theodoros, "Would you like something to drink before you go?" Theodoros smiles and looks at the woman, once again full of pride and certainty standing before him.

"Thank you, but tonight I must decline. I should be on my way home now, but on the evening of the Spring Festival I will come to you." As he goes, Kelenoh watches him. Her body quivers with the promise of Theodoros and she has to brace herself, and sits down on the low wall of the water basin. 'He is coming to me, he is coming to me,' she repeats in her mind, enjoying the feelings his words trigger.

As evening approaches, she makes her way to the city. Stephanos walks ahead of her, two soldiers walk behind. Although she is going to a mournful gathering, she enjoys the walk. It is a quiet, mild evening, and the sun on the horizon almost touches the sea. In the small city, no one is on the streets. Everyone knows about the funeral. Out of respect for Polykrates and his family, the people that not have been invited, have withdrawn into their homes.

When Kelenoh arrives at the palace, she sees a mass of people standing outside waiting for the memorial service to proceed. The people take a few steps back, creating space so she can get to the palace. Kelenoh feels the curious looks of the people and when she passes through, hears their surprised mumbling. Head held high, she walks to the door. Just as Stephanos lifts a fist to knock on the door, it opens and Cleitus lets them in.

The transition from outside to inside is great. Inside the palace it is dark with only a single torch burning in the hallway. The fire bowls have not been lit. Kelenoh pauses for a moment and blinks her eyes to get accustomed to the sudden darkness. She hears a door open and sees Hefaisteon approaching with outstretched arms. "Kelenoh, I am so happy you are here."

While Hefaisteon embraces her, Kelenoh sees Polykrates standing, arms limp at his side, and from the back of the room he looks on with contempt for both women. Over Hefaisteon's shoulder, Kelenoh looks straight at him until he turns his face away and sits down in a chair.

Hefaisteon takes Kelenoh by the arm and leads her to a smaller room where her little daughter lies in state.

As both women stand hovering over the dead body, Hefaisteon says, "Kelenoh, Polykrates doesn't want you to say something when we lay her down in the small cave that we have selected for her. Would you like to say something now, so she will arrive safely into the arms of the gods?"

After a brief moment of silence, Kelenoh looks at Hefaisteon who is nervously squeezing both her hands.

"It would give me peace of mind," insists Hefaisteon, looking desperately at Kelenoh.

Kelenoh takes the hands of Hefaisteon in hers assuring her, "Hefaisteon, she is already with the gods. We will only lay down her body in the cave. She is no longer here. You already know that this fate was decided before she was born. Therefore, you may also know that she has been lovingly carried to her rightful place by the gods. However, I will invoke the assistance of the gods to give you strength and peace, just as I did for your daughter at the moment of her passing."

Laying both of her hands on Hefaisteon's head, she asks the gods to infuse her with strength and peace. She sees the desperate face of Hefaisteon transform into a calm expression. She takes her hands away. Kelenoh holds her in her arms until Hefaisteon gently pulls away and walks to the crib where the body of her little daughter lies.

Silently, she looks at the face of her little girl, then Hefaisteon says, "You are right, she is no longer with us. I have one more question," she stammers, "would...could you help me wrap her body in cloths?"

Kelenoh nods and takes the cloths laid out and ready. She draws nearer to Hefaisteon, looking at her with the hint of a question.

"Yes, I am ready to do this now," says Hefaisteon, answering Kelenoh's inquiring gaze.

When the women are finished wrapping the little dead body, they walk together, hand in hand, back to the large room where, in the meantime, more guests have arrived to honor her daughter.

Hefaisteon walks straight and tall into the room and greets the guests, offering her gratitude for their presence. Kelenoh catches Polykrates looking at his wife with astonishment.

She bows her head, hiding a smile. Hefaisteon walks to Polykrates and says, "Come, it is time to lay our child down in the cave. Could you call Cleitus to let him know that he can take her from her room?"

Hefaisteon gives a signal to the guests that they are going to leave. The guests stand up and wait for Polykrates and Cleitus in the large hall. And when Cleitus comes walking by with the little child in his arms, the female guests break out in tears, lamenting.

Kelenoh looks at Hefaisteon, who closes her eyes for a moment, and bows her head, as though to push back the noise echoing in the hall. Polykrates and Hefaisteon follow Cleitus and the child, then follows Kelenoh and then the rest of the guests.

To Kelenoh, it feels like most of the lamenting is not sincere. Annoyed by this and its effect on Hefaisteon, she straightens her back and starts singing a song. A slightly miffed Polykrates glances back at her, but she keeps on singing. At first, the lamentations of the women drown out her voice. As they continue on the road, Kelenoh hears some of the woman join her and soon the lamenting diminishes entirely and all the women in the company are singing.

Hefaisteon turns her head to Kelenoh and gratefully nods. The procession turns to the right and into the mountains. When Cleitus arrives at the grave in the small cave, the procession stops and spreads out in a semi-circle around it.

Kelenoh looks back and sees the sun disappearing over the mountain tops. Under the dim glow of the setting sun, the little body is laid in the cave by Cleitus. He places the little child on a bed of pine branches and lovingly covers her with more pine branches.

Cleitus steps outside, shares a moment's gaze with Polykrates and Hefaisteon, then turns around again and bows in the direction of the cave. All that are present join him in bowing. It is an intense moment of silence and deep reverence.

Kelenoh's heart jumps up at the sight of this gesture of reverence for life and death, and is struck by a sudden emotion that brings tears to her eyes. A sigh goes through the multitude when they straighten their backs again. Cleitus takes a large stone and with it closes the entrance to the burial cave.

Polykrates signals to Cleitus to come and stand behind him, and then starts descending the mountain. He ignores Hefaisteon who walks behind him and Cleitus. Slowly, the multitude starts moving and in silence the people walk back to the palace.

At the palace, Kelenoh nods goodbye to Hefaisteon, who stands at the top of the stairs looking out with a solemn expression on her face. Stephanos had been waiting for her with the other two soldiers, and all four walk back to the temple.

Chapter 16

The day of the Spring Festival has arrived. Early in the morning, Kelenoh walks to the beach. The sun has not yet risen, but it promises to be a calm, mild day. Kelenoh sits cross-legged in the sand, in conversation with the gods. She thanks the gods for the blessings they have received the past winter months and asks them to be present on this day. A deep peace descends upon her and she knows that the gods have answered.

As she stands up, she hears the sounds of the temple complex. Everyone is very busy on this day. For a short time, she hangs back by the kouros on her right and happily looks at the Temple of Hera. Soon demolition of the temple will begin. Although the temple is clean, the building is no longer worthy to be the Temple of Hera. Before her eyes she sees the new temple rise with the Temple of Hermes and Aphrodite beside it. Her heart swells with pride.

Kelenoh tries to suppress thoughts of Theodoros and his promise that he will come to her tonight, in order to be able to serve the people of the temple complex and of the island as well. She shakes her head and looks out over the beach. Dotting the beach are the many shelters that have been erected for the people of the island, where everyone can sit down later on and eat. Kelenoh instructed Nearchos yesterday to build the shelters, and she is admiring his work.

The shelters were built by driving four poles into a square set in the ground. At the top of the poles, ropes are tied and fastened to cross from one side to the other, from which long linen cloths are draped to shade them from the heat of the sun.

Long tables and benches have been put under them, loaded with food and wine. There will be a spot for everyone, and plenty to eat and drink. Along the edge of the sea, stretching the length of the whole coast, fire baskets have been staked into the ground for light when night falls.

Calm, Kelenoh walks home, ready to dress for the day. As she draws near to the house, she sees Cassandra waiting for her. Together, the women go inside where Selene and Theano are already sitting at the table to have breakfast with them.

After their meal Selene and Theano retire to their rooms to get dressed. Cassandra walks with Kelenoh to get her washed and put into a new, white linen dress made especially for this day.

It is a long dress, so long that it drags over the floor. The dress leaves her shoulders bare and free. A wide golden band is fastened under her breasts. Cassandra combs Kelenoh's hair, so it falls in waves over her shoulders and chest. Using shorter, thinner, golden bands she holds Kelenoh's hair in place so it cannot blow in her face. On top of her head rests a diadem of a snake, the head and tail pinching together at Kelenoh's forehead. Around her arms beautiful, colored, linen bands are wrapped.

The lygos branch Stephanos cut from the lygos tree that morning, lies on her bed. It is a fine branch with budding leaves. Smiling, Kelenoh looks at the branch. The beginning of spring!

She loves the festival and this time of year. Everything that grows and flowers is on the verge of bursting, ready to come forth. There is a quiet tension in the atmosphere, full of expectation, and not only in the air, but also in her! Momentarily, she closes her eyes and feels the kiss of Theodoros. Kelenoh shakes her head. Her mind cannot be wandering to such thoughts; she must be there for the people and tend to the earth to make it fertile once again. As she thinks of the word fertile, she knows that "fertility," will not only be for the earth. Out loud, she expresses her gratitude, "Thank you, beloved gods, for my existence."

Cassandra leaves the room to dress, while Selene and Theano stand by with Kelenoh, waiting for her to return. The three women walk around each other, turning about, admiring one another from all sides.

Selene and Theano are dressed similar to Kelenoh. A little later a red faced Cassandra enters the room and Theano comes to aid, helping to fix the golden bands in her hair.

After Cassandra has been looked at from all sides, Kelenoh says, "Come, I want to be still with you for a moment." Kelenoh leads the way to the small room where they sit hand in hand at the table. With closed eyes they empty themselves, preparing their minds for their service today to the people and the island.

Finished, the women hold each other's gaze, a deep love flowing inside each of them, from one to the other, without any words. Slowly, they stand up, lift their dresses a little to keep the hem from getting dirty, and walk outside. Yufas flutters around the women and makes his presence known. Kelenoh has to laugh at him. Yufas is also happy that spring has arrived.

In front and to the right of the Temple of Hera, the priestesses and people of the island have gathered. To the left, near the stairs that lead to the temple, stands the elite of the island. As tradition and procedure demands, Kelenoh has personally invited them.

Kelenoh glances to the group for a moment and sees Eupalinos is not standing beside Polykrates. Since the last conversation she had with Eupalinos, contact between the two men has cooled off.

Hefaisteon stands behind Polykrates and holds her little daughter by the hand. Kelenoh takes note of how much weight she has lost. Turning her head quickly, she doesn't dare look at Theodoros, fearing she will lose her concentration. However she does look at Rhoikos who waits, calm and dignified, poised for all that is to come.

The soldiers, who protect and take care of the temple, are arranged in two rows from the stairs of the temple to the holy spring. They wear leather breastplates and leather leg protectors. The hair on their heads is kept together with a leather band and each holds a long, upright lance in their right hand.

Silence falls across the square as the four priestesses approach. Kelenoh is the only one to enter the temple and walks through the temple hall to the back where, in a niche, the statue of Hera stands. Singing, Kelenoh removes the flowers and food from previous day and lovingly takes off the winter clothes of the statue. With the statue undressed, she takes a bow and prays in silence for blessings upon the new season.

When Kelenoh is finished, she calls Stephanos and the three young virgin men who were carefully selected by him to execute the ritual. It is a great honor for these men.

Kelenoh tells them to raise the statue of Hera and to bring it outside. Stephanos looks splendid, wearing a silver breastplate and leather leg protectors wrapped with wide golden bands.

The three young men wear white linen garments knotted together on the left shoulder, and around their waists is fastened a silver belt. Kelenoh follows the four men, as two on each side lift the statue onto their shoulders, and carry it into the light.

Cheers ring out from the crowd when the statue comes into view. The men with the statue walk between the rows of soldiers, followed by Kelenoh, Cassandra, Theano and Selene, to the holy spring. When they arrive, Kelenoh raises her right arm. The colorful bands around her arm and the lygos branch are clearly visible to everyone.

Yufas nestles himself under the edge of the spring and waits.

A deep silence suddenly descends, as if everyone is holding his or her breath, tense with anticipation.

At Kelenoh's signal the men put the statue in the water, and proceed to undress themselves.

Kelenoh closes her eyes and connects with the cosmos. She asks the gods to unite Zeus and Hera in order to celebrate the fertility of people, nature and the earth. Then she spreads her arms and opens her eyes.

A sigh of wonder goes through the crowd when they see Kelenoh becoming taller, as she gives the signal to the three naked men to step into the holy water. The first man steps in the spring and lies down under the statue; the other two cover the statue with their bodies. They disappear under water and when the water runs over the edge of the spring and reaches the earth, the crowd breaks out in cheers, clapping their hands.

The ritual is repeated three times, and every time the water reaches the earth, the cheering and clapping increases. Whenever the men and statue emerge, the sun radiates a kaleidoscope of colors in the droplets of water.

The water that runs over the edge imbues the hems of the dresses of the four priestesses. It also washes over the coat of feathers of Yufas who, every time the water reaches him, stretches high on his little feet and shakes off the water with loud trills.

The three men stand straight up in the spring, the statue between them. Two priestesses approach with cloths and hand them to the men and to Kelenoh. At Kelenoh's signal they put the statue on the edge and step out of the spring. Kelenoh wraps her cloth around the statue of Hera, while the men tie their cloths around their loins. Stephanos takes his place beside the young man who was lying under the statue. Two men are positioned on either side of the statue.

At Kelenoh's signal, they lift the statue on their shoulders and carry it back to the temple, passing once again through the rows of soldiers. Kelenoh, Cassandra, Theano and Selene follow.

Their dresses, now heavy from the water, drag over the ground. With every step they take the earth is blessed with the holy water.

Cassandra, Theano and Selene stay back as Kelenoh goes inside the temple with the four men and the statue. Carefully, the statue is put back in its position, after which the men withdraw and Kelenoh stays behind by herself. Lovingly, she dries the statue with the cloth and sings a song of gratitude. Once she is done, she takes a new, linen dress and clothes Hera. By the end of spring the dress will be brown from the moisture retained within the wood.

She sprinkles the head with basil oil and places fresh food at the feet of the statue. She arranges the first spring flowers on a layer of small lygos branches around the food.

Kelenoh sits down on the floor and reconnects with the cosmos, thanking the gods for life.

As soon as she steps outside, a loud cheering erupts. She moves in front of Cassandra, Theano and Selene and raises her arm. A sudden hush sweeps the square and she proclaims, "It is officially spring, the earth will be fertile this year. Treat the earth with love and care, so she, in turn, will provide you with all that you need. Now go to the beach and celebrate the Spring Festival! Sing, dance, eat and rejoice in each other's company!"

Kelenoh blesses the crowd, raising both her arms, palms open to the sky. The crowd bows toward her, then turns around and makes its way to the beach.

Kelenoh stays behind with the three priestesses and the people she had personally invited. Descending the stairs, she motions to her guests.

"Come, there has been a shelter set up on the beach for us too. I will lead the way." She grabs Yufas, holds him on her arm, and walks to the beach.

When she reaches the kouroi she halts for a moment, looking to the left where the people sit under the many shelters busily talking, laughing and eating. Someone plays music and further down along the beach there is dancing. Kelenoh feels happy and is grateful to the gods for the love she receives from them. She turns right onto the beach where, far from the people of the island, a shelter for her and her guests has been erected. Kelenoh smiles seeing her own chair, which is usually sitting in the dining hall, has been placed at the table for her.

Silently, everyone sits down and a priestess pours the wine. The silence is filled with awkward tension, but Kelenoh is too absorbed in her thoughts about her first fertility ritual, to notice and stifle the tension.

Yufas sounds off a loud trill to warn her to be alert. Kelenoh looks up and the tension hits her as a blow. She takes a sip of wine to regain consciousness and to find out what is going on.

She scans the people at the table. Cassandra, Theano and Selene sit quietly, staring ahead of themselves. From them, Kelenoh senses only calm and love. Looking over to Polykrates she is shocked by his angry stare directed at his wife, Hefaisteon. Hefaisteon looks down, powerless against this man. Eupalinos devours a honey cake, neither disturbed, nor even interested at all in his surroundings. Kelenoh feels his emptiness. From the posture and expression of both Rhoikos and Theodoros, it is clear they are uncomfortable. Kelenoh catches them looking at each other with great empathy. Feeling the integrity of both men, an impulse of love floods her.

Kelenoh makes a silent inquiry, 'Where does this anger of Polykrates come from?'

'Jealousy!' The unexpected answer hits her hard. Kelenoh looks at Yufas hoping for some clarity.

She doesn't understand. 'Why would Polykrates be jealous?'

'He is jealous of everyone who gets attention. He wants all the power and prestige for himself!' she hears.

'Which power, which prestige? He is the Ruler of Samos. Nobody is more powerful than he.'

Kelenoh feels as much confusion as she did the day she met Theodoros, unfamiliar with the feelings stirring within her. She would rather stand up from the table and withdraw herself, but her duties are not yet over for the day. She must take care of her guests. Kelenoh takes another drink of wine and looks to Polykrates. "Polykrates," she says, "may I ask you something?" The sudden question shocks the people sitting at the table. All look in her direction. The silence is broken. Polykrates glares at her and nods.

"Do you have enough men available to build the new altar and the Temple of Hermes and Aphrodite? Likewise, will there be enough hands to demolish the old temple of Hera and build the new one?"

Kelenoh looks straight at Polykrates with all the love she possesses.

Polykrates stands up, his face contorting with confusion. He possesses hate for her and is befuddled at the loving, humble manner with which she addresses him. He coughs into his fist a few times, places his hands on his back and postulates, "According to me, we still have to look at the designs for the Temple of Hermes and Aphrodite and the new altar. They have not yet been approved by me."

Polykrates false pride almost makes her laugh, but she holds it in.

"You are right, how dull-witted I must be. We postponed looking over the designs due to the loss of your daughter. My apologies."

Kelenoh looks for a moment to Hefaisteon, hoping for a reaction. Hefaisteon seems numb. A little smile appears on her face when she looks at Kelenoh, but that is all. Kelenoh intends to speak with her very soon.

She directs her attention to Polykrates once more and says, "Is it convenient for you, and also for you," she quickly glances to Rhoikos and Theodoros, "to look at the designs the day after tomorrow? Tomorrow I must be present in our fields for the blessing of the seeds that will be sown."

The three men give her an affirmative nod. Then Polykrates adds, scoffing, "I didn't expect you would forget that I hadn't seen the designs yet."

Kelenoh looks at him, ignoring his remark and speaks, "Will you be able to answer my question, the day after tomorrow, as to whether or not you have enough men for the building of the temple?"

Polykrates nods and sits down.

"Let us then eat and enjoy this blessed food," Kelenoh says.

After the meal Kelenoh gets up, sets Yufas on her shoulder and walks in the direction of the other tables where the celebration is still underway. In front of the kouroi she stops and motions to a few priestesses and says to them, "Listen well to what I am going to tell you, because I want you to pass this on to everyone who is presently on the beach. My voice doesn't have the volume to reach everyone."

She raises her right arm, the signal she wants to speak. It takes a little time before even those seated at the first few tables in front of her are completely quiet.

"Today we celebrate the fertility of the earth and all that lives. Therefore, let us love each other, embrace each other, and enjoy what the gods have bestowed upon us: the gift of family, community, and fellowship. By doing this with all of the love that you have in you, you honor the gods and yourself. I greet you. Celebrate, dance, sing, and be thankful to the gods and this land, because they take care of our livelihood."

Kelenoh gives a signal to the priestesses to approach the people and give them the message. With Yufas still on her shoulder, she walks back to her table, feeling her heart pounding. Her tasks for the day are completed.

She slows down and pauses to look around for a moment, giving herself time until hear heart beats quietly again. Theodoros! He will come tonight. She takes Yufas off her shoulder and puts him on the beach. She sits down in front of him and asks, "Yufas, am I ready to celebrate this love with my body?"

Suddenly surrounded by an uproar of laughter, Kelenoh looks about confused. Then she hears, "You are the Woman of Hera! It is about time you act as the Woman of Hera, not only with your mind but also with your body!" The voices stop and Kelenoh remains seated a little longer. Feeling ready for anything, she stands up, stretches her body, and straight and tall walks back to the table where her guests still sit. Here blue eyes are clear and calm. She looks at everyone one by one, and for the first time she looks straight at Theodoros.

She takes her seat and looks again at Theodoros. He gives her a reassuring little nod and she realizes he knows she is insecure. Her feeling of love for him grows, and it starts burning within her body.

Slightly rattled, she grabs her cup of wine and takes a drink. Her 'out of sorts' manner doesn't go unnoticed. Polykrates looks at her attentive brow and asks, "Is something bothering you?"

Cassandra, Theano and Selene start giggling which incites an angry glare of Polykrates in the direction of the priestesses. He doesn't like to be laughed at. Kelenoh looks at him and says, "Please don't resent my priestesses. It is not our intention to keep you on the outside of things. You are right. Something does bother me. I will tell you what it is." She pauses; holding her breath, then lets it out, revealing all. "I am in love and because I don't know the feeling very well, it makes me uncertain."

Theodoros looks at her with puzzlement in his eyes. She knows his question. She didn't want Polykrates to know, why is she telling him now?

From within the calm of her mind Kelenoh answers him. 'It is better he hears it from me than from anyone else.'

A smile appears on Theodoros' face and Kelenoh knows he is understands her reason for divulging the truth.

Polykrates eyes frenetically dart around the table and then his gaze rests at Theodoros.

"Yes," says Kelenoh, "I love Theodoros."

Laughter and shouts of approval erupt at the table. Everyone stands up, taking his or her cup of wine in hand. Even Eupalinos joins in raising his cup. Rhoikos gives his son a congratulatory slap on the shoulder and with a laugh in his voice says, "I am so happy to hear this, especially on this special day."

All hold their cups high, pointing them in the direction of Kelenoh and Theodoros. Rhoikos voice booms, "We give a toast to Kelenoh and Theodoros—and to love!"

Everyone takes a drink of wine. Kelenoh's face blushes from embarrassment by all the attention. She, who knows what is good for others, does not know what to do where she is concerned, especially in matters of the heart.

She looks at Yufas and hears the cross voice of Yufaa who says, "You are the Woman of Hera, behave yourself likewise! Stop putting yourself down. This uncertainty is not fitting a high priestess." He orders, "Take control of your emotions now!"

Aghast, Kelenoh stands up and straightens her back. Her face, that was red a minute ago, has changed to pale white.

Theodoros looks at her, alarmed. She is able to bring something of a smile to her face and gives him a calm little nod. Then she says, "Please excuse me everyone, I am called to converse with the gods. Selene, please take your zither and play a song. Sing songs of gratitude and enjoy each other's company."

Kelenoh takes Yufas from the table and put him on her shoulder. She walks to the right, in the direction where the island curves, far away from the shelters and celebrating crowd.

The sun has almost set in a backdrop of orange, grey and black.

When she no longer hears the sounds of the crowd, she sits down and puts Yufas in front of her. Kelenoh closes her eyes and merges her consciousness with the cosmos. With the sound of the sistrums she raises her head and asks, "Why do I become so uncertain of myself when I come in contact with love or aggression?"

"Kelenoh, emotions are present in every human being. These emotions can sometimes wash over you so strongly that they overpower your clarity of mind, and try to lead their own life.

Love and hate are strong emotions. Since you are a strong woman, you have a tendency to want to control those emotions. You want to know what they mean, and then decide for yourself what to do with them. That is, of course, your right. You may choose, as you will.

However, know this, surrender between two people, having complete trust in each other, is only possible when you trust yourself."

Laughter breaks out around her.

Suddenly, Kelenoh yells out, angry. "Stop! You are laughing about something that is very important to me!"

"Kelenoh, you know so much and yet so little. Be one!"

Tears role over Kelenoh's cheeks, she doesn't understand and cries over her own powerlessness. "Help me, I don't understand."

"Kelenoh, learn to trust that what you feel is good, without analyzing the feeling. When you feel love, then it is love. When you feel anger, then it is anger. When you feel uneasiness, it is unease. That is all. Don't try to rationalize it."

Kelenoh allows the answer to sink in and then says, "Here is my problem: I can know exactly how other people are feeling. However, when it comes to me, I start to question because I don't know if what I am feeling is really from myself or from another. Since I am unsure as to where the feeling is originating, I start dissecting it and trying to figure it out."

"Close your eyes, Kelenoh. You already know what to do to solve this, because you have already done it. You have already identified the problem, thus there is an open door through which the solution may come.

Just now you felt anger toward us, because you thought we were laughing at you. Without thinking you reacted. So you do know how to do it.

It is important that you allow yourself to feel what you are feeling and not suppress it.

Likewise, refrain from analyzing, for oftentimes when you do this, you distort the original feeling.

By thinking you don't know what you are feeling, you perpetuate a sense of uncertainty. Let go of that. You know the feeling very well."

When Kelenoh hears the faint sistrums, she knows the gods are withdrawing.

She remains still, eyes closed, on the beach.

Suddenly, the voices come back and she hears, "Go now, our child, we are proud of you." Kelenoh opens her eyes and tears run down her cheeks. Her love for the gods is unparalleled.

It is dark around her. The sun has set and she starts trembling from the cold. Wrapping her arms around her, she reflects on what the gods have just told her.

The gods are right. By believing she was unsure of her feelings she only created more uncertainty and confusion.

She stands up, spreads her arms and thanks the gods for what they have said. A sense of unity rises up in her. She recognizes this feeling; the same feeling she had on the last day she spent in the vaults.

It becomes clear to her again how important it is to hold on to this union within, the unification of mind and feelings, and how easy it is to be disturbed and to lose the sense of union.

Out of the corner of her left eye she sees a light. She looks to the side and sees Stephanos standing with a torch in hand, carrying something over his arm. Quietly, he has been waiting for her to finish. Cassandra has called to Stephanos to retrieve her. Kelenoh knows suddenly, and she feels a deep love for Cassandra.

Kelenoh stands up and walks to him. As she draws closer she sees him carrying a shawl. He wraps it around her shoulders. They look at each other for a moment, tears well up in Kelenoh's eyes.

"Thank you, Stephanos; this shawl is just what I needed." Together they walk back to the others.

When they reach the shelter with her guests, all eyes are intensely fixated upon her. Kelenoh searches for Theodoros' eyes to reassure him.

There appears a radiant smile on his face, accompanied by laughter that sparks a sense of aliveness inside of her. She almost cannot wait until all guests have gone and she can finally be alone with Theodoros.

Tension at the table is now different from that at the start of the evening. It is now filled with expectation; everyone wants to know what the gods have said. Kelenoh stands up in front of her chair and says, "The conversation with the gods had to do with myself. I needed help and that is what I have been given."

Kelenoh feels the disappointment, especially from Polykrates.

"I am sorry that I have failed to be a good hostess this evening."

She looks around the table and says, "I hope that everyone had enough to eat and drink. I shall retire now, but please enjoy the remainder of the evening and love one another."

Kelenoh nods curtly to Cassandra, signaling her wish for Cassandra to accompany her. Before leaving, she turns to Selene and Theano for a moment, flashing each one a smile.

"Selene, please play music for the guests, and enjoy your moon and stars."

"Theano, dance, that everyone may be filled with gratitude for the fertility of the earth."

Kelenoh and Cassandra walk home in silence. At home, in the kitchen, Cassandra sets a pot of water on the fire and helps Kelenoh out of her dress. When the water is warm, Cassandra adds some lavender and washes Kelenoh.

Once Cassandra has finished, Kelenoh sends her away. "Thank you, Cassandra, for sending Stephanos to me. That was exactly what I needed. You may go now and enjoy the rest of the evening's festivities."

Relaxed, with eyes closed Kelenoh lies on her bed. The day was good, life is good, and she feels thankful.

When she opens her eyes, Theodoros is there, standing in the opening of the doorway. With ardor and full self-confidence she spreads her arms and says, "Come to me, Theodoros; let us celebrate the gifts of the gods with our bodies."

That night Kelenoh becomes a complete woman.

Chapter 17

When Kelenoh wakes up the following morning, Theodoros is already gone. She turns on her side and smells the odor still present in the sheets. Smiling, she thinks back on last night; two people merged together, becoming one.

She sighs, knowing it is time to get up, but her body feels so relaxed and satisfied, that she lingers in bed to reminisce a little longer. It came so naturally and she can hardly understand why she had so much difficulty to accept his love in the first place.

Her daily struggle to stay tethered in communion with the gods and unified within herself, which is necessary for the tasks required at the temple, makes her realize how difficult it can be when being in a loving relationship with another person. On the other hand, last night proved that it could be effortless. She realizes she is thinking again, but she can't escape thinking about how the weight of her responsibilities is always pressing upon her. Kelenoh turns on her back and tries to direct her thoughts to the day. Suddenly she says out loud, "I have to concentrate so much to stay in a loving relationship with myself, that it leaves little space to love someone else."

With a shock, she sits up straight. Is this her problem? Or is she making this a problem? The beautiful feeling of last night begins to disappear, replaced with a feeling of loneliness and the burden of her responsibility. Though muffled through the walls of her room, she hears a peacock screaming.

She throws the sheets off, gets up and calls Cassandra who shortly enters in with a radiant smile. Her smile soon fades at the sight of an angry and disturbed Kelenoh. Frightened, she hurries toward her. "Is everything all right? Did something happen last night?"

"No, it is all right. Please help me bathe and get dressed. I have to go to the temple and then to the fields."

Cassandra helps Kelenoh in silence and amazement because she doesn't understand her reactions. And Kelenoh has no desire to talk, let alone explain things to her. When she is ready, and without a word to Cassandra, Kelenoh leaves and walks off with long, determined strides, straight up to the temple. The people she passes along the way pause from their labors, bewildered at the Woman of Hera who walks by with a fierce look in her eyes and does not turn her gaze to greet them.

Kelenoh feels a strange anger within her. It confuses her. She abandons her time of seclusion where she usually directs her attention to the gods, and unifies with the cosmos. She has even left Yufas at home. She is fed up with everything! She has a compelling urge to just to run away, take a boat and sail from the temple complex and the inhabitants of the island.

The first thing Kelenoh sees when she reaches the temple is a large group of people standing around, waiting for her help or for healing. She runs up the stairs, disappears into the temple, and sits down in her chair. She forces herself to calm down by placing her right hand on her chest to slow down her rapid breathing.

She now shifts her attention to the people who patiently wait outside until she calls them. Suddenly, she feels contempt for the people who, almost in a lowly slavish way, depend on her. Kelenoh frightens herself. Where has her love gone for all that lives? What is happening to her?

Suddenly she misses Yufaa. She gets up and, to everyone's surprise, runs out of the temple hurrying home to get Yufas. He is sitting calmly on the table when she arrives, as though he had known all along she would return for him. When Kelenoh does pick him up, he doesn't make any noise. Kelenoh sits down at the table, looks at the bird desperate for an answer, "Yufaa, what is happening?"

"Kelenoh, you are too much in your mind while turning off your emotions, which throws off your inner equilibrium. I already warned you of this in Egypt. Remember what you once said you should repeat to yourself when in doubt you could handle it all. You said then, 'Trust the gods and yourself.' Remember that the gods will never leave you. It is you, who rejects their assistance."

"What should I do now?"

"Kelenoh, you already know the answer. I understand you are confused, so again, I urge you to be vigilant in your communion with the gods each day."

Kelenoh sets Yufas on the table, walks to her room and sits down in the middle of her bed trying to stop the feeling of panic. She closes her eyes to connect. Gradually, she feels herself calm down and when she opens her eyes, she is Kelenoh again, the Woman of Hera and one with everything.

Slowly, she stands up and suddenly remembers the people waiting for her. She picks Yufas up and hastens to the temple, this time looking around, greeting everyone she passes with a smile. The people are still standing before the temple and now, a few priestesses are going around with a pitcher of water, offering them something to drink.

Kelenoh approaches the group and stands in front of them apologetic, "I am sorry that you had to wait so long."

Happy to feel a deep love again, tears roll down Kelenoh's cheeks, and with her thoughts she embraces the whole group. A sigh of relief comes out of the group as though they all had shared one breath. Kelenoh suppresses a laugh welling up in her. What a strange morning. She straightens her back and calls the first people to her.

After lunch, Kelenoh goes to the fields. She sits down in the middle of them, connects to the earth until she becomes wholly one with it. She sends out love, and asks the earth if it wants to accept the seeds that are ready to be sown and be brought to blossom. The whole afternoon is spent blessing the seeds and the fields and instructing which seeds go into what field.

At the end of the afternoon, Kelenoh retreats, taking time to reflect upon what happened in the morning. She is reminded that it is imperative she connect with the gods every day. When she skips this, the consequences are great. She may not yet lose her abilities, but she seems to be easily susceptible to lose her love for life. Her feeling of panic has made her very conscious of the fact that it are her responsibilities which come first, and that she will have to live accordingly.

Before she closes her eyes to ask the gods for strength, she looks at Yufas for a moment. Gratitude for the presence of Yufaa washes over her. She is not alone; a piece of Yufaa is tangibly with her. Yufas utters a trill and she hears an encouraging voice, 'Kelenoh, you can do it.'

Closing her eyes, she thanks the gods for their presence, and the insight she has been given. Her next task, she determines, is to find Cassandra, and apologize for her behavior that morning.

Kelenoh finds Cassandra in the Temple of Hera, preparing the temple for the next mornings' service. The regularly scheduled service that morning was put on hold because of the Spring Festival and most of the priestesses didn't get any sleep. Cassandra continues working quietly, even though she knows that Kelenoh is standing behind her looking on. Kelenoh begins to feel disturbed, as she doesn't like to be ignored.

She straightens her back and sends the disturbing feeling away, resolving to apologize. She walks to Cassandra and puts her hand on her shoulder. Cassandra turns around and looks at Kelenoh. Kelenoh looks into her eyes and says, "Sorry, Cassandra, for my behavior this morning."

Cassandra, looking straight at Kelenoh, nods and says, "It is good," In her eyes Kelenoh can see that it is not really 'good.' She has hurt Cassandra and something between them has been broken.

She takes Cassandra by the shoulders with both hands and wants to say something more, but no words come when she opens her mouth to speak. Kelenoh is struck silent. She lets go of Cassandra and takes a step back. Somewhat reluctant to leave, she says, "Good, I am going to the dining hall now, if anyone needs me, you know where I am."

The voices of the priestesses resound throughout the dining hall as they prepare the evening meal in the kitchen. The voices are cheerful, telling stories of the events of last night. Kelenoh smiles proudly and sits down in her chair to prepare herself for the meeting scheduled for tomorrow with Polykrates, Rhoikos and Theodoros.

The construction of the new Hermes-Aphrodite Temple will soon begin and Kelenoh feels a nervous expectation, yet all the while looking forward to it. The temple complex will, with the building of these two new temples, become even more beautiful, although it will be a long time before the Temple of Hera is fully erected.

While in the middle of her thoughts, the dining hall fills up with people who have finished their work for the day and who desire to enjoy their evening meal with Kelenoh. When there are no seats left at the table, Kelenoh starts a song of gratitude for the food. A deep calm and peace settles over the dining hall.

The following day, hours after the morning service in the temple, Kelenoh is preoccupied helping the people in need. Once every person has been tended to, she leaves the temple and goes on her way to the dining hall to meet with Polykrates, Rhoikos and Theodoros. She smiles to herself, remembering her question to Polykrates whether he has enough men for the construction of the temples and the altar. Of course he has enough men. It is at his commission that the temples are being built. This time, to break the tension which had been felt by everyone last time at the table, she will give Polykrates the feeling that it was he who was giving the orders.

Theodoros! It will be the first time she will see and talk to Theodoros since their night of love. She hadn't heard from him, but admits that she hadn't much time to think about him either. Now she will soon see him again. Her body starts coming alive at the thought of him. For a moment she surrenders to the pleasant feeling, and then forces herself to let it go. She must concentrate on matters having to do with the temple complex.

For a brief moment, anger and bitter dissatisfaction with her responsibilities rise up again. Shocked, she sits down on the edge of the basin and closes her eyes. For the second time that day Kelenoh connects with the gods. Upon opening her eyes, she meets eye contact with a few of the priestesses who are staring at her from just beyond. Kelenoh feels their fear and their reverence. She nods at the priestesses and beckons to them. They come near and stand before her. Kelenoh asks, "Where are you going?"

"We are going to the laundry," one of the priestesses answers. The others stand, hands behind their backs, eyes looking down.

Please give Leatis my regards and tell her I think you are all doing a great job. I am very grateful to you."

Smiles appear on the faces of the priestesses. Kelenoh stands up, and one by one she takes their hands, wrinkled by frequent washing, into hers. "Are you happy with your work or would you rather do something else?"

The priestesses all start talking at the same time. Kelenoh raises her hand laughing, "Stop, one by one please."

Each tells of how happy they are with their work, and how easy it has become since they are able to rinse the laundry from the plank bridge placed in the middle of the river. With their fear now gone, they continue on their way, strolling merrily in the direction of the Spring Road and on to the laundry.

Kelenoh follows them with her eyes and ruminates, 'A distance is growing between the priestesses and me. They have to know what keeps me occupied and I have to get them more involved. I have to take care not to lose contact with them.'

The dining hall is empty when she enters. Sitting down in her chair, she waits for Polykrates, Rhoikos and Theodoros. Beside the table is a smaller table set with wine and cakes for her guests.

She doesn't have to wait long before Polykrates noisily enters in with his four companions. He then promptly sends all four back outside. And without greeting her, he goes and sits down at the other end of the long table across from Kelenoh. She looks at him and says, "Welcome, Polykrates." Polykrates gives her a little nod, acknowledging he has heard her.

"How is your wife?"

"Good," is his brusque response.

"I would like to talk to her."

"That is not necessary," says Polykrates.

"Well, what would she like?" says Kelenoh, keeping her voice calm.

"She? She does not need it," he scoffs.

Kelenoh keeps silent and hopes to come across Hefaisteon by herself, or to view inside Hefaisteon without her awareness of it, but that is something she'd rather not do. She lets it rest for now.

Rhoikos and Theodoros enter; they greet Kelenoh with the customary greeting of putting their hands together before their chests and making a little bow. Kelenoh tries to look into Theodoros' eyes, and when their eyes do meet, Theodoros winks at her. How wonderful to see him again. Both men then greet Polykrates. He motions for them to come and sit on the lengthwise side of the table.

While the designs for the Temple of Hermes and Aphrodite and for the altar are laid out and systematically arranged on the table, a priestess pours the wine and then offers it to Kelenoh, and then to the guests.

Polykrates passes by them with his cup of wine in hand. He examines the tablets silently. Theodoros approaches him and says, "When you need an explanation, please let me know."

Kelenoh watches Polykrates, who appears offended because he wasn't the first one greeted by Rhoikos and Theodoros. For a moment, she is confused and uncertain, not understanding his over-sensitive behavior.

"Don't analyze it, it belongs to him," she hears Yufaa say.

She walks to Polykrates and asks, "What do you think?"

Polykrates answers, "This temple is much larger than the old Temple of Hermes and Aphrodite. I had a smaller temple in mind. The altar is good. It is an altar worthy for the Temple of Hera."

Theodoros maneuvers to stand by them and gives an explanation to Polykrates, "You have to realize that we will use this temple for many years during the demolishing and construction of the new Temple of Hera. We determined the measurements based on the need to be able to perform all functions which usually occur at the Temple of Hera, for the complex and for the island to run well."

Polykrates nods and says, "You are right, I approve. You can start the construction. I will send my men to help you with it."

For the first time he looks straight at Kelenoh, "So now you have the answer to your question as to whether or not I have enough men for the construction." He huffs, "I thought it was a stupid question. That is why I didn't answer it the day before yesterday." Polykrates sets his empty cup on the small table, nods, turns around and walks out.

Unfettered by his attitude, Kelenoh turns to look at the designs more carefully. The three of them, Rhoikos, Theodoros and her, hover around the table in silence for a while longer. That is until

Kelenoh feels the touch of Theodoros hand, as he takes hers and
asks, "What do you think of it?"

"I think it is splendid Theodoros, but why are you building this
temple in a slanting direction in relation to the Temple of Hera?"

"If we build it that way, as with the new Temple of Hera, it will
be in a straight line with the new altar."

"I admire you, Theodoros. Your vision and insight are
splendid. Thank you very much."

Kelenoh feels the urge to embrace him and press him against
her, but she realizes where she is and suppresses the feeling. The
only thing she can do is express love and admiration through her
eyes. They look at each other and Theodoros squeezes her hand
as a sign that he understands. Rhoikos coughs, and Kelenoh and
Theodoros break their handhold and look at the older man.

"Pardon me if I am disturbing, but I am here also." Kelenoh
starts laughing, laughter that erupts into a giant roar.

"Sorry Rhoikos, thank you very much for all your hard work
also." She goes and takes Rhoikos by the hand and all three walk
to the small table where Kelenoh pours another cup of wine for
each of them, and also offers them cake.

"I think that Selene should see this design also, since she will
be the priestess of this temple." Kelenoh calls a priestess from the
kitchen and orders her to get Selene. Shortly thereafter, Selene
enters, and in her own modest, silent way, she looks at the design.

"Splendid," she says, looking at both architects. "I almost
cannot wait until the temple will be finished. In this temple I will
be able to worship Aphrodite in a way that she deserves."

Wide smiles appear on the faces of Rhoikos and Theodoros.
Kelenoh catches the glint in Theodoros eyes when he looks at
Selene. What is this? A stitch of jealousy moves through Kelenoh.
She notices how love makes one vulnerable. Is it because when
you open yourself up to another, you open yourself up to their
uncertainties?

She picks Yufas up, goes outside and leaves the three people
behind in the dining hall. She sits down on the edge of the spring
situated across from the dining hall on the other side of the road.
With her left hand, she plays with the water, then picks Yufas up
and looks straight at him. "What just happened?"

Yufas remains still for a minute, then Yufaa answers, "Kelenoh,
when you feel real love for someone, it is both with your mind and

your feelings, just as with everything else you do in your life. It is important, as I taught you in Egypt, to maintain a balance between the mind and feelings. When one or the other dominates, there is imbalance. When someone loves with the mind, it often causes jealousy, possessiveness and anger. When you love only with your feelings, it can cause jealousy, uncertainty and powerlessness. You are caught up in your feelings for Theodoros so much, that it makes you uncertain and that's why you are experiencing jealousy."

Kelenoh thinks about the answer and realizes again how important it is to have one's mind and feelings working in harmony one with another. She sighs. Time after time, she seems to fail at maintaining harmony between her thoughts and feelings.

She gets up and walks back into the dining hall. When she enters, Theodoros looks at her with a question on his mind. She smiles, reassuring him and joins the three people who are still standing near the table looking at the designs.

Not long after, Rhoikos and Theodoros leave. They walk to the open space planned for the new temple, and kick their feet into the tough dirt and patches of grass, happy that they can finally start construction on the new temple. Selene returns to her herb and flower gardens.

Kelenoh walks home where she finds Cassandra working in the kitchen. She stops what she is doing and walks up to Kelenoh.

"Kelenoh, yesterday we were still not right."

Kelenoh nods, "I know."

"I thought about it today and I think that I understand why you behaved like that yesterday, and it is fine with me now."

Kelenoh spreads her arms and the women embrace each other. Kelenoh takes her by the shoulders and says, "Cassandra, I would like to ask you something. Would you gather everyone, who works at the complex, tomorrow evening in the dining hall?"

Cassandra's brow rises, quizzically, "Certainly, but why?"

"I would like the people to know more about what occupies my time, and I wish to inform every one of the changes the complex will endure in the coming years. I notice a distance between me and the people, and I must rectify that.

Chapter 18

When the morning service is over and after tending to the people, Kelenoh starts looking for Rhoikos and Theodoros who have begun work at the new site where the new Temple of Hermes and Aphrodite will be built. The terrain has already been marked out, and Kelenoh is impressed by how large the temple will actually be, as it will fill a large portion of the open square.

Seeing her arrive and looking around, Theodoros comes up to her and says, "When we are finished with the construction of the Temple of Hermes and Aphrodite, there will be a newly defined open square in front of the new Temple of Hera, because it will be further back from where it is now."

Kelenoh nods in acknowledgement, remembering that he had talked about this change with her previously. Back then, he had discussed how the temple would be positioned more toward the west.

"Tomorrow Polykrates' men will come, and then we will begin," he says playfully, while rubbing his hands.

Kelenoh starts laughing, "Eager to get started, are we?"

"I can hardly wait." Theodoros beams.

Kelenoh takes a step back because under his strong gaze, her body is starting to tingle, so by keeping her distance, she can avoid giving in to the urge to fly into his arms. "Are you coming to me tonight?" she asks softly.

Theodoros nods. Kelenoh turns around and walks to the dining hall with a wide smile on her face. Cassandra comes toward her but seeing Kelenoh's face, halts and swallows the words she wanted to say. Instead she presses, "What is the matter with you? You are radiating from head to foot!"

"Theodoros will be coming tonight."

Kelenoh's eyes rest on a field far off in the distance as she holds on to the feeling of love. A few perfunctory moments pass and then she looks to Cassandra, "What did you want to tell me?" she asks.

"I wanted to inform you that I have told everyone to come to the dining hall tonight as you requested."

"Thank you, Cassandra." Kelenoh hooks her arm around Cassandra's and together the women stroll to the dining hall where lunch is ready and waiting.

After her meal, Kelenoh isolates herself and returns to the beach. Together with Yufas she sits down in the sand to the left of the kouros. The last days have been full of her obligatory high priestess' duties and Kelenoh has the need to be alone for a little while. Still, she stares out over the sea; the familiar sounds of the complex can be heard from behind her. She takes a few deep breaths of sea air and gets ready to become one with everything around her.

The clear little eyes of Yufas tilt up at her and she hears the voice of Yufaa speak, "Become one with nature and your surroundings, this will give you the energy whenever you need it."

In a brief flash, she sees herself sitting at the Nile again where she had learned to master 'becoming one.' She closes her eyes, merges with all life around her, and feels whole again.

Filled with energy, Kelenoh buys some more time alone on the beach as the sun sets. Quickly, she gets up, puts Yufas on her shoulder and hurries home. On her way, she encounters several inhabitants of the complex already on their way to the dining hall.

At home Cassandra is waiting for her. She helps her bathe and get dressed. A short while later both women are on the road, headed to the dining hall. Yufas, very content, sits perched on Kelenoh's shoulder and he sounds off his loud trills which calms Kelenoh. It is good what she is doing.

Everyone is standing in the dining hall when she arrives. Kelenoh's chair has been placed on a platform so all can see her. Pausing before her chair, she turns around to give a signal with her hand that everyone may be seated.

She remains standing, opens her arms and says, "It is great that we all have come together. I have decided to have a joint meeting every month from now on. I wish for you to be well informed about what keeps me busy around here, and to answer any questions that you might have."

Kelenoh sits down, scanning the faces around the hall, and feels everyone's enthusiasm. Her gaze falls on Stephanos. He looks straight at her, righteousness shining from his eyes. However, there is something not quite right. She uses her gift of vision and looks inside him. He is nervous and has an important question for her. Kelenoh stirs in her seat and feels there is something else the going on.

When Kelenoh feels it, she can't help but laugh quietly. He is in love! 'But with whom?' She surveys the hall and her eyes settle on Theano, whose head darts around looking for someone, looking for Stephanos!

Theano and Stephanos! Kelenoh intends to call Stephanos to come to her after the meeting. She realizes she has given him little attention lately. She nods at him and on his face appears a laugh. Then she directs her attention in the hall and begins speaking.

"I am sure you all have seen Rhoikos and Theodoros busy on the open plot of land beside the Temple of Hera. They have made an outline with ropes, to mark where the new Temple of Hermes and Aphrodite will be. This temple, when it is ready, will temporarily serve as the Temple of Hera. We will place the statue of Hera in this temple, as the old Temple of Hera is being demolished and rebuilt, larger and grander, worthy of our Goddess. Both of these temples will be splendid.

"With the help of his father Rhoikos, Theodoros has made some very fine designs. There will be a new altar as well. The new altar will be in the same spot where the altar is at present, near our holy lygos tree, but it will be much larger than the current one."

"A new square will also be built between the altar and the new Temple of Hera. Since the location of the altar is fixed adjacent to the holy lygos tree, it has been decided that the new Temple of Hera will be positioned further back on the lot than where it is now, so as to have enough space for the new square."

"The worn and weathered stone of the Temple of Hera will be demolished. The stones that are still in good condition will be used to build a treasury. The construction of the new Temple of Hera has been commissioned by Polykrates. He has also consented to replace the Temple of Hermes and Aphrodite and the altar. Polykrates has made men available for the construction. The men who are currently hard at work erecting the city wall and digging the tunnel, will become part of the temple building crew when those projects have been completed."

Kelenoh pauses for a moment; it remains very quiet in the dining hall is, everyone is paying close attention. Then looking over to Stephanos she says, "Stephanos, I would like you to determine which of your men will be able to help with construction. This project will take years, and the more men working on it, the sooner it will be finished." Stephanos nods to her in the affirmative, grateful that she needs his assistance.

Kelenoh continues, "It will be very busy at our complex in the coming years, and our quiet life will be turned upside down. I want to ask each of you to keep on with the daily tasks you have been given with your hearts' devotion and commitment. It is important that the temple complex continues to function for the people on the island. It is our benevolent task to assist the people with all that we possibly can, so that they can live happily and that we take care of our animals with love and respect, so they will in turn provide for us. We cultivate our crops with equal love and respect, so they in turn will yield their fruits, feed us and clothe us. We take care of the plants, herbs and flowers, that in turn nature will gift to us her healing secrets and keep us free from disease. We likewise revel in her pure beauty that we might be reminded that all life is sacred. It is our humble and blessed task to do all of this in the grace filled estate of peace and harmony."

Kelenoh is silent and closes her eyes for a moment, scanning herself, making sure she has said everything she wanted to say. She opens her eyes and looks out at the people who stare up at her, wide eyed and full of expectation.

"This," Kelenoh says, "is what I wanted to share with all of you, the new plans for the temple complex. We shall carry on as before and henceforth come together and meet. I give thanks for your dedication and loving service."

Everyone stands up as cheers and applause break out. The priestesses break out into a spontaneous song of gratitude and in no time all join in. Silent, Kelenoh listens and watches the crowd sway from side to side, her heart feeling as though it is about to burst out from her chest with happiness.

When the song fades out and the dining hall is silent again, she says, "If there are any questions now, please go ahead. If you think of something later you would like to ask me, please report it to Cassandra, Theano or Selene. I will answer those questions the next time we get together." The silence remains uninterrupted. There are no questions.

"I thank you all for coming. Go in peace, loving yourselves and all that lives." Slowly, the dining hall empties. Kelenoh remains seated in her chair. She beckons to Cassandra and asks, "Would you please find Stephanos and bring him to me?"

It isn't long before Stephanos stands before her. His dark wild hair is going in all directions. His broad and toned figure is a credit to his strength, but his eyes convey the softness of his heart and love for her. Kelenoh realizes she has taken his love for granted. "Stephanos, I have not talked with you much lately. I am sorry. I have been preoccupied with all kinds of other matters. How are you?"

"Woman, I am well. I have missed our conversations, but I have seen how busy you have been. I would like to talk to you soon when you have more time. I have something to ask you."

"Stephanos, I have time for you now. Go ahead and ask your question."

"Woman, last month I was asked to participate in the games on the continent of Mount Olympus. I would like to participate, if you will allow me."

"Stephanos, what an honor! Only the best men receive an invitation to join in the games." Kelenoh suddenly realizes how little her thoughts have gone to this man. This had escaped her totally.

"Who was it that asked you and when do the games begin?"

"Last month a ship from the continent arrived in our harbor. This ship goes to all the islands looking for strong men who can participate in the games. Polykrates sent those men to me. I told them I would like to participate, but I wanted to discuss it with you first. Soon, they will return to Samos and would like to hear my answer. The games will be held next year in the spring. If you approve, it means that in a short time, I will need to leave for the continent. If you give your approval, I will make sure, before my departure, that men will be available for the construction of the temple."

Kelenoh feels a deep anger boiling to the surface. Polykrates! How dare he do this behind her back! She looks at Stephanos who blinks back at her, hopeful. In Stephano's presence she doesn't let her true feelings show and enthusiastically declares, "Of course you can go, Stephanos! What an honor for you and our island. Just make sure that before your departure, there will be someone to stand-in and take over your duties. You know better than I, who of your men can handle such a task, but let me know who you choose. Visit me before you leave, I would like to bless you and ask the gods to return you to us alive and healthy. I will miss you." Stephanos folds both hands before his chest and takes his leave with a bow.

Kelenoh stays behind, her anger begins to slowly build up at Polykrates. The pressure of her responsibility for the temple complex falls on her as a blanket of lead. She scolds herself for not being alert enough, for being overly occupied with the new temples and with her own confusing feelings for Theodoros.

Theodoros, she loves him, but can she answer to this love as it should be? Her responsibility for the complex and the island are so great that there is actually no room for a love relationship. Kelenoh thinks back to the morning after their first night of love. The same feelings of loneliness, doubt and panic strike again. Desperate, she looks at Yufas and hears the voice of Yufaa encouraging her, "Trust in the gods and in yourself."

Kelenoh closes her eyes and connects to the gods. When she opens her eyes, her doubt and feelings of panic are gone, but the loneliness and the feeling of anger toward Polykrates are still there. She thanks the gods, gets up from her chair and puts Yufas on her shoulder. As she begins to descend the podium, she sees Cassandra enter the dining hall.

"Kelenoh, I have come to see if there is anything you need. I talked to the people and everyone was happy about the meeting. You have spoken well and clear."

Kelenoh nods, acknowledging her, but feeling the meeting is already far behind her. "Thank you, Cassandra. On a different note, could you send someone to fetch Polykrates? I have to talk to him immediately."

Cassandra looks at Kelenoh astonished. Before she had left the dining hall, Kelenoh was radiating happiness and love, and now she stands before her, a woman angry and disheartened. What happened in such a short amount of time? "I will send someone to get Polykrates, but what troubles you? Can I help you?"

"No, please, leave me alone. Go now and make sure Polykrates gets here." Kelenoh is silent and scans the whole of the island.

"He is at the harbor," she says somewhat contemptuously. Casandra, though slightly disturbed by Kelenoh's behavior and tone, obediently turns around and dashes off to find someone who can fetch Polykrates. Of course Polykrates can be found at the harbor, Kelenoh sneers. No doubt, he is waiting for a ship from the continent. Kelenoh jumps at the sudden trill of Yufas. She realizes she is not totally honest with herself; it is her anger that is speaking.

Polykrates has been occupied with the innovative design of a new type of ship, a ship that most assuredly will make Samos famous and well known. A ship he has already named *Samaina*. That is the primary reason why he is at the harbor. Secretly, she admits her admiration of Polykrates' plan. When this ship is a success, he will build a whole fleet. Kelenoh recognizes this as advantageous for the island and its inhabitants.

She admires his perseverance as well. Usually when he has thought of something, he will look for the best people who can help him realize his ideas and plans. In the development of the *Samaina* he sought advice from the Corinthian ship builder Ameinocles. He was the first to think of putting three men on the oars in order to increase the ships' speed. 'You have to give him his due.' Polykrates thought of a system to make a ship sail faster by enlarging the cargo spaces and relocating them where they make the ship more stable in the water. As Kelenoh thinks about these things her feeling of anger diminishes.

Polykrates not only has big plans, but he executes them. She also discovered that he is a lover of culture, overhearing him boast of the feasts held in the palace, where he invites poets and scientists to exchange ideas. How is it then that he can be intolerable to be around? The question leaves her perplexed. Startled, Kelenoh jumps again at the sudden interruption of Yufaa's voice.

"Kelenoh, you ask a question with such an obvious answer. A human being is not only the faculty of his or her mind and reason, emotions play a part as well. If one or the other is grossly out of balance, it is impossible to function optimally as a human being. You know better than anyone the need for balance with both. Only then can one be in true harmony with oneself, other people, nature and their environment. What Polykrates may have in brilliance of mind, he lacks in emotional sensitivity and the ability to connect with others, and life around him."

Kelenoh hears noise at the entrance of the dining hall and quickly turns around. A furious Polykrates rushes in, leaving his men at the entrance. "What gives you the right," he roars, "to call me away from important business you don't know anything about?"

Kelenoh looks at his angry, reddening face and takes a moment to react. Focusing on Polykrates positive qualities lessens her own anger, and now she addresses him with composure. Her silence infuriates Polykrates.

"Did you summon me here to stare at me, or will there be something sensible coming out of your mouth?"

"I wanted to talk to you about Stephanos. I understand that you sent the men from the continent, scouting around for strong men for the games, to him behind my back. Why?"

"Do I owe you an explanation for that? I am in charge of this island and Stephanos is one of my subjects. It seems a great honor for him to represent our island. Think of the fame he can bring us. Furthermore, this is a men's business, what concern, then, is that of yours?"

Kelenoh closes her eyes for a moment, the shouting voice of Polykrates resounds in her head and she has trouble staying calm. "Stephanos works here at my complex. To me, that seems enough of a reason to inform me of your plans for him."

"Your complex? My complex you mean," says Polykrates with a defiant sneer, "you are as much a subject of mine as all the other people of the island. Did you forget it is I who has the last word here?"

"I am in charge of the temple complex," Kelenoh says, "and I am responsible for the people that work here. That gives me the right to be informed when you intend to send one of my men to the continent for almost one year." Kelenoh is able to restrain herself and exudes a quiet confidence, but everything inside of her is trembling from the bottled up anger.

"Now that you know, what is the problem? Before long they will come to get him, I have given my permission. Stephanos himself was very enthusiastic and felt honored. But until now he has not taken action. I hope that you didn't change his mind. The honor of Samos is at risk and you don't have the right to have the people of Samos look like fools on the continent of Greece."

The cap on the bottle of Kelenoh's pent up anger suddenly explodes, and out it comes as her shouts are directed at Polykrates. While pointing her finger at him she says, "What do you think? That I would sell Samos short? You have to know better. I have given enough proof of my loyalty to Samos, the island and her people since my return!"

A pleased look appears on Polykrates face, and Kelenoh realizes she has made a mistake. He has succeeded in making her openly angry.

"So, what I understand is that you agree with my decision to send Stephanos to the continent. So what is the reason for all of this commotion? You want the same as I, the best for Samos. Don't disturb me again with these kinds of trifles."

Polykrates huffs and spins around, his short and portly body radiating an air of victory. Chin up and straight as an arrow, he marches out of the dining hall. Kelenoh remains behind defeated. She walks back to her chair and sinks down. She is suddenly exhausted. All the energy has streamed out of her body. It is impossible to have a sensible conversation with that man. All of a sudden, the face of Hefaisteon flashes in front of her and Kelenoh determines to get in touch with her as soon as possible. Kelenoh feels Hefaisteon is in trouble.

She looks at Yufas who sits on a small table beside her chair. His little eyes are closed, as if he is thinking deeply. Then she hears the voice of Yufaa saying, "Don't be too hard on yourself, Kelenoh. You are a human being, not a goddess. You are not perfect. However, you have forgotten something that I taught you, which is very important. When you think someone is saying something that relates to you, it's usually exposing something about that person. As you become more conscious of this, what someone says to you will hit you less hard. You won't take on their thoughts, feelings, and attitudes. Therefore it is so very important that, when you want to engage in any form of dialogue, you first think before you speak. Always do this in love and while seeking the direction of a higher intelligence. This way is pure and you can help someone to see him or herself."

"When you speak in anger, you are merely operating from the realm of the intellect. When you speak from a place of love, you have come in touch with your feelings. When you operate solely from one without the other, it will be difficult to help someone to see who they are, while at the same time allowing them to *be* whom they are. Sometimes it is better to keep silent."

"Kelenoh, you have the ability to listen to someone because you have the gift of hearing. Furthermore, you are able to speak in love and with a higher intelligence. For a brief moment you fell short of your abilities. Rise up and be mindful once again of the language you use and how you use it. You know as no one else, how much power thoughts and words have. Close your eyes, I will give you energy."

Kelenoh closes her eyes and feels energy streaming back into her body. When she opens her eyes, she looks straight into the face of Hefaisteon. She kneels before her, desperately looking up at Kelenoh.

"Kelenoh, help me! I secretly left the house accompanied by Cleitus and walked via the beach over the Sacred Road to here. To my horror I saw Polykrates leaving the dining hall. I had just enough time to hide behind a wall. Luckily, he went back to the city via the Procession Road, otherwise he would have seen me!" Hefaisteon bursts out sobbing.

Kelenoh glances to the exit of the dining hall for a moment and sees Cleitus standing there, clearly on guard to alert his mistress if Polykrates should return. Kelenoh closes her eyes to tune in to Hefaisteon's needs.

Hefaisteon erupts once again, "Kelenoh, I am no longer allowed to leave the house! I am no longer allowed to meet with you! I don't know what to do! I feel so alone!" Hefaisteon's words spill out in a convulsion of heaves and sighs.

Kelenoh rises from her chair and sits down on the edge of the platform close to Hefaisteon. She takes Hefaisteon's hands in hers, trying to calm her. Kelenoh stays quiet. In the silence of the dining hall she hears Hefaisteon's breathing slow down.

"Please tell me what has happened since we last saw each other," Kelenoh asks in a gentle whisper.

Hefaisteon's square face has become even more defined; her cheek and jaw line are harder and sharper due to her loss of weight. Kelenoh wishes to take her into her arms and to comfort and ease the intense sorrow she feels in Hefaisteon. She hesitates to do so because she remembers that Hefaisteon does not like to be touched. With her mind, Kelenoh expands her aura and surrounds Hefaisteon with it. Hefaisteon's face softens and she starts talking more slowly and clearly.

"Since the day we laid our little daughter in the cave, Polykrates hardly speaks to me. He speaks only of urgent matters and tells me what I am no longer allowed to do. For a period of time, following the death of our youngest, I was too sad to pay any attention to him. I hardly heard anything he said to me. It didn't matter to me what he said or did. I followed your advice to listen to my own feelings. When I felt sad about our daughter, I allowed that sadness to pass through me, rather than keep it bottled in. I did this again and again until I felt settled about her death, until I knew she was alright and in a place where she was loved. I know you told me she was, but I really had to know and feel it to be true for myself."

"Once I found a measure of peace, I began to pay more attention to my other daughter and the duties of being a wife. That was when I became keenly aware of the rules Polykrates had imposed upon me. I was locked in the palace, and I could not find the words and the strength to oppose Polykrates. With my thoughts I often asked you for help, but I didn't know if you could hear me, nor if you were able to do something about it. Today I could no longer stand it. I had to see you and tell you how I have been feeling. Now that I have been able to say this out loud, I am feeling much better."

Hefaisteon is silent and looks at Kelenoh with large inquisitive eyes. The loneliness and despair of this woman overpower Kelenoh. She feels guilty, wishing she had been more attentive.

"Hefaisteon, I have indeed heard you these past months," she assures her, "and I intended to get in contact with you, but I had other business that took precedence. I am truly sorry." Both women sit still, hand in hand, close to each other. It is as if the world has become so small, that all that exists is only between the two of them.

Kelenoh starts in, "Hefaisteon, Polykrates is your husband. His flawed perception thinks that it gives him the right to give you orders. You must remember you are your own self. Try to accept the situation you are in and don't look at what is no longer possible, look at what *is* possible. Look into yourself and figure out what makes you feel alive. Find ways to create opportunity for yourself within the restraints you have been given. Perhaps you discover an interest for painting or modeling clay. When you know what you would like to do, direct your attention to that. Giving time to something you love, will develop your self-esteem. Polykrates words will eventually no longer undermine your sense of self. You will notice that you will not only be helping yourself, but Polykrates as well. When you regain your self-confidence, you will be better able to express yourself and speak your mind and, in turn, Polykrates will respect you for that. Be your strong and confident self. You don't have to do anything else." The women studied each other for a moment. Kelenoh noticed that the despair in Hefaisteon's face had disappeared.

"I will give you energy Hefaisteon. Reflect and think back on what I have told you."

"I don't have to think about it Kelenoh, you are right. And I know something I would like to do. I would like to weave. I took up weaving early in my life, but since my marriage I haven't continued on. I remember it calmed me down and enabled me to think more clearly. I also remember that I often sang when weaving. In fact, that was how I met Polykrates." Hefaisteon paused, a distinct sparkle began to return in her eyes. "I was singing behind my loom when we noticed each other for the first time."

"Great! Hefaisteon, hold on to the feeling of that moment when you first saw each other. That is often the first step in renewing the joy of a relationship. Weaving is a great way to put your thoughts in order. Walk home via the Procession Road, where you will pass our weaving mill. Please take the opportunity to go in and look around. Theano and Selene will be happy to give you any advice you will need to begin weaving again. Theano will share all the recent information on the latest and best of the weaving looms. Selene is an outstanding weaver who makes splendid cloths. I shall signal them with my power of thought for them to go to the weaving mill. When you arrive at the mill, they will both be present. After speaking with them, you can go to our workshop and tell Nearchos I have approved the production of a weaving loom to be made for you. I promise that from now on, when I hear or see you in my thoughts, I will respond and try to help you."

Kelenoh places her hands on Hefaisteon's head and infuses her with energy. "Go now, Hefaisteon, and remember to be kind and loving to yourself!"

Hefaisteon gets up, her once set jaw and the hard lines in her face have become soft and her eyes are once more radiating hope. "Thank you, Kelenoh, for listening and having an understanding heart."

After Hefaisteon left the dining hall, Kelenoh remained seated on the podium for a little while. The emotions stirred up by these conversations, first with Polykrates and afterward with Hefaisteon, hang as a heavy cloud in the dining hall. Kelenoh gets up to look for Roxanna, the head of the kitchen, that she may purify the dining hall with a little bowl of burning sage before it will be used again. She finds Roxanne and gives her the assignment, then leaves the dining hall and walks to the beach to be alone.

There is a bright moon in the firmament. The sea and the sky are a deep blue color, almost black. A gentle wind blows on her back. She spreads her arms and throws her head back, letting the wind play with her hair and touch her body. She heaves a deep sigh. All anger and tension disappear from her. She sits down cross-legged in the sand and closes her eyes.

Suddenly a vision of Pythagoras stands in front of her. Kelenoh looks up and meets the warm gaze of Pythagoras. He sits down in front of her and takes her hands in his. Tears roll down her cheeks. She wishes he was physically there but she knows it is not yet possible as he has not yet finished his studies. She is comforted by the thought that even though he is far away, he will be there when she needs him most. She opens her eyes and says, "Pythagoras, I am so happy you are here! I feel so lonely sometimes, and the life of a high priestess, the responsibility, is hard on me. I need you."

"Kelenoh, be patient for a little while longer. I will return to Samos at a time when you will need me even more. Just know I will always be there for you, as I am now. Don't be afraid to make mistakes. That which you learn from your mistakes can provide great insight into life, sometimes better than if you had done it perfectly. You are a human, not a goddess, even though the people think so and expect much of you. You have just been reminded in your interactions with both Hefaisteon and Stephanos, that you are needed. Cherish this feeling. It will help you better serve the people. Be aware of this need and don't let your mind rule by thinking that other things are more important. You are here for the people, not for the building of a temple! I know you are lonely, people like you and I, who have many responsibilities, are lonely. On the other hand, never forget that you are surrounded by love, both by the gods, as by Yufaa and I. Even if this is not always tangible, we are present. Always! Never forget that, dear Kelenoh."

Silence enfolds them as Kelenoh and Pythagoras stay seated for a short time, hands still folded in one another's. Kelenoh feels comforted by his presence, his strength and calm. She takes a deep breath and wishes she could remain seated like this always. She has the feeling of being in total harmony. Suddenly, she feels Pythagoras's hands glide away from hers. She looks up and sees him disappearing in a mist. "Pythagoras," she calls, "please stay a little longer."

His voice echoes, "You are always in my thoughts. The task you were born for, you can handle. Don't forget that Kelenoh. Trust in the gods and in yourself."

Alone with Yufas, Kelenoh is left behind on the dark beach. Tilting her head up to the moon with a blue-black sky filled with twinkling stars, she remembers the time she sat in the desert with Pythagoras, where he coached her to listen to the music of the night. Stillness fills her, raising her energy and confidence again. Kelenoh gets up and goes to look for Theodoros. She needs to be with him tonight.

Chapter 19

A week later the ship and recruiters, looking for strong men from the islands, arrive on Samos. They have come to get Stephanos. Polykrates entertains them by hosting a large party in his palace. Kelenoh has not been invited again, but of course Stephanos has been. Proudly, Stephanos stands before Kelenoh to ask permission to go.

"Of course you can go, Stephanos, the party is in your honor. Take all the time you need and ask all the questions you may have about the Games, so you know exactly what to expect when you get there, and likewise what is expected of you."

Stephanos nods and with a bow says goodbye to Kelenoh. She sits pensively in her chair. The ship will depart in a few weeks to ensure they reach the continent before the fall storms begin. She will surely miss him.

Suddenly, she is attacked by a wave of nausea. Her body shrinks, her stomach turns and she feels as though she is going to pass out. Cassandra enters just as Kelenoh teeters on the brink of a fall, and rushes toward her. Cassandra catches her, "Kelenoh, what is happening?"

Kelenoh waves to Cassandra with one hand, indicating the need for her to be still for a moment. With her other hand in front of her mouth she tries to stop the wave of food that is rising up. Cassandra helps Kelenoh back into her chair, goes to the kitchen and returns with a cup of lukewarm water. Frightened, she looks at the deadly pale face of Kelenoh, wet with perspiration. After a few minutes some color returns to Kelenoh's face and thankful, she accepts the cup from Cassandra.

"What is it, Kelenoh? Are you sick?"

"No, Cassandra, I am not sick." Kelenoh pauses and breathes deep, "I am pregnant." Cassandra gasps throwing her arms in the air and exclaiming, "Oh my, this is wonderful, and just at this time and cycle. The gods are well disposed to us. Your fertility will bless us. You are a real High Priestess of Hera. Now the new Temple of Hera can be inaugurated as it should."

"I know what to do, Cassandra. Yes, it is great that I am pregnant. The gods will show favor on the people and bless them and the temple complex. Please go get Selene. You will find her in the garden. Selene possesses the knowledge of the herbs needed to end this pregnancy. Summon Theano as well. She is in the clothing warehouse. I need all three of you."

Cassandra embraces Kelenoh, and for the first time Cassandra feels Kelenoh totally surrender herself and crawl up against her. Moved, she takes Kelenoh's head in her hands and kisses her on the forehead. Then, with the clear task before her, goes in search of Selene and Theano.

Kelenoh stays in the empty dining hall. Tenderly, she lays her hands on her abdomen; a smile appears on her face. A song of gratitude wells up in her heart to the gods. She is pregnant! Exactly now, when there are plans for the construction of a new temple for Hera! A little later the three women enter and Kelenoh is surrounded and embraced with so much love she starts to weep.

Cassandra, Selene and Theano look on astonished as they all hold on to her. Kelenoh sobs. They have never seen her cry in their presence. Cassandra lays her hand on Kelenoh's head and asks, "Why are you crying?"

Through her tears Kelenoh looks at Cassandra and assures her, "I don't know, but don't be afraid, it is not out of sorrow I cry; inside I am so happy and grateful. Come, sit down, we have to discuss what to do now. Cassandra, you have to explain to me how we conduct the ceremonial offering. Hestia can no longer explain it to me. You were at her side and aide until her death. Did she talk to you about this? Please tell me."

"I can't tell you, Kelenoh, because Hestia was not fertile."

A hush falls in the room and in the silence, Kelenoh connects with the gods. Though the silence is brief, Kelenoh reemerges with a sense of direction. "Listen," she says, "For now I will retire and ask the gods what I have to do. As soon as I have the answers, I will call for you. Selene, could you gather the herbs needed to return this fruit to the earth?"

The three women get up, embrace Kelenoh and leave the dining hall, talking and animated with excitement. Kelenoh follows them with her eyes, a smile on her face that turns into laughter that makes her shoulders shake. Soon, she is on her way to the beach where she sits down at the feet of the kouros and closes her eyes. She raises her arms, places them together above her head and then lowers them in front of her chest.

In the silence that follows, she hears the voices of the gods. To her surprise, Hestia appears before her. She sits down in the sand and takes one hand of Kelenoh's in hers saying, "Kelenoh, I already told you in Egypt I would come to you when you need me. I am here for you now, but first I want to tell you something." She pauses, and looks directly into Kelenoh's eyes. "The gods and I love you, and are proud of the way you have been conducting your task here on earth. Now go ahead and ask me what you have to ask, my blessed child."

Kelenoh feels deep love from the gods and from Hestia. Tears well up in her eyes. Quietly, she sits with her hand in the hands of Hestia, enjoying the intense moment. Her voice cracks, "Hestia, I am so happy that you are here. I am pregnant and I wish to accurately execute the ritual that the gods and the temple dictate, but I don't know how to do it."

"Kelenoh, we know you are pregnant. This blessed occurrence was preordained. The soul of the fruit that is now in you has voluntarily chosen this experience and knows it will not be born. Listen well to me now, Kelenoh. You know that the priestesses of the temple are not allowed to have children, because their attention must be consecrated and focused on service to the gods, the temple, and the people of the island. When they still do become pregnant, it is a sign of honor to Hera, the goddess of fertility. When the high priestess becomes pregnant, it is a blessing for everyone on the island. Now I will tell you how to conduct the ceremony. It is important that you let go of your fruit at the beginning of a new day at sunrise. A funeral or cremation of someone who has passed on is conducted in evening when the sun sets. For instance, such as the little child of Hefaisteon and

Polykrates, that was laid down in the cave at sunset. The location where you together with three other priestesses have to conduct the ceremony is where the current and soon to be old Temple of Hera now is. Your three priestesses of choice will have to support you. There is a reason the four of you do this, nobody else has to know about it, not even Theodoros."

"Numbers, Kelenoh, are a given certainty. When people listen to the sound of music or a voice, everyone will experience and hear differently. When you look at something, it doesn't matter what, every human will see and feel something different. A number is always the same, and will be experienced by everyone in the same manner. Four is the number of nature and its elements: air, fire, water and earth. This has everything to do with your earth and the temple complex. That is why you have to conduct this ritual with the four of you. It is important you position yourselves in a square; it will strengthen the power of four."

"The circumference of the new Temple of Hera has already been fixed and indicated by ropes stretched out by Rhoikos and Theodoros. This will help you find the four wind directions. It is important that you involve the four wind directions consciously. Not only because of the number four, but because the four wind directions are connected to the four seasons, which of course are important for the earth, the people and the growth of crops."

"You, Kelenoh, will take your place and sit down at the back of the old temple, on the southwest side, where earth is still visible. When the new temple is complete, that area of earth will be the room housing the statue of Hera. It is there you will return your fruit to the earth. Cassandra will stand in front of the temple, the northeast side. Selene and Theano will stand opposite one another, on either side of the temple, at the southeast and the northwest side. The statue of Hera will, through your offering, receive the power to help women who are infertile. The women will be assisted when they touch the statue or bring an offering, for Hera is the goddess of fertility and marriage."

"It is up to you, Kelenoh, to decide when you will bring your own precious offering. You alone determine when you are ready to let the fruit of your womb go. We will be present. I want to tell you one more thing. As long as the people on earth live in harmony with the gods and the cosmos, this harmony will reverberate into the earth body herself, and all life will prosper."

Kelenoh's eyes remain closed as she continues to absorb Hestia's words. She feels Hestia remove her hands from her hand. She opens her eyes to see Hestia disappearing. She wants to cry out something, but her throat is closed and tied up in her emotions. A faint voice comes, brushing lightly against her ear, as though a whispering wind, "Kelenoh, even if you don't see me, I will always be close by you."

Kelenoh wipes the tears off her cheeks and enjoys the deep love the gods send her. She lingers a little longer in their presence before she gets up and goes in search of Cassandra, Selene and Theano. They must know what she has heard from Hestia, and to decide on a time they will perform the ritual. Kelenoh realizes she cannot wait too long. Fall is near and with it, promises of heavy rain. The plot of land, where the new temple will be built shall become a swamp!

A peacock screams from far away. A smile appears on Kelenoh's face as the familiar sound brings her back to herself. She is aware again that she sits on the beach, and her tasks for the day are unfinished. She picks Yufas up and looks into his little eyes for a moment, hoping to hear something from Yufaa. Yufas blinks at her silently and she realizes she is asking too much of the gods. She just had a conversation with Hestia. All that she has to know has been said.

Her attention is now drawn to a little spot in the far distance, gradually moving toward her. She makes out the figure of Stephanos as he is coming from the party hosted by Polykrates. There is something in his posture and way of walking that is different. Kelenoh decides to view inside of him. He is confused, but also proud. The quiet Stephanos, who is usually hidden in the background, has been the center of attention at the party. He is the star of Samos. He has enjoyed it, she sees, but he doesn't know how to handle it. Kelenoh bursts into laughter. Startled, Stephanos looks up and sees Kelenoh sitting on the beach. He raises a hand, the signal that he has seen her. A shy, boyish-like Stephanos makes his way toward her. Smiling, she signals with her hand for him to come and sit down in front of her. "Dear Stephanos, I can tell you had a nice party. Tell me all about it. Were you able to ask questions, and do you know what is expected of you at the upcoming Games?"

Stephanos sits down in front of her and begins to speak. "Woman, I did not know that so many people knew me. When I entered the palace, everyone started cheering. I have to say that it scared me. Everyone was looking at me. I was buried under compliments and I didn't know how to react to all the attention. Fortunately, a servant came to me with a plate full of delicious snacks, so I was occupied. Beautiful music played on through the evening and there were even poets who had written poems for and about me. There were so many people that, at first, I couldn't find the crew of the ship. Finally the man, who had selected all the men from the neighboring islands, came up to me, and I was able to ask him all my questions."

Stephanos is silent for a moment and takes a deep breath. Kelenoh has never heard him speak so much at one time and realizes all of the wine that Stephanos had drunk at the party has made him anxious and chatty. After a deep sigh Stephanos continues talking.

"We talked about the sports I would be able to participate in. I told him that I am good at running, wrestling, boxing and spear tossing, and that I would like to compete in the pentathlon as well. In the pentathlon I will have to throw the discus and spear, do the long jump, running and wrestling. I think that I can master those events well. He was happy to hear that I wanted to compete in so many events and assured me there would be enough time to train and grow to be even better. The place where I am going is called Olympia, situated on the west coast of Greece. There is a village built on the hill of Kronos, where I will receive accommodations and food for a year." Stephanos is silent for a moment and looks bashfully at Kelenoh. Kelenoh waits patiently for him to continue speaking.

"My living quarters will depend on the amount of money I bring with me for my stay. Some participants, who are rich, will stay in the pavilions. The less fortunate will sleep in tents or huts. Participants who have nothing to spare will sleep in the open air. Training sessions, food and drinks have to be paid in advance. The man in charge of the Games will settle all expenses with Polykrates. My costs for accommodation have to be paid by the temple complex. Polykrates told me to tell you. Just as I was leaving, he pulled me aside and told me this, reminding me it is for the honor of Samos. As I walked back to the complex, I thought about it all, and of course I can pay you back from my prize money, if I earn any."

A wave of anger rises up in Kelenoh. What audacity Polykrates has to ask Stephanos! No, not ask, but demand that the temple complex pay the costs of accommodation without first discussing it with her, and then lay that on the shoulders of Stephanos! She suppresses her anger and assures Stephanos with a smile.

"Of course we will take care of the costs of accommodation. Don't you worry about it. Those are matters you don't have to be concerned with. Direct your attention to the sports and events you are going to participate in. I am so proud of you! I give you my blessing as you go to the continent to represent our island."

Silent, they remain seated for a little while, each in their own thoughts. Then, without the slightest warning, Kelenoh says, "Tell me about Theano."

Surprised and wide-eyed, Stephanos looks at her. "You know," Stephanos stammers, "you know that I am in love with her?"

Kelenoh nods with a serene smile on her face. Stephanos cheeks flush with color, "I love her. She makes me so happy and I feel more myself because of her." Bashful, he looks at Kelenoh, not used to expressing his feelings. Kelenoh takes his hand and says, "Stephanos, I am so happy for both of you. Enjoy being together. You both deserve to be happy."

Kelenoh is silent for a moment and watches Stephanos relax into his body, "It is so important to be able to be yourself in a relationship. When both people are able to be themselves, it will add to their happiness. Go now! Go to her, and become one with her."

"Have you found a substitute who can take over your job? I want to release both you and Theano from your duties, so you can enjoy each other as much as possible up until the moment of your departure. I will discuss this with Theano tomorrow."

"Woman, I have found a fine successor. Tomorrow I will introduce him to you. Thank you for giving me time off to prepare for my journey and likewise for giving Theano and I the space to say our good-byes." Stephanos stands up, bows graciously and walks between the two kouroi and onward to the temple complex.

The following day, after the morning service at the temple, Kelenoh ambles down to the Temple of Apollo, knowing Theano will be working there. When she arrives, she looks inside the small temple and pauses to admire Theano who stands at the statue of Apollo. She is small but radiates a joyfulness and a liveliness beyond her size. Kelenoh understands why Stephanos loves her.

Kelenoh watches while Theano carries on a conversation with her beloved Apollo. She sits down on the steps to the entrance of the Temple and waits patiently until Theano is finished. Musing, she looks out at the lemon trees and the homes of the priestesses situated on the other side of the Sacred Road. Yufas nestles himself in her lap and sits with his little eyes closed, enjoying the quiet around them, as she does.

She reflects on her last two years at the temple complex. Since then a lot has happened indeed, she thinks. The complex is more prosperous than ever. What a difference from when she first arrived from Egypt and found everything so neglected. The foundation for the Temple of Hermes and Aphrodite has been laid, clearly defining how big the new temple will be. Construction on the new altar is well underway.

She now sees Theodoros on a daily basis and enjoys his company. Kelenoh has not told him she is pregnant. After one occasion of weakness, upon discovering her fortunate circumstance, she hasn't had any problems with fainting. She feels healthy and energetic. She has decided to hold the fertility ritual and return the little fruit of the earth after the Harvest Festival. Soon, she reminds herself, she will have to discuss her decision with Cassandra, Theano and Selene.

Two men approaching on the road catch her eye. One man is Stephanos and the other is unknown to her. They stop short in front of her. Each takes a bow and Stephanos says, "Woman, I want to introduce you to Epidus. He will take care of my tasks while I am on the continent." Kelenoh stands up and looks into the eyes of Epidus, who, unflinching, looks straight back at her. He is taller and leaner than Stephanos, and from his narrow face radiates an intelligence that appeals to Kelenoh.

"Epidus, it is great that you will take over the tasks of Stephanos. I think we will work well together."

Epidus bows and says, "Woman, it is a great honor to be allowed to do this work, and I will put everything of myself into it, so you will not even notice that Stephanos is away."

Kelenoh bursts out laughing and says, "I don't think you will succeed in that. Stephanos is my friend and for that reason alone I will miss him dearly. Nevertheless, I thank you very much for your effort. Before Stephanos leaves, I would like to have a more detailed conversation with you."

Kelenoh nods to both men and shows Stephanos by her gaze that she is happy with his choice. A smile stretches across Stephanos face and Kelenoh feels his happiness and pride. She follows both men with her eyes as they leave. She sits back down on the stairs. Kelenoh breathes deep and closes her eyes. Yes. The temple complex has surely prospered and wonderful changes have been instituted since her arrival.

Suddenly, something tremors from deep inside her, something she has felt once before. Where has she had this feeling? Kelenoh frantically searches her memory and in a flash she sees herself standing by the harbor in Karnak, at the moment Pharaoh Amasis departed and she received a vision of the Nile colored red with blood, and the death of the Pharaoh Amasis.

A shiver goes through her body. Does she really want to see what is going to happen in the future? The feeling becomes stronger. She notices that Yufas is no longer sitting in her lap. Where is Yufas? Oppression quickly descends on her and silently she pleads for the gods to spare her this vision. Suddenly, the earth moves and Kelenoh flails, finding a grip on the stairs. A loud cry comes from the earth and she puts her hands over her ears. Kelenoh sees the whole temple complex shaking. Her head darts to the left, just as the two large kouroi fall from their pedestals. All the splendidly colored statues along the Sacred Road fall to the ground in pieces. Bewildered, Kelenoh looks around. The temples, the houses, the workshops, everything is falling apart. The people run around in panic trying to look for shelter. She sees Cassandra and Selene helping people wherever they can. Where is Theano? Where is she?

Then the vision stops and Kelenoh catches her breath. She opens her eyes and looks around as though confused by her surroundings. It is so quiet and peaceful as it was before the horrific scenes appeared to her. Where is Yufas?

In shock, she searches for Yufas and finds him sitting beside her, looking at her with clear little eyes. She picks him up and holds him before her eyes. "Yufas, is this the future of the complex?"

Yufas remains silent and from his little eyes run tears. Yufas is crying. With the instinct to protect, she holds the bird against her chest and cries about the terrible vision she had just witnessed. What is the meaning of this? What are the gods trying to tell her? Desperate for answers she calls to the gods, but only silence follows.

Carefully, she puts Yufas beside her on the stairs. She stands up and places her hands on her abdomen. There is new life growing in her and she realizes this gives her comfort and the courage to continue. Startled by a hand placed on her shoulder, Kelenoh jumps. Theano stands behind her, perplexed and concerned, "Kelenoh, you were lost in your thoughts. Is there a problem? Can I help you?" Kelenoh embraces Theano.

"No, Theano, I came here for you and saw that you were in a conversation with Apollo, therefore I sat down on the stairs to wait. I was thinking of how much has happened since my return. Do not be concerned, there is no problem." Kelenoh takes a deep breath and on the exhale, lets go of the terrible vision she was allowed to see.

"What do you want to talk to me about?" Theano asks.

Kelenoh shakes the rest of the vision off and looks at Theano, "About Stephanos."

Theano's face flashes a scarlet color. Kelenoh takes her by the shoulders and asks, "Does that embarrass you? It is fantastic that both of you are in love! I talked about you two with Stephanos last night, when he was returning from the party at Polykrates' home. I am so happy for both of you.

"Listen, Theano, since Stephanos will be leaving us soon, I freed him from his tasks at the complex. This gives him time to prepare for his departure and for you to say your good-byes. I wanted to likewise relieve you of your tasks until Stephanos leaves. Go away with him for a few weeks. Go explore the island. I know of a splendid valley on the north end of the island, where the natural landscape is so beautiful that you feel as though you are in paradise. You can say your good-byes there in peace. Unfortunately, I can't give you any donkeys for transportation. We will need them to work the land for harvesting the crops. Stephanos is already busy packing his belongings. Go to him and make sure to return before the Harvest Festival."

Theano, radiating love, says, "Thank you Kelenoh, I will finish my tasks for today in the temple and then I will go to be with Stephanos."

The women embrace, then they separate and Kelenoh leaves. She turns quickly, not wanting Theano to see her onrush of tears. She hastens to the beach and halts at the foot of a kouros. Kelenoh trembles, and holds onto the leg of the kouros as though her life depended on it. She looks out over the sea and breathes in the waves, quieting her inner self. She sits down, overtaken by a sudden wave of jealousy. How wonderful it would be to go away for a few days with Theodoros, away for a short time from the temple and all its responsibilities. Kelenoh sobs, she feels terribly alone.

Yufas sounds his trill. She picks the bird up and says, "Yufas, I know you are here, but I feel so lonely that I can hardly bear it. Why did I have to see that terrible vision?"

"Kelenoh, breathe deeply and connect to the earth, allow her to replenish your energy."

In a sudden fit of anger Kelenoh lets Yufas drop to the ground and shouts, "I have had enough of it! I want to feel what I feel! I want to be sad because I feel so lonely! I no longer want to connect to the earth!"

Without looking back at Yufas, Kelenoh marches to the sea, raises her hands and starts shouting to the sky, "I don't want to be here any longer. Pick me up. I want to go home, to you." The gods remain silent. In despair, Kelenoh falls to her knees and sobs with her hands over her face. When she is finished weeping, she sits straight up and for the first time in her life feels very drained.

Yufas! She has dropped Yufas! She gets up and quickly walks back to the kouros. Yufas lies still on the ground and a sudden fear captures her. Yufas, she cannot be without Yufas! Carefully, she picks up the motionless bird, puts him in her lap and holds her hands above him.

Fortunately, he is alive and opens his little eyes. Tears come surging forth when she sees the deep love in his little bird eyes. "I feel very bad, Yufas, that I have hurt you," she cries. "I don't know where that sudden anger came from."

"Kelenoh, you know very well where that anger came from. You lost confidence in yourself and thus confidence in the gods as well. Your loneliness has consumed you. Do you remember when you once said, 'I trust in myself and the gods?' You said this for the first time in Egypt and I told you then, to hold on to this as a declaration of truth when things become difficult!"

Yufas is silent and Kelenoh sees herself sitting in front of her little house in Egypt, waiting for Yufaa and Pythagoras, saying these very words. It seems so long ago and surely her life at the time had hardly a care or worry. Kelenoh shakes her head and says, "Yes, I still remember, but at that time my life was somewhat simpler than it is now."

"I know your life is difficult, but realize you chose this life before you were born. You already possess everything you need to fulfill your mission. Know that the gods and I will do everything we can to help you. But that is only possible if you don't reject us!"

The scream of a peacock startles Kelenoh. The sound is coming right from behind her. She turns around and is looking straight into the little beady eyes of the peacock. When the bird sees Kelenoh, he spreads his feathers in full splendor. The colors splash out, reflecting the sunlight and touch Kelenoh's soul. She keeps staring at it until her body starts feeling alive again. A quiet repose settles upon her. She turns her face to the sun and absorbs its warmth.

She is alive!

Slowly, tears roll down her cheeks and she cries without making any noise. Gently, she sets Yufas on the ground beside her, and prepares to unite with the earth.

Chapter 20

The following days are characterized by the harvesting of the crops. It is a hive of activity at the complex. Kelenoh is busy, full of energy, directing everything as to where it should go.

She misses Theano and Stephanos. Once in a while she tunes in to them, catching a glimpse of them enjoying each other and the environment they are in. She is sincerely happy for both these people whom she loves so very much, and that gives her energy. Negative feelings, like anger, fear, jealousy, and lack of self-confidence, make her feel exhausted.

The conversation she had with Epidus went well. He is a substitute worthy of Stephanos. Kelenoh spent time looking inside him and was content with what she saw. He is a hard worker and a person of integrity.

Tuning into Hefaisteon now and then, she feels things are going well with her. Hefaisteon has found herself again in the wake of taking up her old hobby, and weaving the most splendid cloths. Her relationship with Polykrates has improved and Kelenoh sees she has once again embraced the role of mother and enjoys her little daughter.

Kelenoh has become even busier in the mornings as more and more people flock to the temple for healing. News of her abilities has spread, and people come from all over with the hope that they can be relieved of their ailments.

Cassandra and Selene help her wherever and whenever they can. They receive the people and ask them why they have come.

People are divided into groups with those whose problems resemble each other. Sometimes, when the problem is too large or when someone requests it emphatically, Kelenoh will work with a single individual.

In the afternoons, Kelenoh tends to the fields, for the Harvest Festival is upon their door. Within the next two weeks, all must be harvested and stored. The harvest is abundant again, and this winter will be free of fear for lack of food.

She also oversees the construction of the new water cisterns by the vegetable and flower gardens. The foundations of the cisterns are being reinforced with rocks, so not as much water will be lost as was last year, and thus the water, collected from the fall rainstorms, will last for a longer period of time in the spring.

The monthly meetings conducted for the people of the complex are a great success. Now the inhabitants of the temple complex speak up with greater freedom and ask their questions. Kelenoh feels closer to the people and she is noticing that they find it far easier to approach her with their questions or to speak with her.

As she does every evening, Kelenoh sits by a kouros on the beach. On this particular evening, the sky is gray and she is taken by surprise with a sudden feeling of unrest. She looks at Yufas who sits in front of her, and asks, "Yufas, what is happening?"

The bird looks at her, but remains silent. Kelenoh closes her eyes and connects with the gods. The earth moves again and she sees everything around her fall down. "Why are you showing me this?" she asks out loud.

"Kelenoh, you have to realize there are cosmic laws. One of these is the law of cause and effect. We show you this to warn you. Thoughts and deeds of humankind have an influence on what happens to the earth. The same is also true for you."

The gods are silent. Kelenoh finds herself moving into a realm of consciousness where she can actually absorb their instruction. "I am hearing what you say, but I don't understand exactly what you mean," she says after a while.

There is no response. After her prayer of gratitude, she gets up, puts Yufas on her arm and walks home. Cassandra and Selene are waiting for her. They then sit together at the table in the small room and drink warm wine before preparing for the night. In most cases the women recount the events of the day and discuss the tasks for the following day. Kelenoh, however, remains silent and Cassandra asks, "Is something bothering you? Can we be of help?"

Kelenoh shakes her head silently. Suddenly, she looks at Cassandra and Selene and says, "The gods have showed me something and have spoken to me, and I don't know how to interpret it. I need some time by myself to understand what they mean." Kelenoh stands up, embraces both women, wishes them a good night and goes to her room.

▥

The harvest is in. The barns are full of barley, hemp, and food for the winter months. At the complex the mood is changing, all the heavy labor has been done for the upcoming Harvest Festival that will take place the following week. Everyone bustles about with joyous expectancy. All are very busy readying the temple complex, cleaning, organizing and making sure the clothing will be finished before next week's festival begins.

Kelenoh delights in seeing all the happy faces around her. She does await the return of Stephanos and Theano.

She has let go of the vision that the gods have shown her, and trusts, when the time is right, she will know what it has meant.

Kelenoh makes her way to the construction site of the Temple of Aphrodite and Hermes, hoping to see and talk with Theodoros. They have both been so busy lately, that they haven't had much time for any intimacy.

Coming upon the construction site, she sees Theodoros talking to Selene. With a broad movement of his arm, Theodoros explains how the building of the temple has progressed so far, and what has yet to be done. For a moment, she is surprised to see both of them together, but then shrugs. Of course they would run into each other, Selene is a priestess of the temple.

Kelenoh pauses for a moment longer, observing them more intently, and realizes they fit well together. They even resemble each other. Theodoros, with his blonde locks and tall muscular frame, compliments Selene with her trailing blonde hair and petite and slender body. Then she catches the glint in Theodoros' eyes when he looks at Selene, and a fit of jealousy flares up in her.

Theodoros hasn't looked much at her for a long time. Is his love for her over? Was it the plan of the gods for her to just become pregnant by him? Suddenly, she feels sick, her stomach stirring up feelings of loneliness. She turns around and turns with a heavy heart toward the beach. She sits down at the foot of the kouros and with a pale face, stares out across the sea. She clutches her hand around one foot of the kouros, as if to draw strength from the large statue. Then she looks at Yufas who sits in front of her and says, "Yufas, is his love for me over?"

"Kelenoh, the love he had for you was determined by the gods in order to impregnate you. He has accomplished that task, even though he himself doesn't know it. Theodoros is a man who can keep giving love when that love is nourished. Your task as high priestess demands much of you. There has been little time for the both of you; therefore Theodoros' love for you has disappeared."

Kelenoh notices that the hand clasping the foot of the kouros has tensed up from holding on so tight and she has trouble letting go. Stiffened by fear, she takes in Yufas' words. Then she starts trembling and embraces herself. Crying, she rocks back and forth. Something snaps inside of her and on her face appears an expression that lacks compassion and peace. "Then is there no love for me set aside?" she asks in desperation.

"Kelenoh, love is not only between man and woman, it exists in many different forms. The love you speak of is between one man and one woman—yourself and another. No, that love is not a part of your path. Your love is to be for mankind in all its variations. This love is much larger than between two people and will ask a lot of you, but you will receive love in return from the people, and from us. Again, everything is in your power to accomplish this task."

Kelenoh looks at Yufas, but inside she feels something snapping apart. Anger and hatred take possession of her, and a fierce fiery look appears in her eyes. Yufas jumps, startled, when Kelenoh looks down at him and shouts, "Yufas, I don't want to hear any words of love or comfort from you. I feel hatred! I hate Theodoros! And I hate my life at this moment! So leave me alone!"

Yufas remains silent and turns away from her, but she doesn't care. In a flash, she sees that he will do that more often in the future and feels the earth move under her. Is it she who makes the earth move? Is she the cause of the visions the gods showed her? She shakes her head, not wanting to go there in the moment. In all honesty, at present she feels indifferent toward the fate of the temple complex.

Kelenoh rises and walks along the beach. A sudden gust of wind almost makes her fall. She tilts her back up to the sky, clenches her fists and shouts, "Go ahead, do what you need to do, I will not be knocked down! You will not bring me to my knees!" With a proud demeanor she plants her feet firmly into the sand and faces the gusts of wind head on until it finally settles down. Without knowing why, she starts laughing hysterically then falls on her knees and begins to weep.

She cries until the wellspring of tears has been emptied, then stretches out, her left cheek on the sand, looking out to and blinking at the gentle waves. She crawls to the edge of the sea and cools her agitated face with water, then pushes herself up with one hand on her knee. She is exhausted. Kelenoh feels like she is in the body of an old woman who is going to die, although she is only eighteen years old. Slowly, she saunters back to the kouros to pick up Yufas, but the bird is not there.

Panicked, she looks around. Yufas is gone! The bird has never left her alone, and Kelenoh feels such a deep loneliness, that she becomes desperate. In her mind she calls to Yufas and begs, "Yufas, please don't leave me alone, I cannot do it without you." When she looks around once more, she sees Yufas sitting on the pedestal of the kouros. She picks him up and holds him against her chest.

"Yufas, please don't ever leave me alone again, without you I cannot manage." Kelenoh sits down and places Yufas in front of her. She looks at him, hoping to see the loving look with which he usually looks at her. Her feeling of hatred fades out but is quickly replaced with despair.

Then Yufas says, "Kelenoh."

The little eyes she gazes into her are soft and full of love. Kelenoh heaves a sigh of relief and says, "Yufas, I know what you want to say. The gods have not left me, I rejected them. But you, Yufas, please don't leave me ever again."

"Kelenoh, I warned you in Egypt, since you had not finished your training completely, to be careful concerning your weak spots, judging other people for instance. Your hate for Theodoros reveals the tendency to judge others, which is still a weak spot. You don't know what the gods say is the need of the people for their own development and spiritual growth. You don't have the right to judge. The pain you feel is because you think that people are doing something to you, that is really your pain. The why, and bigger picture of their lives is unknown to you, so do not judge. I just explained to you why Theodoros no longer loves you, and why the gods put him on your path. The task that you took voluntarily upon you before you were born is difficult, that is why I am here to help you. Your life is a splendid life. The task you have to fulfill is so enormous. The choice, whether to continue or not, is all yours. You have free will. When you decide to continue with the task you were born for, the gods and I will do everything to support you."

The truth in Yufas' words resonates with Kelenoh, but in actuality, they only further feed those feelings of loneliness and abandonment. In the silence that follows, a calm descends upon her, accompanied by a resolve. "Then," she says, "Yufas, I am the woman of Hera and I will do my best to fulfill this task well."

"Good, Kelenoh. Now return to Theodoros and free him from the ties that bind you two, that he might move forward on his path and be happy with Selene. That is what we want."

Kelenoh remains seated a little longer to unite with the earth, to re-center and fill herself again with energy. She gets up and walks to the construction site of the temple. Selene is no longer there and Theodoros is busy. He has a piece of clay tablet in his hand and explains to the builders how he wants to have things done. She remains standing out of sight, a little distance away, secretly admiring him. She loves him. Kelenoh feels deep pain strike her body. She lays her hands on her abdomen and hears the words of Yufas again in her head that this pregnancy is the only reason she met and united with Theodoros.

Theodoros suddenly looks up from his tablet and sees her standing there. He raises his hand and approaches her. He comes and stands close towering over her. Kelenoh starts shaking, but takes heart, and calms her nerves.

"Kelenoh, I haven't seen you for a long time, how are you doing?" Theodoros looks at her with questioning eyes as he seeks answers. Kelenoh sees that his love for her has disappeared from his gaze. "Is everything alright with you? You are looking pale, is there anything I can do for you?"

Kelenoh straightens her back and looks at him for a short time, memorizing his handsome features. She hesitates and puts aside any trace of emotion that would give her feelings away. Theodoros feels a change in Kelenoh as he waits for an answer from her.

"No Theodoros, there is nothing you can do for me any longer. Everything you had to do, you have done." Not understanding, Theodoros' eyes wander about Kelenoh as he speaks, "Kelenoh, I don't understand what you mean."

Kelenoh nods and says, "Theodoros, I have come to tell you that our love is over." Kelenoh quickly turns around. She doesn't want Theodoros to see her great sorrow. She also doesn't want to put any energy into the questions Theodoros would ask her, or to see his despair, because she knows it is not real.

She feels the need to return to the beach, but has to see Selene. As she walks to the gardens, she recovers, and by the time she arrives, she is totally in control of herself again. Selene approaches her laughing, and after an embrace the women sit down on a low wall. "I came to see how you are doing Selene, and I wanted to ask you something," Kelenoh says.

"How nice, Kelenoh, that you have come to see me. I am doing fine, thank you. Is everything alright with you?" Kelenoh feels the love of Selene and also her concern.

Kelenoh then puts her hand on her abdomen and says, "I am doing fine, and my pregnancy is as well. Do you have the herbs needed to end this pregnancy?"

"Kelenoh, everything is ready. You only have to give me notice as to when we are going to conduct the ceremony. You have to start taking the herbs a few days before, so let me know in time."

"Good! Selene, I will discuss it with all of you tonight. I came to ask you something else. What do you think about Theodoros?" The sudden question confuses Selene for a moment.

"Theodoros?"

When Selene pronounces his name, Kelenoh sees a blush appear on her cheeks. Kelenoh knows enough.

"Yes, Theodoros. I saw you with him this morning on the building site of your temple, and I thought that you would make a very fine couple."

"I really like him and he is sincere, but he belongs to you. Why are you asking?"

"Because I think he belongs to you and not to me."

"I don't know Kelenoh. I don't know him well enough to know exactly what it is I am feeling for him."

"Go to him Selene, get to know him and tell him I have sent you. He will understand."

Joy radiates from Selene's face as she gets up. Kelenoh nods assuredly and says again, "Go!"

When Selene is gone to do her bidding, Kelenoh remains seated on the low wall in the garden a little longer, putting her thoughts in order. To her amazement a deep peace comes over her. 'It is good this way,' she declares. She stares out at the flowers around her, which blur against a backdrop of a gray sky, that is, until Yufas lets out a trill and she regains conscious awareness of her environment. She looks at him and sees the fullness of love in his little bird eyes. She gets up, puts the bird on her arm and says, "Come Yufas, there is more work to do and we have to get to it."

In the evening, Kelenoh, Cassandra and Selene sit in the little room and go over the day. Kelenoh tells Cassandra that Theodoros belongs to Selene from now on, and not to her. Seeing the happy face of Selene, a stitch of jealousy goes through her body again, but she suppresses the feeling, and looks over at Cassandra with a half-hearted smile. Cassandra returns her gaze, astonished, but before Cassandra gets a chance to ask any questions, Kelenoh says, "Cassandra, I don't want to talk about it, it is good as it is. I want to discuss the ceremony with you. I have decided that it should take place the day after the Harvest Festival. Unfortunately, Theano has not returned yet, but she should be back before the Festival, so there will be enough time to prepare ourselves."

Cassandra puts aside her questions and Kelenoh knows she will find a way to query her later on the matter of Theodoros and Selene.

They rehearse the ceremony once more, so they all know where to stand. They decide to take their positions before sunrise, so just as the sun breaks, Kelenoh can return the little fruit to the earth in peace.

Chapter 21

One day before the Harvest Festival, Stephanos and Theano return. Both are radiant with love and everyone enjoys their happiness. Kelenoh scans Theano, and discerns that Theano is very sad about the departure of Stephanos, and also that she is pregnant. Kelenoh sees the cell division has just begun and that Theano, distracted by Stephanos' departure, doesn't pay attention to her body.

There will be two women pregnant at the time of the ceremony, which is a very good omen for the complex. Theano does not yet realize she is pregnant. Kelenoh plans to discuss it with her after the ceremony, and determine with her when to end this pregnancy. Theano, Cassandra and Selene aren't allowed to have children. The four priestesses must be available at all times for the work at the complex, and may not be distracted by children.

Full of energy, Stephanos looks forward to his departure to the continent. He will be leaving the day after the Harvest Festival. In the weeks that Stephanos and Theano were away, a few priestesses were busy preparing everything for him—his clothing, cooking utensils, bandages, et cetera. Everything has been packed and made ready for the long awaited trip.

The day of the Harvest Festival has arrived, and just as she did the previous year, Kelenoh prays for the sun to shine and the skies to be clear, so that it will be a splendid day for all the inhabitants of the island. There is a beehive of activity at the complex. More and more people have heard of Kelenoh, and many have come from far and near to visit her for a healing.

The ceremonial rituals begin. Kelenoh lights the oblation to the gods, and the smoke produced from sweet smelling herbs rises straight up; a sign the offering has been accepted. As the smoke goes up, a loud acclamation breaks out among the populace.

Everyone is cheerful and to her surprise, Kelenoh sees Hefaisteon with Polykrates at her side, amongst those present. They both look relaxed. Kelenoh hopes she will get to speak to Hefaisteon for a moment.

At the end of the day she does get a chance while Polykrates is in conversation with the group of men who are leaving for the continent. Hefaisteon eyes Kelenoh and approaches her, radiating and laughing as she walks to Kelenoh and embraces her. "Hefaisteon, I am so glad to see you so happy."

"Kelenoh, after our last conversation I followed your advice. I started weaving and you were right. I felt much better and therefore my relationship with Polykrates has also improved."

Kelenoh escorts Hefaisteon to the dining room, now filled with people who are eating and drinking. She looks for a quiet spot where they can sit down and catch up. "Tell me everything Hefaisteon, and also how your little daughter is doing."

Before Hefaisteon can say anything, Polykrates enters. He looks around and sees Hefaisteon sitting by Kelenoh. His face grows dark and furious and he marches toward both women. While he stands over them, he takes Hefaisteon by the arm and says, "Come, we are going home."

Before Kelenoh realizes it, she is suddenly sitting at the table by herself. Not understanding, she follows Polykrates and Hefaisteon with her eyes. She sends love to them as they go, especially to give Hefaisteon strength to deal with the anger of Polykrates. Silence has fallen in the dining hall and everyone looks at her. Kelenoh gets up, looks for Selene and says, "Selene, please take your zither and play for us, so we can sing and dance. Everyone," she announces, giving a final word, "enjoy the food and drinks, celebrate and love one other."

Kelenoh exits the dining hall and heads toward the beach to stand by her beloved kouros and thank the gods for another successful Harvest Festival.

The following morning, before sunrise, the four women stand in their positions. Cassandra stands facing the northeast side of the temple, Theano and Selene stand, one on the southeast, and the other on the northwest side. Kelenoh nestles herself down behind the temple, on the southwest side.

Though the other women are out of sight, Kelenoh feels the strength that goes out from the four of them. Her dress lies spread out around her, and she has wrapped an extra cloth around her. The ground whereon she sits is cold and moist; the early morning dew is still upon the blades of grass. Fall is fast approaching.

When the sun casts its first rays over the island, Kelenoh closes her eyes and connects to the gods. She feels the presence of Hestia standing beside her, and that gives her comfort. She directs her attention to her body and to the little child in her abdomen. With the power of her mind, she orders the little fruit to come out. A stitch of pain shoots through her and she feels something starting to flow out from her vagina. It feels warm. Hestia's hand reaches out and gently rests on her shoulder and she hears, "Kelenoh, you have accomplished it, you have returned your fruit to the earth."

Eyes still closed, Kelenoh remains seated a little longer until the sistrums start jangling in the distance. Shaking, she pushes herself up on her knees and carefully covers the spot where she was sitting with earth and marks it with rocks, set around it in the shape of a square. For a brief moment Kelenoh's body feels empty and she has the inclination to lie down and not stand up. She feels exhausted. A peacock's scream echoes across the complex. It seems that the sound is coming from every side of it. A smile appears on her face. She summons all her strength and rises to her feet, noticing that Hestia has disappeared.

Slowly pacing herself, and with one hand still clutching her abdomen, she walks to the front of the temple where the three women are waiting for her. In silence they embrace each other and all four, with arms linked, walk home together. Cassandra already has set out warm water with lavender to wash her, and Selene prepares a mixture of herbs for Kelenoh to drink in order to strengthen her body.

One hour later Kelenoh stands next to Theano at the harbor to say goodbye to Stephanos. There are many people arriving at this early hour. The last things are brought aboard the ship. Kelenoh watches as Stephanos searches for a good spot for his luggage. Stephanos looks up and sees both women. He raises his hand, signaling he will come to them soon. Kelenoh and Theano look for a quiet spot where they can sit down for a short time and observe the activity around them. It isn't long before Stephanos stands before them, nervous and excited.

Theano stands up and cups his face with her hands, tears welling up in her eyes. Kelenoh remains seated, looking admiringly up at Stephanos and Theano, until Stephanos looks at her and asks, "Woman, is everything well with you? You look very pale." Kelenoh stands up and nods at him reassuringly.

"Thank you Stephanos, for your genuine concern. Everything is well with me." Kelenoh takes a pouch and gives it to Stephanos.

"Stephanos, here is the money for your stay in Olympia; you don't have to sleep in the open air. Do you have everything you need for your journey and your stay?" Stephanos nods and accepts the pouch.

"Thank you, Woman. The priestesses have taken care of everything and have packed for me."

Suddenly Kelenoh jumps, startled by a loud sound. Someone is blowing a horn, warning that the ship is about to leave. Kelenoh nods at Stephanos, "It is time for you to go," she says, "take care of yourself and show the people how good you are. Samos is proud of you."

Stephanos brings a fisted hand in front of his chest and takes a bow. "Woman, I thank you for everything, and I will make certain that Samos will be proud of me."

Stephano turns around, embraces Theano, and whispers something in her ear. Kelenoh sees Theano fighting back tears and turns around, allowing them their space to say a final good-bye. When she looks up again, Stephanos is walking to the ship. He doesn't look back. She moves to stand beside Theano and squeezes her hand. Together, the two women watch as the ship slowly sails away from the port until Stephanos is no longer visible.

Arm and arm they walk back along the Sacred Road near the beach toward the temple to begin morning service. As they walk, a hard wind starts blowing and the first rain of the fall pummels the earth in large sheets. Kelenoh immediately connects to the gods and asks them to steer Stephanos ship safely to the continent before the real fall storms commence.

At the Temple of Hera, Cassandra and Selene wait for both women. Cassandra and Selene embrace and console Theano. As Kelenoh looks on, a warm feeling of love for these women, for her dearest friends, flows through her. After the morning service and the healing of people that followed, the women walk to the dining hall for their meal. Cassandra walks beside Kelenoh and asks, "May I ask you a question after our meal?"

Kelenoh nods at Cassandra, "Yes, of course." She already knows what Cassandra has in mind to ask.

After their meal, Cassandra and Kelenoh quietly walk to the beach and sit down at the statue of the kouros. It has stopped raining, but the wind is still very audible. Both women wrap their shawls tightly around them. Kelenoh looks at Cassandra and says, "Please, ask your question."

"Kelenoh, you told us two nights ago, very casually, that Selene from now on belongs to Theodoros. I don't understand, can you explain what you mean?"

"Cassandra, the gods have spoken with me and explained that Theodoros had come along my path so that I would become pregnant. They also explained to me that he belongs to Selene, that it was time to let him go, and that is what I have done."

"Just like that?" Cassandra can hardly believe her, "but, Kelenoh, you love him."

Kelenoh bows her head, feeling the truth in her words she searches for a response. A few minutes pass and then Kelenoh looks up at her with sad eyes, "No, Cassandra, it was not easy. I have to admit that I felt hate, jealousy and despair, that I had enough of my life and that I did not want to go on."

Cassandra looks bewildered at Kelenoh. "What happened then, that you were able to tell it to us so calmly?"

"Cassandra, that is between the gods and me. I don't want to say anything more about it. It is good like this." The silence closes in on them as the two women sit together a little longer until Kelenoh abruptly gets up and says, "Accept the happiness of Selene and Theodoros, Cassandra, because the gods have willed it so."

Kelenoh feels Cassandra struggle with this, but is also honored for a moment by her token of compassion. She takes Cassandra by the shoulders and says once more with firmness, "It is good as it is. Come, stand up, I have to go. I want to visit with Theano, to see how she is doing and discuss a matter of importance with her."

Cassandra gets up and looks quizzically at Kelenoh. "Tonight I will tell you what I speak of," answers Kelenoh.

Without waiting for Cassandra to say anything more, Kelenoh spins around and walks away. She suddenly feels irritated by Cassandra and this anger quickly boils to the surface. 'What right does she have to know everything about me?' she asks, her thoughts raging.

A sudden and chaotic sound of sistrums and voices descend upon Kelenoh. She braces herself against a column from the Temple of Apollo. Trembling, she sits down on the steps and waits until it quiets down inside of her so she can hear the voices.

"Kelenoh," the voices come clearly now, "Cassandra is with you to help and protect you. She loves you; that gives her the right."

The voices are silent for a moment, and then she hears, "Be careful Kelenoh, to not push away the people that love you. It will make you very lonely." Kelenoh closes her eyes and shakes her head. She does not want to hear about such things anymore. The voices stop talking abruptly, this time without the sound of sistrums that usually accompany a farewell before they leave.

She is startled for a moment by the sudden silence, but decides not to think much of it and continues on into the Temple of Apollo to look for Theano. When she sees the pale and tear-stained face of Theano, Kelenoh walks quickly to her. She takes Theano's face in both her hands and says, "Theano, be not forlorn. Stephanos will arrive safely on the continent and he will have a great time there. Come, I will take you to the beach, and we will have a long walk. It will benefit you and there is something I must talk to you about." In silence the women walk to the beach and then along the sea to where the stretch of sand ends. There, they sit down, leaning their backs against a wall of rocks that block the wind.

Theano tosses ideas in her mind and raises a quizzical brow to Kelenoh, "You want to talk to me about something Kelenoh? Please tell me. Now is a good time for I feel calm again."

Kelenoh takes Theano's cold hands in hers, pauses for a moment, and then states, "You are pregnant." Just as soon as a blush appears on Theano's cheeks, it disappears, turning to ashen white; she knows what is to become of this pregnancy.

Kelenoh sees all kinds of thoughts race around in Theano's head, and gives her time to absorb the news. The surf breaks on the shore and crashes upon the small rock peninsula stretched out in front of them. Theano stares out across the sea, and after some time turns to Kelenoh, "So," she says, rather melancholy, "we were both pregnant at the time of the ceremony?"

"Yes!" Kelenoh tempers her enthusiasm. "The temple complex has been very blessed this year by our pregnancies!"

A faint smile appears on Theano's face. "Kelenoh, I already had the feeling that something was different in my body, but my thoughts have been with Stephanos more than myself. Thank you for paying attention to me."

Theano, looks down, places a hand on her lower abdomen, rubbing it gently. She swallows back a lump in her throat. "I will go soon to Selene to ask her for the herbs to discontinue the pregnancy."

"Do you want me to go with you, Theano? You don't have to do this alone."

"No Kelenoh, I have the need to be alone. I have to process what is happening in my body and prepare myself for the coming days. However, I would like you to be present when I return the fruit to the earth." Kelenoh nods and embraces Theano. The women cling to each other for a moment, as each one releases their burdens into the comfort and love that they share.

Kelenoh rises, "The gods have blessed you. Thank them for that. I shall leave you alone now. When the time is right for you, I will be with you."

Kelenoh wraps her shawl somewhat tighter around her shoulders. Her raised arm acts as a shield against the cold wind on her face. Battling an even more fierce wind, she drags herself back to the complex.

In the evening, the four priestesses sit together, warming themselves around the kitchen hearth. Kelenoh openly tells

Cassandra of Theano's good fortune. Selene remains quiet, beaming at her friend Theano, who already informed her of the pregnancy. As she tells Cassandra, it is as though she, Cassandra, shrinks beneath her and she, Kelenoh, rises above her. Kelenoh notices her feelings turning away from Cassandra, and strangely enough it pleases her to do so. Kelenoh determines that from now on, she will walk in front of Cassandra instead of beside her.

Far away she hears the sistrums, but pretends to not pay attention to them. Yufas' back is turned to her as though the bird ignores her and does not want to look at her. Cassandra doesn't say a word. Suddenly, there is tension in the small little room.

Selene breaks the tension, "Why are we so silent?" she asks. "Why, this is a splendid gift from the gods to our dear Theano. We should celebrate!"

With her happiness brimming over, Selene jumps up and pours a cup of warm wine for everyone. Then she serves them, and when she hands a cup to Theano, she gently touches her cheek. A few tears appear in Theano's eyes from the warmth of such a lovely gesture.

The women stand up, raise their cups and as if out of one mouth call out, "Thanks be to the gods!"

Chapter 22

The years have passed by, the temple complex and the island are more prosperous than ever. The tunnel of Eupalinos has been completed, and just as Kelenoh had envisioned, the laborers did meet in the middle of the mountain with a difference of almost one meter. She could hear the cheering when the two groups reached each other.

The walls and gates around the city have been completed as well. The Temple of Hermes and Aphrodite had been fully erected and is now in use. The old Temple of Hera has been demolished and the foundations for the new Temple of Hera have been laid and the columns positioned in place, with the exception of the outer row of columns. They will be positioned later, when the roof is completed.

The old stone and debris of the demolished temple has been hammered into small pieces. Some of it was spread out along the beach. The remainder of the debris had been reused to repair and fill in the ancient roads around the city. The wood from the temple was preserved and stacked in the kitchen to be used as firewood to prepare the feast meals for the Spring and Harvest Festivals.

The new altar is splendid. It is built on the same spot where the previous altar had been, in front of the holy lygos tree. Now a wall, in the shape of a *u*, was also constructed in front of it, so bystanders would be protected against the fire during ceremonial offerings.

A sorrowful event struck the complex and the island when Stephanos came back from the games injured. Practicing the javelin throw among fellow contestants, he was hit in his groin. When he returned to Samos, the wound was inflamed to the point that he could no longer be saved. Attacked day and night by a fever, he lay in his bed hardly conscious of his surroundings, his whole body shaking and trembling. Theano never left his side, holding his hand, and comforting him as she could. Selene exhausted her knowledge of herbs to reduce his suffering. Even Kelenoh, with all her healing power, was not able to save him. It was Stephanos' time to go.

Kelenoh spoke with the crew and heard that Stephanos had won two laurel wreaths, one for wrestling and one for running. The crew praised Stephanos for not only being a great athlete, but a great man as well. He quickly earned the respect and admiration from all on the continent. Epidus permanently took over the responsibilities of Stephanos.

Theano had been inconsolable after his death, and lost all her liveliness. From the day of Stephanos' death and on, she could often be found in the Temple of Apollo. She became a driven priestess, dedicating herself wholly to service. Kelenoh removed her from her duties in the weaving mill, so she could devote all her time to the Temple of Apollo, where she found peace.

Oftentimes, Kelenoh would see Theodoros and Selene walking or sitting and talking for hours on the beach. She feels the deep love between them and can now look at them without pain. In spite of this, Kelenoh herself has become stern these the last few years, more reserved and rarely smiling, her outbursts of laughter no longer echoed throughout the temple complex.

She had fewer and fewer conversations with the gods, instead breaking away to do things on her own. The monthly gatherings in the dining hall were abolished. Her relationship with Cassandra had not improved either. It had become one of silence. Kelenoh knew that she was no longer in balance. Through the years she gave up on putting any effort into a daily practice that allowed for the maintaining of her sense of harmony and heart within herself. It became easier for her to conduct affairs of the complex and of the people with the sole use of her intellectual mind. Her mind had won.

She handles her tasks and keeps herself standing. She has turned off her feelings to protect herself and to survive. Faithfully, she accomplishes her tasks and duties the temple complex demands of her, nothing more. In the past she tried to dissuade the fear of the people, but she gave up on that as well.

She became pregnant twice more by men who were working on the construction of the temple. At random, she selected the men who attracted her attention at the time, men that were not afraid of her. Most people fear her and refrain from looking into her eyes—eyes that have grown more stern. She terminated her pregnancies in the shroud of silence at the time when she felt it was necessary, before suspicion would arise among the complex inhabitants, taking herbs and using the power of her mind.

In addition, she began to appear more often at the complex without Yufas. The bird had turned away from her and instead of dealing with it, she let him be, no longer caring. Kelenoh's natural self-confidence was replaced with haughtiness and a sense of pride. When she walked around the complex, her posture was straight and stiff. The joyful, happy child that always ran, eager to experience life, had withdrawn. Seeking solitude, she started detesting large groups of people.

She became proficient in the carving of small statuettes. They all have the same theme; they are statuettes of pregnant women who embody the fertility of Hera. Sometimes the statuettes are given to women who want to become pregnant. For Kelenoh the fabricating of the statuettes is a respite. She is totally alone. No one is allowed to disturb her when she is busy carving in her home, in the small room behind the kitchen. Her need to be with herself is met in this way.

Today a ship has sailed into the port, bringing a message for Polykrates. Pythagoras is on his way to the island! As soon as Polykrates hears of the ship, he sends someone to the temple complex to tell Kelenoh that Pythagoras is returning. Kelenoh listens to the message and feels two opposing feelings stir in her. The first is anger, simply for the reason that Polykrates didn't make the effort to tell her himself. Then, joy—a joy that she hasn't felt for a long time.

Pythagoras! Her Pythagoras is returning. Now all will be well again. Surely Kelenoh is aware that the way she has handled herself and performed the work of the temple complex in the past years has not been ideal. First thing she does upon hearing the news, is swiftly walk home to tell Yufas. For a short time as she picks the bird up and looks into his eyes, there is the familiar contact, like they have had before. Yufas gazes back at her and says, "He is returning, I know it already. Kelenoh, listen to him. It is your last chance."

Kelenoh puts Yufas on the table and with defensiveness in her voice questions him, "What do you mean, my last chance?"

"You know exactly what I mean, Kelenoh."

The small room, where Kelenoh and Yufas sit, fills with an uncomfortable silence. Kelenoh gets up, paces up and down, and then sighs, her face and shoulders softening.

"Yes, I do know what you mean. I know I have neglected the gods and you. I know that I am not in harmony and out of balance. But Yufas, I do my best, and the temple complex functions well, doesn't it? The harvests are abundant, everyone has food and drink, I resolve problems that arise, I heal the sick, I do what I can."

"Yes, Kelenoh, you speak of it well. You do what you can, but your heart is not involved."

"Yufas, you know as no one else, how hard I have fought to remain in balance. I made different choices, because I could no longer manage. I had the feeling that I would not survive."

"Kelenoh, I know everything about you, and I realize that you were sent back to Samos too early due to Hestia's untimely passing. You had to take over the weighty task of high priestess. However, the gods and I were there to help you, and reminded you often, but you rejected us. I know you have chosen the easier way, but does that make you happier?"

"Easier?" Kelenoh raises her tone. "You call it easier, Yufas?"

"Yes, Kelenoh, if you had done your tasks united in mind and feeling, they would have been more difficult in the beginning, but in the long run easier, since love would have been returned to you. Now you are lonely, and the people are afraid of you, shrinking beneath the power you possess."

Kelenoh stops abruptly, looks at Yufas and leaves the house. With clenched fists she marches across the Procession Road, turns left at the Sacred Road, and arrives at the beach. She stops by the kouros, wraps an arm around its leg, and inhales the sea air deep into her lungs.

Her joy over the return of Pythagoras is gone. Dismayed, Kelenoh turns her head downward. She is trying her best and it feels like it is never enough. The urge to run away from the temple complex and leave everything behind re-emerges. Tears of anger and disappointment roll down her pale pink cheeks.

Suddenly, Hestia stands before her. She takes Kelenoh by the hand, caressing the top of it gently, and consoles her, "My child."

At the meeting of their gaze, the anger and despair disappear. Sobbing, she collapses into Hestia's arms. When she has finally stopped crying, Kelenoh looks up at Hestia and sees silent tears streaking down her cheeks. Kelenoh takes Hestia by the hand and pleads, "Hestia, help me!"

"Kelenoh, we are always here to help you. You opened yourself up by listening to Yufas; therefore you gave us the chance to come to you. Renew your faith and trust in yourself and in the gods, Kelenoh."

Kelenoh hears what Hestia is saying, but she feels totally empty after her crying spell and doesn't know what to say or to think. Defeated, she stares at the sea and doesn't notice that Hestia has disappeared. When she does notice that she is alone again, anger and despair resurface. Once more she clenches her fists, rattling them up to the sky, and cries, "Yes, just go ahead and leave me alone. I will take care of it myself!"

Furious, she turns around and stomps back to the complex. She doesn't see the frightened faces of people that pass her by, nor how they try to avoid her.

In the dining hall, the tables are already prepared and the priestesses and soldiers pour in to have their meal together. As she enters, the dining hall grows still. Everyone feels Kelenoh's anger. Afraid of attracting her attention and receiving a dose of it, they evade her gaze and remain silent. Habitually, Kelenoh starts reciting the prayers of gratitude before the meal. There is no singing. Lately, there hasn't been much singing. Kelenoh is totally unaware of what is happening around her, she has shut herself off completely to everything and everyone.

After the meal, Kelenoh makes her rounds over the fields to examine the crops. Suddenly, in the midst of the crops, a memory of her and Selene as small children running through the fields flashes before her eyes, and she feels the happiness of the child that she once was. She halts, shakes the memory from her head and says out loud, "What do you want me to do with this? What are you telling me? Must I become like a child again? I am no longer a child, so don't bother to parade before me something I no longer am."

Holding her head high, she continues walking through the fields and tests the crops. Not a single person crosses her path and suddenly she realizes she is alone. Astonished, she looks around and thinks, "Where is everyone?"

The scent of the crops passes under her nose and she is conscious again of the sun and the wind. The colors that surround her take on a vibrancy. Happiness swells inside as she absorbs all of the beauty nature offers her and she thinks, "Good, I am alone. That is fine. I don't need any people."

The happy feeling is short lived as she realizes that there is still much to do this day. Making haste, she leaves the fields and goes to the weaving mill to take stock of the progress made with the clothing for the coming winter months.

Standing in the open doorway of the weaving mill, she hears the sociable chatter and singing, but when she enters, a shadow is cast and silence falls. With a scorned brow and cross voice Kelenoh shouts, "Talk and sing with each other! I find it extremely offensive when you become silent upon my entering."

She brushes past the women to the back of the weaving mill where the shelves are and where new clothing is stockpiled. Behind her she hears the priestesses start talking in hushed and cautious tones. A single voice stands out above the rest, singing a song.

By the shelves she sees Hedeas, Theano's replacement. She is busy folding the clothing that she then puts neatly on the shelves according to size. Suddenly, Kelenoh misses Theano and plans to make a stop at the Temple of Apollo to visit her.

Hedeas' face flushes at the sudden presence of Kelenoh. Kelenoh is unable to hide her aggravation, at the sight of a nervous and timid Hedeas. Slowly, Kelenoh walks along the shelves, running her hand across the fabrics. The fabrics are soft and a feeling of pride fills her. There is abundance, and everything seems accounted for. Kelenoh turns on her heels, slightly startling Hedeas and asks, "How far along are you with the dresses for my priestesses?"

"The fabric is still in the loom, but almost finished," answers Hedeas shyly, while looking at the floor. Kelenoh suppresses the urge to step forward and shake Hedeas out of her submissive behavior. She doesn't bother to ask any more questions, turns and walks out of the mill without a final word.

Theano, she has to see Theano. Through the entry of the Temple of Apollo, Kelenoh eyes Theano, occupied with arranging flowers by the statue of Apollo. Theano looks up when she hears someone approaching, and a smile appears on her face when she sees that it is Kelenoh.

"Kelenoh, how nice of you to come and visit."

She lays the flowers on the ground and walks to Kelenoh with outstretched arms. Kelenoh takes Theano's hands and suddenly feels moved by her love. The two women embrace, then Theano pulls back and says, "Is there a special reason you have come by, or are you just coming to have a look?"

"No, no special reason. I was just in the weaving mill and I was missing you. Come, let us sit on the stairs in the sun for a moment."

Theano takes Kelenoh by the hand and they walk out to the stairs. They sit in front of the temple, sharing silence between them for some time. Theano breaks the pensive mood. "Kelenoh," she asks, "is something bothering you, can I help you?"

"No, Theano, all is well. I only have the need to be with you for a moment; that is all."

More time passes before Kelenoh stands up and says, "Thank you for keeping me company, but now I must continue on. I have to go to the Temple of Hera to see if everything is ready for the service tomorrow." Kelenoh turns around and feels Theano's eyes following her. She isn't inclined to explain what is going on inside of her. She knows that Theano understands.

The following day after the morning service, and after healing the throngs of people from the complex and the island, Kelenoh goes to rest at the holy spring. Sitting down on a low wall, her left hand plays in the water. Her mind wanders back to all of the people that came by in the morning. Masses of people seem to disturb her more and more. Likewise, she feels more and more that the people are pushy, rude and demanding of her. She closes her eyes, remembering her anger stoked to the point of almost killing a man, a man who refused to leave after she told him she could not help him. She shook with fear of her own power, but more so, at the fact that she was willing to do it.

Yufaa once told her she would acquire the power over life and death, but that he hoped she would never have to use that power. In the end, such a decision would be up to her. Kelenoh's brow furrows and her eyes turned dark. She intends to use this power if the people continue to be pushy and rude, even if it is to just teach them a lesson. She has had enough of it! Every day is the same, bound by her duties and service to the people. She makes herself ready for them, listens to their trials, offers them solutions, and heals them. On and on it goes, all this without gratitude and appreciation. She is tired. Everyone wants something from her. And who is there for her?

Suddenly startled by a sound, Kelenoh looks up and sees someone approaching in Egyptian travel clothing. Yufaa! She was just thinking of him and at the same time someone from Egypt comes up the road. Could it be someone from Karnak?

The man approaches Kelenoh, and then takes a bow. As she scans him from head to toe, her hopefulness is replaced with a feeling of contempt. Kelenoh looks at him haughtily. The man's words tumble nervously out of his mouth, as he states where he is from. He comes from Memphis and Kelenoh's disappointment sinks into her stomach. He is not from Karnak. Silent, with a blank face, she looks at the man repeating in her head, 'from Memphis.'

Suddenly, the face of the priest from the temple of Memphis appears before her. It was the haughty priest she encountered on her return to Samos when they anchored in Memphis. Just seeing his face makes her feel angry, as she was at that time. Here she sits, as haughty now as the priest was then. For a moment, Kelenoh is frightened by the thought, but shakes her head and says, "Tell me why you have come."

"I came to bring you a present from the priest you visited a long time ago. He sends his greetings and instructed me to tell you that he took your words to heart. Everyone is now welcomed in the temple."

Are the gods playing a game with her? Are they trying to tell her something? Kelenoh doesn't want to think about such things, and looks at the man standing before her. He reaches to take something from the pocket of his coat. The something glistens between his fingers. She holds her left hand out and the man puts a small bronze statuette of a little bear in it. Kelenoh holds it up, examining the statuette as it shimmers in the sun. The little bear sits on his bottom and holds his paw in front of his mouth, as if he is eating from a jar of honey. His other paw rests between his two stretched out hind legs.

It is a splendidly detailed statuette. Kelenoh admires the craftsmanship, and looks at the man to say something, but the man beats her to it and says, "Woman, I have to also tell you, on behalf of the priest, that he thinks the little bear resembles you. He remembers first seeing you and thinking you to be very lovely, but when you became angry, you became as tall as a bear."

"Thank you for this present. I accept it, and I am happy to hear that the priest listened to me and the temple in Memphis is now open to everyone. That is how it should be. That is why there are temples. Would you be so kind as to convey my gratitude to the priest?" The man nods and Kelenoh notices he is very tired and his traveling clothes are soiled.

"Come." She stands, "I will bring you to Epidus. He will accompany you to the guesthouse where you may refresh yourself. After that, you can share a meal with us in the dining hall. Epidus will give you a tour of the property and of course you may stay as long as you like."

The man bows and says, "Thank you for your hospitality, but my stay won't be very long. The ship I came with will be leaving on the morrow. We are on our way to Delphi to visit the Pythia and ask the oracle about the problems presently being experienced in Egypt. Tonight we are the guests of Polykrates, because..."

"Polykrates, of course you'd rather spend the night at the palace," Kelenoh snaps, "and you want to visit the Pythia to ask her advice? Ha! I could save you that voyage, but I suppose you have to do what you have to do."

Without waiting for the man to respond she starts walking. When she notices he is not following her, she flips around to see him, head turned to the ground, standing in the same spot. Kelenoh beckons him and says, "Come, I was going to bring you to Epidus."

On their way to Epidus, Kelenoh sees one of Polykrates' men walking quickly toward her. He bows from afar, stirring within Kelenoh an uncomfortable feeling, a feeling that the man's gesture is insincere.

When he stands before her, she straightens her back, lengthening her spine and shoulders to appear taller, so it is she who looks down at the man. He averts his gaze from looking directly into her eyes. "Woman," he says, "I have come to bring you a message from Polykrates. Amasis, the ruler of Egypt has arrived on Samos and Polykrates wishes to extend an invitation to you and Epidus for a celebration in honor of the Pharaoh Amasis this evening."

The man from Egypt, standing behind her, brings a hand to his face and suppresses a laugh. Infuriated, Kelenoh twirls around and barks, "Why didn't you tell me that Pharaoh Amasis was on the ship that brought you to Samos?"

"Because I had a message for you from the priest of Memphis; my only task was to deliver that message, nothing more, and I have done that."

Kelenoh feels rammed in the back by the man from Egypt, whose entire demeanor has now changed. He stands, arms crossed, smug, with no trace of the timid behavior he displayed earlier. Kelenoh also notices his stutter is gone. She has underestimated this messenger and suddenly feels uncertain. Preoccupied and lost in herself lately, she has again failed to pay attention to what was happening around her.

Kelenoh bends her head for a moment, takes a deep breath and says, "Epidus and I will come to the palace tonight. Would you thank Polykrates for his invitation?"

With a little nod to the man dispatched to carry forth Polykrates invitation, she says good-bye and turns around. She can feel him bow disdainfully in her direction behind her back. Kelenoh turns her head and stares down the man, with flaming eyes. Startled, he looks away and his face breaks out in nervous red blotches. He turns around quickly, glancing back over his shoulder as his fast-paced walk breaks out into a run back to the city.

Kelenoh continues on taking the man of Egypt to Epidus. She tells Epidus about the invitation from Polykrates for that evening, and then leaves the men to go to the beach. Kelenoh stops at the kouros and looks for support from the statue by putting her head against its leg momentarily.

Amasis! Tonight she will see the pharaoh again. Images of when she first encountered him rise up in her mind. She recalls feeling disappointed when she set eyes on the pharaoh in Karnak, and then recalls her feelings of shame and guilt for having judged him so readily. She hears Yufaa's voice consoling her, saying she shouldn't be too hard on herself. She was still a child at that time!

A silent scream comes forth from her mind. She starts laughing out loud hysterically. She lifts her skirt and runs to the sea. She falls down on her knees at the edge of the water, placing her hands on her face. She bends her body forward and begins to sob. To Kelenoh, it is as if it is not only her body that is crying, but her soul is crying as well. In waves of sorrow that she has suppressed over the years, she descends into expressing her most pent-up feelings—her great responsibility as high priestess, her loneliness, how the expectations from the people are overwhelming her. Whatever the need, she, Kelenoh, will meet it. Whatever the problem, she, Kelenoh, will solve it. Whatever the ailment, she, Kelenoh, will heal it. Whatever they want, Kelenoh will be there for them!

She removes her hands from her face and puts them in the sand in front of her. Leaning on her hands, she looks down at the water, mesmerized by the gentle sea washing over them. It feels comforting, though she feels she is empty inside. Suddenly, a hand sets itself on her shoulder. Startled, Kelenoh looks up into the loving eyes of Theano beside her. Yufas sits on her shoulder. Yufas! Theano takes Yufas off her shoulder and gives him to Kelenoh. Theano lays her hand on Kelenoh's cheek, and then turns around, walking away without saying a word. Confounded, Kelenoh looks at the bird, which cocks its head side to side, looking back at her with questioning little eyes.

Silently, they look at each other. Everything has already been said. Kelenoh knows she is not in balance, but is no longer able or knows how to find harmony within herself once again. For self-preservation and in her own best interest, she performs her tasks with the sole use of her intellectual mind—enough to get her through, but no more. She knows she has turned off her feelings in order to protect herself. For her, it has become the only way to lead the temple complex and keep herself going.

Yufas utters his sounds, and now Kelenoh looks at him more consciously and with all her attention on the bird. Tears well up in her eyes, as she is touched by the love that is streaming from his little eyes. It is as if he wants to say, "Kelenoh, I understand."

Kelenoh takes a deep breath and says, "Yufas, I have neglected you lately, but I am so glad you are with me now."

Yufas remains silent. Kelenoh puts him on her shoulder, and together they slowly make their way back to the temple complex.

Chapter 23

That evening, two soldiers escort Kelenoh and Epidus to Polykrates' palace. It is a pleasant evening; a warm, little breeze plays with their hair and dances around their bodies. Kelenoh feels tense, but at the same time looks forward to meeting Pharaoh Amasis. She is curious about him. The palace is bustling. Music and chatter can be heard even from a distance.

From the top of the stairs, Polykrates sees them arrive. He stands, chest stuck out, chin held high, with scrutinizing eyes looking down upon them. His clothes and the many ornaments he has on are rich in color and Kelenoh can't help but think of a strutting peacock when she sees him. She takes a moment and looks inside of him. She can sense how much he despises her out of sheer fear of her powers and capabilities. Polykrates descends the stairs only so far that he still towers above them and greets Kelenoh and Epidus with a jovial gesture. "Welcome, Woman of Hera and Epidus. I have been waiting for you. Come, I would like to introduce you to my friend Amasis."

They walk inside, and to her surprise Kelenoh spots Hefaisteon in the hall. She wants to go over to Hefaisteon, but Polykrates prevents her by grabbing Kelenoh by the arm. Anger surges through Kelenoh; she doesn't like to be touched and certainly not by Polykrates.

Hefaisteon looks at her with a sad spiritless expression, and then quickly turns around and walks away. Not understanding,

Kelenoh follows her with her eyes. On Polykrates' face appears a triumphant smile and sinister laugh. "Ha ha! Woman," he says, gripping her arm more tightly, "we have to go in this direction. I will introduce you to the pharaoh."

The first thing Kelenoh notices as they turn a corner to the large room, are two long tables loaded with food, fruits and drinks. Then she directs her attention to all the people who amble about. Scanning for Pharaoh Amasis, she finds him seated at the far end of the room. He is even shorter then she remembers, although not quite as short as Polykrates.

Polykrates forges a path through the crowd to the pharaoh and then presents Kelenoh. Kelenoh nearly loses her footing when Polykrates pushes her in the back toward the pharaoh. Her anger flares up, but then she suddenly realizes the meaning of his actions, and takes a bow.

Bowing is so unfamiliar to Kelenoh that it makes her unsure. Epidus, faithfully standing behind her, feels her confusion. He steps beside her, bows and says, "Pharaoh Amasis, what an honor it is to meet you."

In the meantime, Kelenoh has time to recover and with a smile on her face she says, "Pharaoh Amasis, did you have a good journey?"

Amasis pretends to not hear her question and says, "So, you are the Woman of Hera, I have already heard much about you." He glares at her, hands folded together, twiddling his fingers as if he is judging a camel.

Kelenoh shivers and has difficulty keeping a friendly smile on her face. She turns her head toward Epidus and whispers, "Epidus, would you please get me a cup of wine?" As she follows Epidus with her eyes, she takes a few deep breaths, regaining composure, then looks directly at Amasis. She is surprised to see him becoming uncertain under her gaze.

"Yes, Pharaoh Amasis, I am the Woman of Hera. Do you have a question for me? May I help you with anything? Or," she pauses, "do you presume to know everything about me that there is no need to know more?"

Amasis swallows a sip of wine and as he stares back at her. In his small beady eyes there appears a slyness that catches her off guard for a moment. Fortunately, Epidus comes back, cup of wine in hand. She thanks him and quickly takes a drink, realizing that she has to be on guard with Amasis. Everything in her body and mind is on high alert. She notices Polykrates, on the sidelines, grinning sadistically, taking pleasure in what he perceives as Kelenoh's vulnerable state.

Pharaoh Amasis turns his nose up at her, and scoffs, "No, Woman, I don't have any questions for you. Nor do I need you to help me with anything. I can help myself very well. And, yes, I do know who you are!"

"Of course, you are the pharaoh. I wouldn't expect anything less of you. You know!" Kelenoh holds her gaze fast on the pharaoh, her face and body standing defiant.

A red blush of anger appears on Amasis' astounded face at her response. Although Kelenoh realizes she shouldn't, she keeps looking at him, her eyes burrowing deep into his soul. Amasis flinches, suddenly uncomfortable, and looks down and away. He directs his anger at Polykrates, asking him, almost hissing, "You had promised me a fine evening. Where is the music? Where are the poets?"

Polykrates frantically searches the room for the musicians. He looks angrily at Kelenoh, as he brutishly pushes past her to retrieve them. Kelenoh looks back calmly. She has the feeling she has won this silent power struggle. Amasis has seemingly lost his interest in Kelenoh and mingles with the other guests.

In the corner of the room, Kelenoh eyes the man who gave her the little bear that morning, his face is stricken with sheer terror. From his vantage point, he was able to watch and follow the conversation between her and Amasis. Kelenoh's feeling of victory suddenly disappears, overtaken by a feeling of impending danger, a feeling so strong that her body stiffens. She convinces herself silently, 'The gods are with me, nothing can happen to me,' and dismisses the feeling of danger.

Kelenoh looks around in the room, hoping to see Hefaisteon, but the woman is not there. She walks to one of the tables and chooses a few little snacks. Kelenoh doesn't feel like eating a lot, she would prefer to call Epidus and leave. However, she is an invited guest and it would be very impolite to leave this soon.

From a distance she discretely watches Amasis and Polykrates speak with each other. Once in a while they glance in her direction and she realizes both gentlemen are talking about her. The threat of danger raises its head again and Kelenoh connects with the gods to arm and defend herself against whatever is the scheme of these two men.

Strengthened by the gods, she looks at both men, who have stopped their discussion and stare at her, wide-eyed and shocked. Then they turn around and continue their intense discussion without looking at her.

Kelenoh has had enough of it and seeks out Epidus. She wants to go home. When she looks to say good-bye to her host, Polykrates, he is nowhere to be found. Kelenoh finds Cleitus and asks him, "Would you thank Polykrates for his invitation and hospitality, and Cleitus, would you greet lady Hefaisteon for me. Please tell her that I hope to talk with her soon." Cleitus gives her a grim-faced nod, and just as his mistress, she detects a distance. This servant of Hefaisteon once arranged for her and Kelenoh to meet, sympathizing with her plight, now looks at her as if she were an enemy.

With a heavy heart Kelenoh walks with Epidus and the two soldiers back to the temple complex.

The following morning, Kelenoh is confronted again with the man she had sent away several times yesterday. Once again, she sends him away, determining his problem was of such a nature that it would be best solved by him. Kelenoh does her best to explain to him her reasons in a calm, low tone of voice, but the man refuses to go. Three times he returns to her, each time more demanding than the last. Kelenoh feels anger rise in her like never before. She has had more than enough of always being ready to help everyone else and now someone, this persistent man, stands before her, not wanting to even help himself!

Kelenoh feels herself become taller, and on her face appears a grimaced expression. She hears and sees Cassandra's contorted face in her periphery turn ashen white, and heave a terrible scream.

Kelenoh closes her eyes, connects with the cosmos, and gives the order to end the life of this man. To the horror of all present, the man falls down dead at Kelenoh's feet.

The buzz in the temple ceases, it grows instantly silent. Then some people fall to their knees and start screaming. Kelenoh looks down at the man lying in front of her, and then out at the multitude gathered in front of her that is starting to panic. Kelenoh raises her hands and the multitude obeys her signal, becoming quiet once again. She feels the fear of the people that hits her, as though a blow to her diaphragm and says, "This man has called forth his own death, because he refused to do something with his own life. Consider well that it is important for everyone to accept his or her life as it is, to seize the opportunities that present themselves, and to improve his or her situation wherever and whenever possible." She turns to Cassandra, ordering her to call a few soldiers to carry the man away.

Theano and Selene, who have been busy at the temple square helping the people waiting in line to see Kelenoh, hear the screams in the temple. They run up the stairs, stop at the entrance, and see the lifeless body. They glance at each other, looking to the other for an answer as both don't understand what they are seeing. Cassandra approaches them and tells them what happened. The three women embrace, and then Cassandra leaves to get a few soldiers who can carry the man away.

Kelenoh silently observes the scene, her three friends embracing one another, and for the first time in her life she feels excluded by them. She is alone.

She looks back at the crowd in front of her, moving from face to face, all are staring at her with wide, terrified eyes. The urge to run away overwhelms her. Kelenoh turns around and sits down on her chair, waiting until the soldiers arrive to take the man away. Her fingers and knuckles turn red from gripping the arms of the chair tightly. It is the only thing which is keeping her from bolting.

She closes her eyes and connects to the gods, asking for energy and peace. She hears sistrums, but not the voices of the gods. A sense of calm returns to her. When Kelenoh opens her eyes, she sees that many people have left the temple. She also realizes that what just happened will be known all over the island very soon. She feels a paralyzing fear from the people still around, unable to make a quick exit.

Cassandra returns with the soldiers. The soldiers pick the man up and take him away. She positions herself beside Kelenoh again, standing silent. Kelenoh notices she doesn't dare look at her.

Kelenoh stands up, raises her hands once more in an angle over the people and removes their fear from them. For the rest of the afternoon, she continues helping them as she can. When everyone has been seen and the temple has been emptied of those seeking healing, she beckons Cassandra, "Come, we will go look for Theano and Selene."

In her mind she scans the temple complex and outer surroundings and sees the two women sitting on the beach by the kouros. It isn't very long before the four women are sitting together. The silence is as a shroud about them. Selene is the first one to dare to speak, "Tell us, Kelenoh, what happened between you and that man?"

Kelenoh looks at the women one by one and says, "This man used me as an instrument, because he didn't really want to live, that is all." After a short silence Kelenoh continues, "He provoked my anger, therefore I connected to the cosmos and had him picked up. If the cosmos would have disagreed with my request, the man would have been kept alive."

Cassandra reacts first, "Kelenoh, I am very much startled. I stood beside you and watched as you sent him away repeatedly, but then suddenly you became someone else, you grew taller before my eyes and in an instant the man was on the ground, motionless.

A hint of disapproval laces Cassandra's words, "I know you have the power over life and death, but I didn't expect you would ever use it." Cassandra stares blankly out to the sea as though she is reliving the scene. "I saw fear all around me. The people shrunk back in fear of you. You took a man's life. However, now that you have explained to us how it works, I understand better. But," she stammers, "how do we explain what happened to the people of the island?"

"This cannot be explained to the people, Cassandra. And it is not necessary either. This is between me and the gods."

Kelenoh looks at the small group of women and realizes something has changed between them. She is no longer one of them. They do not look her in the eyes. Kelenoh rises from her seat and excuses herself, "I want to be alone for a little while, let me know if you have any further questions."

She turns around and treads wearily to the far end of the beach where a mountain descends into the sea. There she sits down in the shade. She misses Yufas and intends to take him with her more often. He is the only one who understands her. A feeling of bitterness rises up in her, which causes a sudden rush of anger. Without thinking, she stands up, places her bare hands against a rock and starts beating it wildly. She doesn't shout, but tries to release the pain and anger she feels inside on the mountain. When her hands start bleeding, she stops. Kelenoh looks down at her hands, blood dripping on the sand.

Inside of her something starts trembling. She throws her head backwards and from her abdomen a feeling of desperation rises up and out in a primordial scream. She falls down on her knees, the sound of her scream echoing back on the rocks behind her.

Suddenly, she remembers this sound. An image of Hefaisteon flashes in front of her, an image of her heaving the same scream when she first heard her little daughter was going to die. Kelenoh starts laughing hysterically, until the laughing changes into a soft weeping. The sky has grown dark by the time she gets up. She drags her feet to the edge of the sea and rinses her hands in the salt water.

The grayish-white moon glows just enough to light her path back to the complex. Slowly she walks home to be with Yufas.

In the small room she sits down at the table and looks at the bird. Not a word is spoken. Spoken words would feel as empty as her soul.

Chapter 24

Today, less people have come to the temple than the day before. The news of the dead man had done its job. Kelenoh heals and helps just as usual. The average person wouldn't notice anything different about her, even after what happened the previous day. When she has finished, she walks to the beach and sits down at the feet of the kouros.

She hears a noise behind her, looks over her shoulder and sees Epidus approaching hastily. "Woman," he calls out, "Pythagoras has arrived on Samos!"

A feeling of joy streams through Kelenoh. Pythagoras! "Thank you, Epidus, for bringing me this message."

Epidus bows and excuses himself, running off to tend to his many duties. She closes her eyes, a prayer of gratitude wells up from inside of her. She remembers Pythagoras' words when they parted in Egypt, "I will be there when you need me most."

How true were those words. Did he know at that time how difficult her life would be and how lonely she would become?

Kelenoh turns her attention to a silhouetted figure that suddenly appears over a sunlit hill. She squints, trying to make out the person walking toward her. She can't see who it is, but with her thoughts she connects to them. Pythagoras!

His face and smile flash before her eyes, and she knows he can feel her. He has aged considerably. His once full black head of hair and beard are streaked with grey. Kelenoh jumps up and for the first time in many years, runs. Her heart pounds in her chest as she races toward him.

When their hands finally touch, they stare at each other long and deep, emotions rising to the surface as tears. As they hold on to one another, the silence surrounds them, and their souls melt together, becoming one. Pythagoras and Kelenoh sit cross-legged in the sand, facing each other. Pythagoras' low, baritone-like voice is comforting to her, "Dear Woman of Hera," he begins, "how are you doing?"

Kelenoh laughs at his formal address and says, "Pythagoras, welcome to Samos. I am so happy you are here! Have you finished your studies? Will you stay here long?"

A shadow falls across Pythagoras' brow, his eyes gloss over with sadness. Kelenoh doesn't notice, and blinks at him full of childlike expectation.

"Kelenoh, I will stay on Samos for as long as you need me. I have finished my studies in Babylon. I will tell you more about that later on. "First," he speaks softly, placing his hand over hers, "I want you to tell me how things are going here."

"Oh, Pythagoras, there is so much to tell you, but I think I will show you and give you a tour of the complex. We can talk along the way." Kelenoh looks away, embarrassed. "I don't have to tell you anything about myself, you already know." Quiet tears roll down Kelenoh's cheeks. Pythagoras takes Kelenoh's hands and sets them in his. Kelenoh feels his peace and energy flow into her. She stares into his brown eyes, though sunken in his aged face, they are clear and sparkling with love. For a moment, she feels genuinely happy.

Pythagoras gets up and helps Kelenoh to her feet. They walk between the kouroi toward the terrain of the temple complex. They pass by the treasury and the Temple of Apollo, and then pause at the old Temples of Aphrodite and Hermes that have been demolished and reconstructed to be a second treasury. Pythagoras declines the offer to see the inside. He doesn't care about earthly goods.

They arrive at the newly built altar, the heart of the complex. Pythagoras takes considerable time examining its construction, but remains silent. Kelenoh looks at him wide-eyed, with expectation, but the only reaction she gets is an approving little nod. Pythagoras halts on the square in front of the new temples of

Hermes and-Aphrodite and of Hera, scanning the structures. His eyes rest for a long time on the Temple of Hera before he finally says, "This Temple of Hera is exactly the same temple I saw when in Egypt."

Kelenoh nods and says, "The day I arrived on Samos I had a vision to build that temple here. Fortunately for me, Polykrates already planned to build a new temple and approved my design when I explained how I wanted it. He also agreed on constructing the new Temple of Aphrodite and Hermes, and a new altar."

Kelenoh points to the roof of the Temple of Hera. "The frieze has yet to be put up on top. Sculptors are still working on it. The outer row of columns for the temple, designed to support the roof, also still has to be put in place, but the inside of the temple is almost finished. At this time they are working on the wall that will be behind the temple to protect it. Come," she says, "I will show you the inside of the Temple of Hera."

Kelenoh is overcome with the atmosphere of the temple when they step inside. The blue-black marble floor, the bare red-brown walls, the small columns with gold leaf that support the ceiling, and the cella, painted a splendid deep-blue, take her breath away.

To her joy she sees her marble chair has been finished, custom made according to her exact measurements. They will be able to celebrate the Harvest Festival for the first time in the new temple. The chair is set on the left-hand side of the building against the back wall. To the right of it, an opening leads to the room where the statue of Hera will stand, exactly on the spot where she buried her first fruit in the earth.

Tomorrow, the statue of Hera will be transferred from the Temple of Hermes and Aphrodite. Proudly, Kelenoh spreads her arms, spins around a few times and then stops short in front of Pythagoras, beaming.

"It is splendid Kelenoh. This temple suits you." Pythagoras face is unmoved. The display of wealth does not mean anything to him.

Kelenoh approaches him laughing and says, "I know, Pythagoras, that this doesn't mean much to you, nevertheless, I am so happy that I can show it to you, and you will be with me to celebrate the Harvest Festival. Come, let's go to the dining hall, you must be hungry."

It is quiet in the dining hall. The hour for lunch has already passed. Food is still set out at her place at the table. She goes to the kitchen and asks for an extra helping and a drinking cup for Pythagoras. They sit in silence for some time, deep harmony flowing between the two of them.

"Pythagoras," Kelenoh starts, "do you already know where you are going to live?"

"I will be living in a cave just outside the city. This cave looks out over the temple complex. In front of this cave is an open space that I will use to teach anyone who is willing. My possessions are being taken there right now. I wanted to see you first."

Suddenly, they are disturbed by a noise at the entrance of the dining hall. Looking back, they see Polykrates storming in. With a face distorted from anger, he marches toward them. Pythagoras and Kelenoh heave a deep sigh at the same time, which causes Kelenoh to almost burst out laughing. Pythagoras gives her a warning glance, but Kelenoh pretends to have seen nothing. Her happiness cannot be broken now that Pythagoras is back.

Polykrates marches right up to the table beside them, and slams both hands down. He glances back and forth between the two of them, and then directs his attention to Pythagoras and huffs, "I had to hear from strangers that you are back on Samos. Did you not think it worthwhile to report to me first?"

Pythagoras looks quietly at Polykrates and says coolly, "Polykrates, Ruler of Samos, it was and is not my intention to pass you by. My priority lies with the temple complex and Kelenoh. That's why my first steps on the island were to her and this place. Does it suit you that I make an appearance to you by the end of the day?"

"I expect you tonight in the palace."

After an intense stare at both of them, Polykrates whips around and leaves the dining hall. When he is completely out of sight, Kelenoh starts laughing loudly. "Pythagoras, you said that very well."

Her laugh disappears when she sees Pythagoras' serious expression. "Kelenoh, please be careful. You cannot mock Polykrates."

Kelenoh brushes off his admonition with more laughter and says, "Come, let's go to the fields. I will show you the harvest and the rest of the complex."

It is busy on the fields. Everyone is working hard to get the crops harvested.

"Kelenoh, why is there no singing?"

Ashamed Kelenoh looks down, saying nothing, until she lifts her head and admits, "Pythagoras, you are right, in these last few years I lost my joy and that had its influence on the inhabitants of the complex."

Kelenoh walks toward Epidus who is in charge of the harvest, and instructs him to start singing a song of gratitude so the people can join in. Epidus looks at her; it has been a long time since he has seen a spark of joy in Kelenoh's eyes.

"Woman, it will be a pleasure to sing." Soon the song is echoing over the fields. Pythagoras and Kelenoh continue walking toward the vegetable and flower gardens. They stop in front of the water cisterns.

"Kelenoh, this is a good improvement," Pythagoras remarks. Kelenoh looks at the still empty cisterns and feels proud of Pythagoras' praise. Selene is bent over, busy in the flower garden, but stops when she eyes Pythagoras and Kelenoh approaching.

"Pythagoras, you are back!" Radiating love, she hastens toward them and greets Pythagoras with a bow.

"Selene, would you please go fetch Cassandra and Theano and tell them that Pythagoras has returned? We are going to our house now, please join us there."

Surprised, Selene looks at Kelenoh. She hasn't spoken in such a happy tone for a long time. "Of course Kelenoh, we will be there soon. Now I understand what prompted the singing in the fields."

Selene turns around laughing, and then goes looking for Cassandra and Theano. Pythagoras looks at Kelenoh and says, "I have returned just in time."

Kelenoh nods, enjoying the happiness within her. "Come, let's go to my house."

They are greeted with the high trills of Yufas as they enter the house. The bird skips back and forth excitedly. When Pythagoras walks into eye range of the bird, Yufas becomes silent, lowers his head, and rests his wings. Kelenoh sees tears in his little eyes.

"You are being greeted by your friend Yufaa," notes Kelenoh.

Pythagoras picks up the bird, raising him to meet his gaze, and smiles, "Yufas, you have become a splendid bird! When I last saw you, you were still very small." Pythagoras carefully puts the bird back on the table and Yufas brushes his little head against Pythagoras' arm.

After a short while, Cassandra, Theano and Selene join them, their faces red from running. They greet Pythagoras with a synchronistic bow. Theano stares at Pythagoras with a childlike smile on her face. "You are back," she whispers.

"Casandra, Selene," he says, pausing for a moment and giving Theano a nod, "Theano! Yes, I am back, and I am happy to see you all in good health."

Light on her feet, Cassandra fetches everyone wine and all five of them sit at the table, enjoying each other's company.

The complex is lively with ceremony and celebration the following afternoon as the statue of Hera is transported from the Temple of Hermes and Aphrodite to the new temple. Only the inhabitants of the complex are present at the inauguration of the new temple. Proudly, Kelenoh walks behind the statue being carried into the new temple by four strong men. Kelenoh directs them to place it in the room behind the cella, ensuring that it is put exactly on the spot where her first fruit was buried. She sends everyone away and consecrates the room with a little bowl of burning sage.

Kneeling, she lays flowers at the foot of the statue. For the first time in a long time, the people waiting outside the room hear Kelenoh singing. Hearing her melodic voice, some start crying and fall on their knees in homage to the gods.

The moment Kelenoh steps outside, a collective cheer rings out and a song of gratitude swells into one unified chorus among all gathered for the celebration. Kelenoh radiates loveliness. For the first time in years she observes a quiet and harmonious state within herself and with the gods. Yufas, who sits on her shoulder, feels it and sounds off a happy trill. Hearing Yufas trills, tears come to Kelenoh's eyes and a feeling of gratitude for her life streams through her, watering her very soul.

She did it! The temple she saw appear before her on the first day she arrived at the complex, is now almost finished and will be used to celebrate the Harvest Festival for the first time. Once the crowd has dispersed, Kelenoh searches for Epidus, wanting him to act as escort to the cave of Pythagoras. Epidus selects two more men to accompany them. Epidus leads the way, followed by Kelenoh, with Yufas on her shoulder, and the two soldiers behind her. All walk over the Procession Road in the direction of the mountains.

It is quite a climb to get to the cave. The path veers to the right, and then it is a steep ascent to the top. As they near their destination, Kelenoh sees Pythagoras sitting on a rock in front of the cave, eyes closed, hands on his lap, meditating. She stops for a moment to take in the joyful sight in front of her.

Pythagoras embodies calmness itself. He blends into his new environment in complete harmony. Pythagoras opens his eyes and stretches out his hands and says, "Woman, welcome to my home."

Kelenoh runs the last few meters to Pythagoras and places her hands in his. "Pythagoras, I am so happy that I can touch you and that you are so close to me now."

Very still, they stand across from each other and for a short while disappear into each other's eyes. Yufas, perched on Kelenoh's shoulder, makes himself known with a loud trill. He wants to be a part of this reunion too! Laughing, Kelenoh and Pythagoras let go of each other. Then Pythagoras points to a rock situated across from where he had been sitting, suggesting to Kelenoh she can sit down there. Epidus and the soldiers separate themselves and go sit on a lower ledge of the slope a little distance away from them. There they will wait until Kelenoh is finished.

Before Kelenoh sits down, she walks with Yufas to the end of the open field. Pythagoras follows them. From where she stands, Kelenoh has a panoramic view of the island and can see the whole complex. It is as though it is lying at her feet. Her heart nearly stops. Her breath is caught in the grasp of such awesome beauty. She looks to her left and sees a glimpse of Polykrates' palace and a small section of the city. Stretched out straight in front of her is the sparkling harbor of the temple complex. To the right of it, spreading the length of the land, all the way up to a mountain that ends in the sea, one can see the whole temple complex. The fields are dotted with people harvesting the summer yield.

The new temple can be seen high above it all, even with its unfinished flat roof. The two kouroi and the row of statues along the Sacred Road seem small from this new perspective. The colors of the statues, hit by the noontide sun, shine upwards toward the bright blue sky.

"Pythagoras, you have chosen a splendid place to live." Pythagoras nods. Kelenoh looks back at the open field where Pythagoras wants to teach his lessons. The summer is almost over and the grass is already turning yellow. Around the open space is a row of trees. It is an ideal place to teach. Kelenoh heaves a deep sigh that makes Pythagoras laugh, which in turn sets Kelenoh off into a laughing fit. Pythagoras doesn't laugh very often, and his deep hearty laugh is contagious.

"Yes. Kelenoh, this is exactly the spot where I have to be now. I relish it when I wake up, walk outside and can see the whole complex, knowing that you are so close to me."

Kelenoh glances at the entrance of the cave. In the light of a torch she sees the lectern, the rest being hidden in the dark. Pythagoras catches her looking and says, "It is a good place to live and work."

Kelenoh interrupts him, "I know what you are going to say. It is your domain and you don't need anyone spying on you. I respect that Pythagoras. It is sufficient for me to sit here outside by you."

Once again laughter erupts on Pythagoras' face. "I know I don't have to explain it to you. You know who I am and how I think."

Yes, Kelenoh knows that Pythagoras needs to have a space where he can be totally alone. During his years of study in Egypt, as well as in Babylon, he lived in solitude. She looks at his face, a face that emanates only peace. His broad square face has become wrinkled through the years. His larger lower lip hangs a bit more than his upper lip, and his brown eyes, clear with learned wisdom, are framed by black-grey curls. Kelenoh sighs again, relieved. She now feels happy and content with her life.

There is a sudden change in the mood of the atmosphere and Pythagoras calls her to attention, "Kelenoh," he says, with a firm tone, "I have to warn you about Polykrates. Stay away from him and be careful in the words you choose to use toward him."

Kelenoh laughs dismissively, "Pythagoras, I am not afraid of him, and the gods are with me. For years I have tried to understand that man. He is very intelligent. He gets everything done that he envisions. I mean, just look at the splendid fleet he has built. The design of the *Samaina* is absolutely brilliant. Just look at the improvements he has made to the city, the tunnel he had constructed to supply it with water year round. The wall he had built around it, the construction of the temples at the complex. Yes, I admire him for doing all of this. However, as a human being he is unbearable. I compare him to a peacock, strutting about in his colorful and decorated garments. His social intercourse is not understandable. He is nice to people who agree with him and from whom he needs something."

Pythagoras nods, "That is exactly the reason why I admonish you, be careful what you say to him. He has a lot of power, Kelenoh."

"Pythagoras, I am not afraid of him." Kelenoh says, somewhat unnerved. Embarrassed by her tone, she quickly apologizes and locks eyes with him again. "I have to return to the complex now. I have to go inspect the progress at the weaving mill to see whether our festive clothing for the Harvest Festival is ready, and whether there is sufficient clothing for the winter. After the Harvest Festival, I will have lots of time to converse and be with you."

Kelenoh gets up and doesn't notice the worried expression on Pythagoras' face. She beckons Epidus and the two soldiers to be on the ready, then places her hands in Pythagoras' hands and closes her eyes. This time, it is not only the energy of Pythagoras that flows to her, but she feels that her energy flows to him as well. For the moment, she feels total bliss. When Kelenoh opens her eyes, she sees deep love in Pythagoras' eyes. "Until tomorrow," she says and makes her way down the mountain.

Chapter 25

The harvest is in. Once again, nobody will suffer hunger this winter, for the barns are stocked full to the brim. Tomorrow is the day of the Harvest Festival and everyone is busy tidying up the complex, and decorating it for the many visitors that will come for the Festival. Kelenoh is also busy, involved in every department, desirous to make the Harvest Festival extra beautiful and special. It will be the first Harvest Festival held in the new Temple of Hera and also the first with Pythagoras in attendance.

Since her initial visit, Kelenoh has hiked to Pythagoras' cave every day. However, on each occasion her time was cut short by her demanding schedule. Unable to go to the beach regularly, the Kouroi have been left unattended. The large statues, that had been her comfort over the years, have become superfluous. Today Kelenoh won't be able to go see Pythagoras. After her lunch she decides to stroll down to the beach and give her friends a long overdue visit. She puts her arm around the left leg of the right kouros, and inhales the sea air deeply.

As she lays her head against the leg, Kelenoh thanks the gods for the abundant harvest and for her life. Yufas, who has been by her side on a daily basis, sits in the sand at her feet. Kelenoh crouches down and looks at the bird. Fearful little eyes look back at her. Kelenoh asks, "Yufas, are you afraid?"

"Kelenoh, I fear for you, be careful."

"Yufas, you sound like Pythagoras. Of what should I fear? I am happy and feel like nothing can touch me. You know the gods are with me, don't you? Come, let's go to the weaving mill to have a look at my new dress."

At the weaving mill, Kelenoh first examines the shelves to see if there will be enough clothing for everybody at the complex for the approaching winter. The shelves are stacked high with folded garments and she gives the women, who have worked so hard, a compliment. In the hall where the weaving looms are, it remains silent. The women are not used to this Kelenoh who gives compliments, and Kelenoh feels their fear of her. She bows her head sadly, knowing she has only herself to thank for that. She scans the room and looks at all the women in front of her. To her dismay, the women turn their heads away. They seem to be afraid of her eyes and the power that goes out from them.

Kelenoh suddenly remembers the incident with the man, whose life she had taken. It is evident that news of it was still circulating in hushed tones throughout the complex. She had heard the stories. It had been said that she had killed a man with her eyes. Nobody knows she connected with the gods and sought their approval beforehand. They only saw that with one look the man fell down, dead. Kelenoh gives the women a friendly nod and turns around. Hopefully, she sighs under her breath, this incident will be forgotten over time. She resolves to be more alert in the future and to give the people the attention and love as she did in her first years at the temple complex, in harmony with herself and the gods.

Once again she feels in equilibrium with herself, and a feeling of happiness flows through her. She walks to the back room to have a look at the dresses for herself, as well as for Cassandra, Theano and Selene. The four dresses are laid out on the table, all finished. They look splendid, and Kelenoh runs her hand over the soft woven fabric. She is looking forward to tomorrow.

Back at the house, she encounters Cassandra who sits meticulously polishing her golden belt, golden pin and silver headdress. The silver headdress is the one Kelenoh will wear tomorrow in the form of a snake ring. It is the sign of the Woman of Hera. The golden belt will be secured under her breasts. The golden belts and the silver pins of her priestesses are already polished and shine in the light of the torch.

"They are looking splendid, Cassandra." Cassandra nods but doesn't say anything. Kelenoh has the inclination to embrace

Cassandra, but she decides against it. She knows Cassandra, and that it would frighten her. Kelenoh hopes the connection they once had can be renewed in the future.

The next morning the four women rise early. The atmosphere is tense, as all anticipate the events to come. The Harvest Festival has arrived!

Carefully, they dress themselves. Cassandra helps Kelenoh into her garment and fixes the hair on top of her head in curls, leaving a few loose tendrils to fall over her shoulders. Lastly, she crowns Kelenoh with the snake ring.

Kelenoh closes her eyes, feeling the energy of the ring. Cassandra takes a few steps back, looks at Kelenoh from a distance, and then nods in approval. Epidus enters with a lygos branch for Kelenoh and lygos wreaths for Cassandra, Theano and Selene.

Not a single word is spoken. Everyone seems lost in her own thoughts. Ready to go, they exit one by one and make their way to the dining hall to assemble with the other priestesses for the morning service.

As the priestess are busy singing, that resounds through the temple, Kelenoh moves reverently with Yufas on her shoulder to the space behind the cella. Carefully, she undresses the statue of Hera and silently asks the gods for blessings upon the day.

After the service, the priestesses go outside. With her lygos branch in hand, Kelenoh walks out to the top of the temple stairs with Cassandra, followed by Theano and Selene not far behind. Before them are the soldiers with spears in hand, standing in rows to accompany them to the altar. Epidus, in full regalia, stands proudly in front. Kelenoh feels a stitch of sadness pass through her; though she likes Epidus, she still misses Stephanos.

She gives Epidus a nod of approval. He straightens his shoulders, lifts his chin, instantly growing taller before her. Kelenoh smiles, and then directs her full attention to the people who are approaching the area slowly. There are less people than last year and Kelenoh intends to do whatever she can to regain the trust of the island's inhabitants.

She sees her priestesses directing everyone to their places until the procession commences. The women of the island look beautiful wearing their new clothes and, hanging on their arms, their baskets filled to the brim with flowers and produce of the land. It is a colorful whole, Kelenoh muses.

Kelenoh misses the cozy chatter and laughter she used to hear from the crowd while standing there. Uncertain for a moment, she looks back for some support to the three women behind her. They shrug their shoulders. They don't know what is going on either. Yufas picks her ear as if in warning to keep paying close attention. She turns back to the crowd, connects to the gods and beseeches them for help. The people are not allowed to notice her uncertainty, it will make them uncertain as well. When her sense of calm returns, she pours it out over the crowd, and to her joy the people start talking and laughing.

At the sudden eruption, Kelenoh catches sight of Polykrates amidst the crowd with a self-satisfied expression on his face. He looks to everyone for admiration because of what he has done for the temple complex. Hefaisteon trails closely behind him. Thank goodness she is here! Kelenoh hopes to be able to talk to her today, even if it is for only a few minutes. She tries to make eye contact with Hefaisteon, but she looks down, avoiding any contact with Kelenoh.

A shiver travels up Kelenoh's spine. Something is not right.

She sees Pythagoras nearing with a few of his students and shakes off the uneasy feeling. His serious expression brings a smile to Kelenoh's face. It takes her a while to find Rhoikos and Theodoros, standing indiscriminately in the back of the crowd with Eupalinos right behind them. She smiles at the men, though unsure if they see her, as she can see that Theodoros is trying to locate Selene. He stretches his neck to find her. She turns to Selene and tells her where Theodoros is standing.

Selene's face blushes pink and Kelenoh thinks back to the time, already many years ago now, when she had a conversation with the gods that showed her Selene was the woman for Theodoros. The gods were right. Selene still blushes when she sees him.

It is time to start. She sees the priestesses looking in her direction, awaiting her signal. She raises her left hand and everyone rises to their feet. Kelenoh, Cassandra, Theano and

Selene descend the stairs and walk through the row of armed soldiers. At the end of the row, Epidus stands at the altar with a torch. Kelenoh takes the torch from Epidus and lifts it high, signaling that the people may come forward and lay their offerings on the altar.

The train of people slowly starts moving. The altar becomes filled with flowers, herbs and other produce of the land. Kelenoh is deep in communion with the gods and doesn't notice Hefaisteon standing hesitatingly at the altar. She throws her offerings quickly on the altar, disappearing into the crowd just as fast.

When the procession has passed, Kelenoh takes the torch in her left hand and lights the offerings. When the fire spreads, Kelenoh knows something is wrong. A terrible stench reaches her nose and she covers her mouth in an effort to not throw up. The smoke does not rise straight up like a pillar as usual, but flies in all directions.

When the stench reaches the people, and they see the smoke doesn't rise up, a wave of shock moves through the whole crowd and a woman starts lamenting. Frozen, Kelenoh stares at the fire. Yufas sticks his little head under the pin of her dress. Kelenoh hears vague little coughs and realizes that the bird is nauseous too.

Suddenly she knows. Hefaisteon! Inwardly she canvases the crowd and sees Polykrates looking at the altar with a triumphant grin. Where is Hefaisteon? Kelenoh searches with her inner eye and finds Hefaisteon lying on her knees under a lygos tree near the Imbrasos River, with her face in her hands crying. A feeling of compassion for the woman overtakes Kelenoh.

Suddenly, the peacocks start screaming and Kelenoh shivers at the sound. Pythagoras, where is Pythagoras? She needs him! When she meets his gaze from among the crowd, his admonishments finally hit her. Almost in a panic, she tries to connect with him in her mind and hears, "Go on, Kelenoh, have the statue of Hera picked up and do what you have to do."

She looks at Epidus who stands beside her, face ashen white, and orders him to fetch the statue of Hera. Cassandra comes near her with a cup of water, and thankfully, she swallows a few refreshing sips. As the statue of Hera is carried out of the new temple, Kelenoh hears a few people cheer, but not wholeheartedly. Kelenoh hides her sadness, straightening her back and lifting her chin, putting on an air of calm and confidence. As the statue passes by her, she joins from behind, following it to the end of the row of soldiers. She is now close to tears.

The row closes in behind her, followed by the priestesses and then the islands' inhabitants, as they all slowly walk to the beach. Once all are on the shore, she orders the statue to be placed in the sea. The tension breaks when, to her relief, the statue stays near the beach and doesn't float away. Cheers and exclamations of triumph ring out from the people and Kelenoh takes a deep breath before she orders the women of the island to throw the rest of their gifts and offerings into the sea.

The crowd is silenced by Kelenoh's raised hand. Connecting with the gods, Kelenoh begs them to help her. She slightly moves her hand and a big backwards wave takes all the offerings and the statue of Hera into the sea. Nervously, Kelenoh stares into the water. Will the statue return? Again she moves her hand and a big wave washes the statue back onto the beach. Kelenoh weeps. The statue of Hera is back! Samos shall have the protection and blessing of the gods another year.

Trembling from the stress, Kelenoh blinks from the light reflecting on the surface of the water. She feels as though she has been emptied and the thing she would love to do most is lie down on the beach and never get up again. Through her tears, she watches the soldiers cover the statue with lygos branches.

Cassandra comes closer with cloths and a new dress for Hera. Together, they remove the branches and dab the wood dry as good as they can. Kelenoh tries to say something to Cassandra, but she is unreachable. She would like to crawl into Cassandra's arms for a short time and be a child once more. Even so, she is an adult now and knows Cassandra also feels stress from the people around her, and has enough to do performing her duties and taking care of herself at the moment. Cassandra dabs with a controlled face and doesn't so much as look at Kelenoh even once.

When the statue of Hera is practically dry, they dress it together. Kelenoh nods for Selene to play on her zither. Kelenoh starts a song of gratitude. It takes a while before everyone joins in the refrain. A few moments of reflective silence pass when the song ends and Kelenoh orders the statue to be brought back to the new Temple of Hera.

With the statue back in its permanent home, Kelenoh places flowers, herbs, grains and her lygos branch at its feet. Eyes closed, she thanks the gods for their assistance, and for the blessings that the people of the island have received in the last few months. Hands pressed together in prayer, she asks the gods to keep helping and blessing the people and all that lives on the island.

Her task complete, she lingers for a time on her knees in front of the statue. Looking up into Hera's eyes, she suddenly feels the urge to run away from it all. Where is the joy she recently felt since the return of Pythagoras?

Her mind suddenly flashes back to a mystery unsolved: Hefaisteon's actions. Why would she throw herbs on the altar that caused such a heavy smoke and stench? The answer comes immediately, 'She did this by the order of Polykrates.'

Kelenoh feels her body become icy cold, remembering the multiple warnings of Pythagoras that she should watch out for Polykrates. In her thoughts, she seeks contact with Pythagoras. She sees him walking on the way to his cave. When he feels her, he stops, turns and says something to his students. They continue in the direction of the cave and Pythagoras sits down at the side of the road on a rock. "Kelenoh," she hears him say, "Nothing can be changed anymore. I will be leaving. I have instructed my students to pack my things."

"Polykrates has started to disparage us to the people of the island. There is nothing that can stop him. I will go with a few of my students to the Kerkis Mountains here on Samos to hide in a cave where he cannot find me. I fear for my life. I see you are frightened Kelenoh. Don't be afraid of what is coming. We always will be connected. Remember that!"

Full of horror, Kelenoh listens to Pythagoras and then watches as he sends her a gesture of blessing, gets up and continues his way up the mountain. Her body stiffens up, she cannot move. Yufas soft tapping against her ear with his beak eventually snaps her out of it. She starts feeling some life in her body again, and then gets up carefully. She shakes her body back and forth to get the circulation going again, and walks back into the cella.

To her surprise, she sees Cassandra, Theano and Selene waiting for her. The women glance awkwardly between each other for a moment, then Cassandra turns around "Come," she says, "let's go home. We shall no longer attend the banquet in the dining hall."

As the women pass the dining hall, they hear the banquet in full swing. Suddenly, Kelenoh hears Polykrates, who raises his voice above the clamor and yells, "Long live the gods and Samos!"

Kelenoh doesn't feel anything hearing his voice, not even a trace of anger toward him. She is empty. It doesn't bother her any longer what Polykrates says. Now Kelenoh needs all the strength of her mind she can muster to get home.

When they arrive, Kelenoh goes straight to her room. She stops Cassandra midway, as she comes near to help her with her clothes, "No, Cassandra, I will do it myself this time. I want to be alone."

She takes the snake ring off her head and places it carefully on the dresser. One by one, Kelenoh removes the pins from her hair and shakes her curls loose. She loosens the belt and the pin on her dress, and then slides it off. Reverently, she lays the dress on her bed and walks to the dresser with the mirror above it to rub her face with olive oil.

Suddenly, she hears a hissing behind her. Kelenoh looks back over her shoulder and sees a large, fat, dark-brown-blackish snake come slithering from under her bed. For a moment, she is paralyzed with fear, unable to utter any sound out of her mouth, then her screams fill the room as she takes a step forward, but the snake already has gotten her and sets its teeth in her left ankle.

Cassandra, Theano and Selene immediately come running into her room to see what is happening. It is as if time has stood still for a moment. Cassandra makes haste, grabbing a pan from the kitchen and attacks the snake. The snake loosens its hold on Kelenoh's ankle and slithers to a corner of the room.

The women lay Kelenoh down on the bed, all the while keeping an eye on the snake. Kelenoh knows she is going to die. Selene stays with Kelenoh. Cassandra and Theano run outside to look for help. They run and yell toward the dining hall, knowing Epidus is there. Epidus gets up quickly and with a few other men they look for sticks.

When they arrive at Kelenoh's home, they enter cautiously with the sticks at the ready. When they see the snake, they use all their power to beat it to death. Kelenoh opens her eyes and sees Epidus take the snake outside, its lifeless body hanging on a stick.

She closes her eyes again and concentrates on what is happening in her body. She feels the venom ascending and spreading through her limbs. Pretty soon she will no longer be able to move. Her muscles will be paralyzed and her organs will, one by one, lose their ability to function. Her tongue starts swelling; she won't be able to speak any longer. She panics for a moment. She is going to die!

So this was what Pythagoras meant when he told her not to be afraid of what was going to happen. He knew already! Kelenoh surrenders. It doesn't make sense to try to resist this venom. Yufas, where is Yufas? She doesn't see him! A strange little squeaking sound comes close to her ear, and she knows Yufas sits beside her head on the bed, crying.

Selene sits beside her bed, holding her hand, and with her other hand, she carefully dabs Kelenoh's forehead. Kelenoh tries to look at her and sees that Selene's face is wet from her tears. Selene cries without making a sound. Dear Selene, her beloved childhood playmate with whom she shared her stories and problems.

On the other side of the bed, Kelenoh sees the tear-streaked face of Theano, looking desperately at Selene, as if she doesn't understand what is happening. Theano, oh, blessed Theano, who always washed her and took care of her during her childhood. At the foot of the bed, stands Cassandra with a grim and distorted face. Cassandra, with whom she felt so safe during her childhood, and in whose arms she often crawled. Her sisters! How much she loves them, but she isn't able to say it any longer.

Kelenoh realizes she doesn't have to say it. They know it, this love is mutual. A man enters the room accompanied by Epidus. Kelenoh doesn't recognize him. He wears a spotlessly clean grey coat with stiff pleats on the front. It is Polykrates' physician. Kelenoh sees him shaking his head to Epidus. There is nothing to be done. He leaves the room without ever touching Kelenoh or having a good look at her. It is not necessary; everyone knows what the poison of this snake brings about. Kelenoh closes her eyes. Her tongue has swollen so much by now, it fills the back of her throat and she starts to choke. The faces around her begin to blur between the lines of life and death. In an instant all becomes black around her. Kelenoh is dead at the age of thirty-two.

Kelenoh's body is burned that same night on the beach. Epidus cuts a lygos tree with his own hands and makes an altar of it. All three priestesses, Cassandra, Theano and Selene wash her body, and then wrap Kelenoh in her pleated coat from Egypt. Theano and Selene are crying. In contrast, Cassandra's face is unmoved.

When the body had been wrapped and is lying on the bed, Cassandra removes herself, leaving Theano and Selene alone. After quite some time passes by, Selene heads out in search of Cassandra, as it is time to carry Kelenoh's body out to the beach. She finds a distraught Cassandra on the ground near a cistern at the vegetable garden. Selene waits until Cassandra's crying lessens, and then softly touches her shoulder. Startled, Cassandra looks up and then starts weeping once more.

"Cassandra, may I hold you?"

Cassandra nods and Selene stoops to wrap her arms around her. After a little while, when her crying subsides, Selene says, "Come Cassandra, we have to carry her away." Cassandra nods and slowly rises to her feet.

Epidus and a few soldiers stand ready. They arrive back at the house; they have brought with them a bier to take Kelenoh away. Carefully, they lay Kelenoh on the bier. Epidus and the soldiers lift the bier up onto their shoulders, and then start walking in the direction toward the beach.

Cassandra, Theano and Selene follow and when they reach the dining hall, a multitude of people are waiting there for them. Nobody has to be notified of the cremation; all who were present for the Harvest Festival are still at the complex and join in the memorial.

Polykrates stands front and center surrounded by his men. There is no emotion to be read on his face, but anyone standing near him could easily see his trouble in holding back a snicker. His men around him have faces white as sheets, as though their consciousness had been struck with some terrible guilt. Fear of the actual snake itself is still in their bodies. For it was they who, by the order of Polykrates, had captured the poisonous serpent, and then threw it into Kelenoh's room. Afterwards, they ran away as fast as they could. Prior to the capturing of the snake, they had left food under Kelenoh's bed to attract the snake, and to make sure it would stay there.

When the bier passes by, the women of the island start lamenting. The sound swelled and echoed across the complex. Some of the priestesses hold their hands against their ears knowing Kelenoh wouldn't have liked the mournful cries.

During one of their monthly meetings, she once explained to them that when you feel sorrow in your heart, crying was permissible because that was real. However, crying only because it was considered proper protocol was hypocritical. She instructed the priestesses to always listen to their feelings, and then it would be fine to lament.

The priestesses form a row behind Cassandra, Theano and Selene. Behind them the people of the island join the line and follow. Polykrates and his men walk up front, with Rhoikos, Theodoros and Eupalinos behind them. Nervously Polykrates looks around. He is searching for Pythagoras and thinks it strange that he is not there.

The procession reaches the beach, and the crowd gathers around the bed of lygos branches. Cassandra, Theano and Selene take Kelenoh's body carefully off the bier and lay it on the branches. With torch in hand, Epidus hesitates to light the pile. Cassandra maneuvers to stand beside him, places her left hand over his right hand, and together they light the pile. The lygos branches quickly catch fire and the smoke streams straight up into the air.

Somewhere in the crowd, a woman lets out an ear-piercing scream. It is Hefaisteon. Polykrates sends his men over to take her away. Hefaisteon's screams fade out into the distance as she is dragged away from the crowd.

Selene picks up her zither and after a few sad strums, Cassandra starts singing a song to honor the deceased. When the fire has gone out, Cassandra, Theano, Selene, Theodoros and Epidus stay behind to wait as the crowd disperses.

Kelenoh, the High Priestess of Hera on Samos, has passed away. The following morning at sunrise, Cassandra, Theano and Selene, accompanied by Theodoros and Epidus, disseminate Kelenoh's ashes into the sea as a symbol of a new beginning.

Now the story has been told.

Epilogue

After Kelenoh's death, Pythagoras went into hiding in the Kerkis Mountains and lived in a cave for a time. Several weeks later one of his students, who wouldn't be recognized by the people in the city, went to the complex to bring back Theano.

Pythagoras, Theano and a few of his students fled to Italy where they settled in the small town of Crotona. There he established a school attended by both men and women. Pythagoras and Theano later married, and settled to start a family.

Selene remained at the temple taking care of Yufas. He would often accompany her in the gardens and during walks to the beach in the evenings.

A few months later, a big earthquake shook the Island of Samos, just as Kelenoh had seen in her visions. The temples and the whole of the complex were destroyed. The large kouroi fell down, as did the statues along the Sacred Road and broke into pieces.

During the earthquake, Cassandra and Selene tried to save as many people as possible, but both of them perished, as did Yufas.

Kelenoh was the last High Priestess of the Temple of Hera who possessed the ancient knowledge of how to connect with the gods and with the cosmos, in order to help the people on earth. With her death, the esotery of secret wisdom disappeared from Samos and from Greece, and eventually, it also disappeared from Egypt.

Pythagoras took his philosophy to the continent of Europe, and Plato, one of his students, later wrote down this philosophy.

During one of my vacations on Samos, I learned about the flight of Pythagoras and Theano from some of the locals. I saw and felt myself what had happened to Cassandra, Selene and to Yufas. It was not shown to me what happened to others, such as Rhoikos, Theodoros and Epidus. It is likely that they survived the earthquake.

Hillie Kuipers

Glossary

Akhetaton City on the east bank of the Nile, founded by Pharaoh Akhenaten, ca 1350 BC.

Amasis II Pharaoh of Egypt from 570 -526 BC, 26th Dynasty. The last great ruler of Egypt before the Persian conquest.

Ameinocles Ship builder who helped Polykrates to build the *Samaina*. Not likely the historical Ameinocles.

Amenhotep III Ninth pharaoh of the 18th dynasty, 14th century BC.

Amenhotep III, Temple of One of the temples at Karnak, built by Amenhotep III.

Aphrodite Greek goddess of love. Venus is he Roman equivalent.

Aphrodite, Temple of One of the temples of the Samos Temple Complex.

Apollo Greek god of music, truth, prophesy, healing, the sun, poetry and more.

Artemis and Apollo, Temple of One of the temples of the Samos Temple Complex.

Artemis   Greek goddess of the hunt, animals, but also
                         of childbirth and virginity. Daughter of Zeus
                         and twin sister of Apollo.
Assyria   A kingdom in Eastern Mesopotamia, located
                         east of Egypt, just north of Babylonia. In the
                         time of Pharaoh Amasis II it had conquered
                         most of Mesopotamia.

Babylon   Capital of Persia, situated I modern-day
                         Iran and Iraq.
Book of Death   Ancient Egyptian funerary text.

Cassandra   One of the priestesses of the Temple
                         Complex of Hera, assigned as a personal
                         assistant to Kelenoh.
Cella   Inner chamber of a temple.
Chonsu Pa-Chered, Temple of
                         Chonsu (=Chons, Kons or Khonsu), god of
                         the moon, son of Amon and Mut. Chonsu is
                         considered a child deity. Located in the
                         Karnak Temple Complex.
Cleitus   Servant of Hefaisteon, the wife of
                         Polykrates.
Cockatiel   A medium sized parrot-like bird with
                         characteristic tuft and an orange-rose
                         round spot on each side of its face.
Colossi of Memnon   Twin statues, depicting Amenhotep III in a
                         seated position. They are 18m/60ft high,
                         and they are located at the west bank of the
                         Nile at the memorial temple of Amenhotep.
Corinth   City in the Greek Peloponnese region, about
                         78 kilometers/48 miles west of Athens.
Crook and Flail   Insignia of the Pharaonic authority.
Crotona   Modern day Crotone, town in the south of
                         Italy where Pythagoras founded his school
                         ca 530 BC.

Deir el-Medina   Town on the west bank of the Nile where
                         the artisans, craftsmen and workmen lived
                         who were employed to work at the tombs

and memorial temples in the Valley of the Kings.

Epidus   Leader of the soldiers at the Samos Temple Complex after the demise of Stephanos.

Eupalinos   Engineer and builder of the underground tunnel and aqueduct on Samos Island.

Fertility Festival Spring Festival, celebrating the fertility of the land and of women.

Harvest Festival A festival celebrating the abundance of the crops.

Hedeas   Priestess of the Hera Temple Complex, head of the clothing warehouse, after replacing Theano.

Hefaisteon   Wife of Polykrates, ruler of Samos.

Hera   Wife and sister of the god Zeus. She was the supreme goddess, patron of marriage and childbirth.

Hera, Temple Complex of

Also known as the Heraion, situated at the south side of Samos Island, not far to the west from the present town of Pythagorion.

Hera, Temple of   One of the largest temple in the whole of Greece according to Greek historian Herodotus (5th century BC). Temples of Hera on Samos date back to the 8th century BC due to the fact that she, according to legend, was born there under a *lygos tree*.

Hermes   Son of Zeus, messenger of the gods.

Hermes, Temple of One of the temples of the Samos Temple Complex.

Hermes-Aphrodite Temple

One of the temples of the Samos Temple Complex, replacing the old temples of Aphrodite and Hermes.

Hestia   Second last High Priestess of the Temple of Hera on Samos, followed by Kelenoh.

Imbrasos River   River that flows just west of the Samos
                        Temple Complex and exits there in the
                        Aegean Sea. According to mythology, the
                        site of this river was the place where Zeus
                        and Hera celebrated their wedding.

Kadesh   City in Syria, battle ground between Egypt
                        and the Hittites in 13th century BC.

Karnak   Ancient Egyptian city, situated in Upper
                        Egypt at the east bank of the Nile River,
                        about 1.5 miles north of Luxor, 800 km/500
                        mi north of the Mediterranean Sea.

Karnak, Temple Complex of
                        The main temples are dedicated to the gods
                        Amon-Ra, Mut and Montu (or Khonsu). The
                        majority of the complex was built around
                        1500 BC, it took well over 2000 years from
                        start to finish. Pharaohs were responsible
                        for building and maintaining the temples
                        and surrounding structures. It is the largest
                        temple complex in Egypt, containing over
                        25 temples and chapels.

Karpathos   Greek island in the southern Aegean Sea,
                        east of Crete.

Kawari   A girl from Nubia assigned to assist Kelenoh
                        during her stay in Karnak.

Kerkis Mountain   A 1433m/4701 ft. high mountain in the
                        western part of Samos.

Kohl   Ancient black eye cosmetic.

Kouros   Free standing statue of a nude male young
                        man. Originally thought to be a
                        representation of Apollo. Plural: kouroi,
                        female counterpart: kore.

Kronos Hill   Located directly east of the Temple
                        Complex in ancient Olympia.

Lane of the Sphinxes
                        Avenue of human headed sphinxes,
                        connecting the temples of Karnak and
                        Luxor.

Leatis   Priestess of the Hera Temple Complex, head
                               of the Laundry.

Letopolis   Ancient Egyptian city at the beginning of
                               the Nile Delta.

Listening Ear, Temple of the
                               Also called the Chapel of the Hearing Ear in
                               Karnak. Open to the populace of Thebes
                               with an entrance through the eastern outer
                               wall.

Luxor, Temple Complex of
                               Situated in Upper Egypt at the east bank of
                               the Nile River, about 1.5 miles south of
                               Karnak.

Lygos tree   Vitex agnus-castus, the "chaste tree."
                               Dedicated to Hera.

Malachite   Green colored mineral, used as pigment in
                               green paints and mascara.

Megara   Greek town, halfway between Athens and
                               Corinth.

Memphis   Ancient port city in Lower Egypt, at the
                               west bank at the mouth of the Nile delta,
                               about 20 km (12 mi) south of modern-day
                               Cairo.

Mount Olympus   Highest mountain in Greece, traditionally
                               the home of the Greek gods. Accessible from
                               the town of Litochoro on the east side of the
                               mountain.

Mut, Precinct of   Smaller Temple Complex at Karnak
                               dedicated to the female Deity Mut, wife of
                               Amon-Ra. Situated south of the main
                               temple.

Naucratis   City in ancient Egypt in the Nile delta area.

Nearchos   Master Craftsman at the Hera Temple
                               Complex.

Nefer   Egyptian hieroglyph for *good, pleasant,
                               beautiful.*

Nubia   Region in Southern Egypt.

Olympia   Ancient Greek city with a sanctuary,
                        containing several temples and buildings,
                        the largest temple being dedicated to Zeus.
                        The site of the ancient Olympic Games,
                        located on the west coast of the
                        Peloponnese peninsula.

Polykrates   The ruler of Samos at the time of Kelenoh,
                        from circa 538 to 522 BC. He brought
                        prosperity and fame to the island; he was
                        considered a fierce warrior and an
                        enlightened tyrant who didn't think twice
                        to get rid of people who were standing in
                        his way.

Portico   A porch leading to the entrance of a
                        building.

Procession Road   Road at the Hera Temple Complex, parallel
                        to and north of the Sacred Road.

Pylon   A gateway of very large dimensions at the
                        Karnak Temple Complex.

Pythagoras   Greek philosopher and mathematician from
                        Samos, ca. 570-495 BC.

Pythia   The oracle of Apollo in Delphi.

Ramses II   Third pharaoh of the 19th Dynasty, 13th
                        century BC.

Ramses III   Second pharaoh of the 20st Dynasty, 12th
                        century BC.

Ramses III, Temple of

                        Temple in the Karnak Temple Complex,
                        built by Ramses III.

Ramses III, Tomb of   Mortuary Temple of Ramses III at
                        Medinet Habu (Luxor), on the west bank of
                        the Nile.

Rhodes   Greek island in the southern Aegean Sea,
                        north-east of Crete.

Rhoikos   Sculptor and architect in 6th century BC
                        Samos.

Rosetta   Egyptian port city of the Nile delta.

Roxanna   Priestess of the Hera Temple Complex, head
                       of the kitchen.

Sacred Road   Road in the Samos Temple Complex that led
                       all the way from the City to the Hera
                       Temple, about 6 kilometers (4 mi) in length.

Sais   Ancient Egyptian town in the Western Nile
                       Delta.

Sakkara   Ancient Egyptian city along the Nile River,
                       about 30 km (19 mi) south of modern-day
                       Cairo.

Samaina   Ship built on Samos, commissioned by
                       Polykrates, with a new configuration of
                       rowers and cargo space to make it more
                       stable and faster.

Samos   Greek island in the eastern Aegean Sea, just
                       off the coast of Turkey, north of Patmos and
                       south of Chios.

Selene   One of the priestesses at the Temple
                       Complex of Hera, assigned as a personal
                       assistant to Kelenoh.

Spring Festival   Festivities dedicated to Hera and Zeus, to
                       implore the gods to make the land fertile
                       and grow abundant crops.

Stephanos   Head of the soldiers at the Samos Temple
                       Complex.

Theano   One of the priestesses at the Temple
                       Complex of Hera, assigned as a personal
                       assistant to Kelenoh.

Thebes   Ancient Egyptian city on the east bank of
                       the Nile, about 800 km (500 mi) south of
                       the Mediterranean Sea, where modern-day
                       Luxor is now.

Theodoros   Sculptor and architect on Samos. 6th century
                       BC.

Thutmose III   Sixth pharaoh of the 18th Dynasty, 15th
                       century BC.

Thutmose III, Temple of

Temple in the Karnak Temple Complex,
built by Thutmose III.

Thutmose III, Tomb of

Mortuary Temple of Thutmose III at
Medinet Habu (Luxor), on the west bank of
the Nile.

Valley of the Kings Valley with the tombs of pharaohs and
nobles from the 18th to 20st Dynasty, located
on the west bank of the Nile, opposite
Thebes (modern-day Luxor).

Yufaa   High Priest at the Karnak Temple Complex
during the time of Pharaoh Amasis' reign,
who initiated Kelenoh in the esoteric
wisdom of Egypt.

Yufas   Bird that was a gift from Yufaa to Kelenoh.

Zeus   Ruler of the gods of Mount Olympus, god of
sky and thunder, often referred to as
"Father of gods and men."

About the author

Hillie Kuipers was born in Losser, the Netherlands to a working-class family. Most of her life she worked in the care giving industry. She also produced and presented a program at a regional radio station.

Hilly has two grown children, Sonja and Erik. She presently lives on the Greek island of Samos in the eastern part of the Aegean Sea.

Hillie Kuipers has two published books in the Dutch language, *Kèlenòh* (2008), and the prologue to her first book, *Terug naar Samos* (Return to Samos) (2015).

If you would like to contact the author, please visit the website www.mountolympuspublishing.com.

www.ingramcontent.com/pod-product-compliance
Lightning Source LLC
Chambersburg PA
CBHW031827090426
42741CB00005B/155